THE PRINTED PAGE IS EVERYMAN'S UNIVERSITY

THE CIVILIZATION OF THE AMERICAN INDIAN

COURTESY, DEPARTMENT OF HISTORY, STATE OF SOUTH DAKOTA

Sitting Bull at Fort Randall, 1882

New Sources of Indian History
1850-1891

THE GHOST DANCE - THE PRAIRIE SIOUX
A Miscellany

STANLEY VESTAL

UNIVERSITY OF OKLAHOMA PRESS
NORMAN, 1934

New Sources of Indian History—1850-1891 by Stanley Vestal
Copyright 1934, by the University of Oklahoma Press

SET UP AND PRINTED BY THE UNIVERSITY OF OKLAHOMA PRESS, PUBLISHING DIVISION OF
THE UNIVERSITY, AT NORMAN, OKLAHOMA, U.S.A. FIRST EDITION SEPTEMBER I, 1934

To
JOHN COLLIER
Commissioner of Indian Affairs, U. S. A.

In admiration

PREFACE

THE HISTORY OF THE WEST, AND PARTICULARLY THE history of the American Indian, shows many gaps and, in general, requires coördination and more complete documentation. In fact, considering the large number of unpublished sources and available eye-witnesses who might be consulted, the general high level of excellence maintained by our historians is remarkable. My five years' research among the Sioux Indians in preparation for the writing of my biography of Sitting Bull uncovered much fresh material. Of course it was impossible in a one volume biography to present all the documents and publish all the statements of Indians which led me to accept the view of Sioux history there put forward. These materials, however, seemed much too valuable in themselves to be cast aside when the biography was completed. They seemed worthy of publication. Hence this miscellany.

The Sioux occupied a territory about as large as the State of Texas. The Western Sioux, with whom this book has chiefly to do, were at the very center of the culture area of the Plains Indians, so that what we learn of them is significant to a greater or less degree for all the surrounding tribes. Comparatively little has been done upon the northernmost Western Sioux tribes, with which I am chiefly concerned. Another book, therefore, seems justified.

The first part of this volume consists of some sixty papers having to do with the Ghost Dance among these Sioux and with the military campaign of 1890-91. I have arranged these papers chronologically in groups so as to present in turn the views of officials of the Indian Bureau, officers of the United States Army, Sioux Indians, and white citizens. Hardly any of these papers have been published heretofore and most of them are items of private correspondence. They are reproduced here from the originals or from true copies of originals prepared by myself, and for permission to use them I am indebted to the following friends: Lieutenant-Colonel George P. Ahern, U.S.A., Retired; Mrs. Irene Beaulieu; Mr. Lewis F. Crawford, former State Historian of North Dakota; Mr. Lawrence K. Fox, Department of History, State of South Dakota; Mr. Robert P. Higheagle; Dr. V. T. McGillycuddy; and—especially—Mrs. Sibley McLaughlin.

The second part of the book consists of information with regard to Sioux Indian history, compiled from statements of Indian and white eye-witnesses of the events narrated. The first section has to do with Indian warfare, the second with treaties and negotiations, the third with notes on individuals, and the fourth with Indian Chronology.

For assistance in compiling this portion of the book, I am indebted chiefly to the following informants: In Canada—Mr. Francis J. Audet, Chief of the Information, Public Archives of Canada; Mr. George A. Gooderham; Colonel Cortlandt Starnes, Commissioner, Royal Canadian Mounted Police; Mr. W. M. Graham, Commissioner, Department of Indian Affairs. In the States

—The Librarian, U. S. Army War College; the late Colonel W. H. C. Bowen, U.S.A., Retired; Mr. Moses Old Bull; Chief Henry Oscar One Bull; Chief Joseph White Bull; Mr. John M. Carignan; Mrs. W. A. Falconer; Mr. George Bird Grinnell; Hon. Frank T. Kelsey; Mr. J. Dallas McCoid; the Librarian, Wyoming State Library; Miss Grace Raymond Hebard; the Honorable C. J. Rhodes, late Commissioner of Indian Affairs; Mr. Willard Schultz; Mr. O. S. Upchurch; Mrs. J. F. Waggoner; Mr. A. B. Welch; Mr. Frank Zahn; and, in addition, to most of the Indian informants mentioned in the text and preface of my *Sitting Bull* and *Warpath*.

I wish also to thank my publishers, the Houghton Mifflin Company, for their generosity in waiving rights under their contract with me to permit publication of this book by the Press of the University of Oklahoma.

STANLEY VESTAL

Norman, Oklahoma

TABLE OF CONTENTS

PART I

DOCUMENTS PERTAINING TO THE GHOST DANCE AND THE DEATH OF SITTING BULL

PREFACE *Page vii*
I. OFFICIAL PAPERS.
  (a) *Papers prepared by officials of the Indian Bureau.*
    1. Report of John M. Carignan (undated), referring to four letters listed below as "Exhibits A, B, C, & D." *Page 1*
    2. Letter from Philip Wells to Major James McLaughlin, October 19, 1890. *Page 5*
    3. "Exhibit A"—McLaughlin to Carignan, November 21, 1890. *Page 7*
    4. "Exhibit B"—McLaughlin to Carignan, November 27, 1890, 4 P. M. *Page 8*
    5. Carignan's reply to McLaughlin, November 27, 1890, 10:30 P. M. *Page 9*
    6. Henry Bullhead to McLaughlin, December 9, 1890. *Page 11*
    7. Louis Primeau to Charles DeRockbrain, December 12, 1890. *Page 11*
    8. "Exhibit C"—Carignan to McLaughlin, December 14, 1890, 12:30 A. M. *Page 13*

9. "Exhibit D"—McLaughlin to Carignan, December 14, 1890. 4:30 P. M. *Page 14*
10. McLaughlin to Afraid-of-Bear (Bullhead) and Shavehead, December 14, 1890. *Page 15*
11. Report as to ammunition in hands of Indian Police, after the fight on the morning of December 15, 1890. *Page 16*
12. Report of casualties of Indian Police and "Hostiles," December 15, 1890. *Page 18*
13. Pass issued by McLaughlin, December 21, 1890. Endorsed by Wm. D. Hodgkiss. *Page 19*
14. Telegram, Major McLaughlin to Commissioner of Indian Affairs, Jan. 9, 1891. *Page 20*
15. Secretary of the Interior to John M. Turner, January 19, 1891. *Page 20*
16. Major McLaughlin to Colonel W. F. Drum, February 10, 1891. *Page 21*

(b) *Papers prepared by officers of the U. S. Army.*
17. Colonel W. F. Drum's Report to Asst. Adj. General, Department of Dakota, December 17, 1890, enclosing No. 18. *Page 22*
18. Extract from Orders No. 274 by Colonel W. F. Drum, December 14, 1890. *Page 25*
19. Captain E. G. Fechet's Report to Post Adjutant, Fort Yates, Dec. 17, 1890. *Page 26*
20. Colonel W. F. Drum to Major McLaughlin, February 26, 1891. *Page 33*
21. Colonel W. F. Drum to Major McLaughlin, August 20, 1891, enclosing No. 22. *Page 34*
22. Letter from Captain Jesse M. Lee to Colonel Drum, August 20, 1891. *Page 34*

23. Major George P. Ahern to General ―――――,
June 20, 1929. *Page 36*

II. UNOFFICIAL PAPERS.
(a) *Papers prepared by Sioux Indians.*
24. White Buffaloman to Sitting Bull, November 11, 1890. *Page 38*
25. Brings Plenty to Sitting Bull, (undated). *Page 39*
26. Gall to Major McLaughlin, November 29, 1890. *Page 40*
27. Spotted Mountain Sheep to Kills Standing, December 7, 1890. (Translation). *Page 41*
28. "I Saw the Ghost Dance at Standing Rock," by Robert P. Higheagle. *Page 42*
29. "The arrest and killing of Sitting Bull," by John Loneman. Translated and recorded by Robert P. Higheagle. *Page 45*
30. "Note on Crowfoot," by Robert P. Higheagle. *Page 55*
31. Grass and Gall to Major McLaughlin, December 15, 1890 *Page 56*
32. Little Soldier to Major McLaughlin, December 31, 1890. *Page 57*
33. One Bull to Major McLaughlin (by Carignan), January 6, 1891. *Page 58*
34. Laurence Industrious to One Bull, March 4, 1891. *Page 59*
35. Many Eagles to his Sister, March 5, 1891. *Page 60*

(b) *Papers prepared by white citizens.*
36. Mary Collins. A Short Autobiography. (A Missionary's account). *Page 61*

37. Grait Manitoo to Sitting Bull, November 19, 1890. *Page 73*
38. V. E. Parr to Major McLaughlin, November 21, 1890. *Page 74*
39. Agent McLaughlin's Work (News clipping), November 22, 1890. *Page 74*
40. Abstract of Petition from La Grace, South Dakota, December 2, 1890. *Page 75*
41. Some man in Georgia to Sitting Bull, December 8, 1890. *Page 76*
42. J. A. McDougal to Major McLaughlin, December 31, 1890. *Page 77*
43. H. R. Lyon to Major McLaughlin, January 6, 1891. *Page 78*
44. John M. Turner to Major McLaughlin, January 8, 1891. *Page 78*
45. Newspaper clipping. *Chattanooga Times*, January 11, 1891. *Page 79*
46. John M. Turner to Major McLaughlin, January 13, 1891. *Page 79*
47. John M. Turner to the Hon. Secretary of the Interior, January 13, 1891. *Page 80*
48. Arthur W. Tinker to Major McLaughlin, February 20, 1891. *Page 80*
49. Dr. V. T. McGillycuddy on the Ghost Dance. *Page 81*
50. C. N. Herreid on Sitting Bull (newspaper clipping), September 13, 1891. *Page 90*

(c) *Papers prepared by Mrs. Catherine S. Weldon, and others regarding her.*
51. W. J. Godfrey to Major Roberts, July 11, 1889, enclosing No. 52. *Page 92*

52. Mrs. Weldon to Chief Red Cloud, July 3, 1889. *Page 92*
53. News story about Mrs. Weldon and Sitting Bull (undated). *Page 96*
54. Newspaper clipping on Mrs. Weldon and Sitting Bull. *Bismarck Daily Tribune*, July 2, 1889. *Page 97*
55. Mrs. Weldon to Major McLaughlin, April 5, 1890. *Page 98*
56. Mrs. Weldon to Major McLaughlin (undated). *Page 100*
57. Mrs. Weldon to Major McLaughlin, October 24, 1890. *Page 102*
58. Mrs. Weldon to Sitting Bull, November 20, 1890. *Page 103*
59. Mrs. Weldon to Sitting Bull, November 23, 1890. *Page 105*
60. Mrs. Weldon to Sitting Bull, December 1, 1890. *Page 107*
61. Mrs. Weldon's address to the Indians—"My Dakotas," (undated). *Page 111*
62. Miscellaneous notes in Sioux and English in Mrs. Weldon's handwriting, found in Sitting Bull's cabin after his death. *Page 115*

PART II

INFORMATION WITH REGARD TO SIOUX INDIAN HISTORY, COMPILED FROM STATEMENTS OF INDIAN AND WHITE EYE-WITNESSES

PREFATORY NOTE *Page 121*

I. INDIAN WARFARE.

(a) *Notes on the Sioux wars with white troops and tribal enemies.*

  1. An Officer's Tribute to the Plains Indians.
                                                Page 131
  2. Comparative Casualties as between U. S. Troops and Indians during the Sioux Campaigns, 1865-1876. *Page 132*
  3. Note on the Ways of Warriors. *Page 141*
  4. Sitting Bull as a Medicine Man. *Page 142*
  5. Note on Sitting Bull's shield. *Page 152*
  6. George Bird Grinnell on Torture in Indian Warfare. *Page 156*
  7. War Story: A Brave Crow Warrior is Killed. *Page 158*
  8. Movements of the Hunkpapa Sioux Camp from the Spring of 1870 until the Custer Fight, 1876. *Page 159*
  9. Old Bull's Battles. *Page 167*
     (a) South of Arrow Creek; Fight with the Crow. *Page 167*
     (b) On the east side of the Rosebud, 1873. *Page 168*
     (c) Baker's Fight, August 14, 1872. Mouth of Arrow Creek. *Page 168*
     (d) On Scarf Creek. *Page 170*
10. Chasing Horses in Camp. 1871. *Page 171*
11. Sitting Crow is Killed. 1873. *Page 172*
12. A Fat Enemy Killed. 1874. *Page 173*
13. Note on Curly Horses. *Page 174*
14. The Fate of the Horse-Thief. *Page 175*
15. Taking Enemy Horses. 1875. *Page 177*

16. Note on the Reynolds Battle. Powder River, March 17, 1876. *Page 178*
17. List of Indian Survivors of the Custer Fight. Standing Rock Agency, 1929 *Page 180*
18. Note on the Custer Fight. *Page 181*
19. Indian criticism of Major McLaughlin's book, *My Friend the Indian.* *Page 181*
20. "Young Sitting Bull" is Killed. December 17, 1876. *Page 181*
21. Note on "Sitting Bull's Boys." *Page 183*
22. Note on The White Horse Riders. *Page 183*
23. Note on the Fox Warrior Society. *Page 184*

II. PROBLEMS OF PEACE.
24. The Great Treaty Council at Fort Laramie, 1851. *Page 185*
25. The "Treaty of Laramie" at Fort Rice, 1868. *Page 219*
26. The Silent Eaters, 1869. *Page 231*
27. Trade with the Slota, 1873. *Page 233*
28. How the Sioux made friends in Canada, 1877. *Page 236*
29. Chief Joseph's People join Sitting Bull, September, 1878. *Page 240*
30. The Sioux account of how Sitting Bull's surrender came to be made, 1881. *Page 245*
31. Note on Louis LeGare. *Page 260*
32. Sitting Bull as Prisoner of War, 1881-1883. *Page 263*
33. Note on Fort Randall. *Page 297*
34. The Mysterious Red Coat. 1884(?) *Page 300*
35. Note on the Delegation to Washington from Standing Rock, 1888. *Page 301*
36. Note on the Signing of Treaties. *Page 303*

37. "Sitting Bull and an Indian Boy," by Robert P. Higheagle. *Page 304*
38. Indian Tales of Standing Rock Agency. *Page 306*
39. The Swan Song of the Sioux Nation. *Page 309*
40. Grasping Eagle's report of Sitting Bull's words on being told that he was to be arrested. *Page 309*
41. Note on Sitting Bull's Pipe during the Ghost Dance excitement. *Page 311*
42. Note on the so-called "Squaw-Men." *Page 312*

III. NOTES ON INDIVIDUALS.
43. Note on Chief Makes-Room. *Page 314*
44. Note on Chief Four Horns. *Page 317*
45. Note on Chief Crazy Horse. *Page 320*
46. Note on Chief Red Cloud. *Page 324*
47. Note on Crow King. *Page 327*
48. Note on Little Assiniboin. *Page 334*
49. Note on Mrs. Eubanks. *Page 338*
50. Note on Frank Grouard. *Page 339*
51. Note on Isaiah. *Page 339*
52. Note on Chief Running Antelope. *Page 340*
53. Note on Kicking Bear. *Page 340*
54. Note on Chief John Grass. *Page 341*
55. Note on Sergeant Shavehead. *Page 342*
56. Note on Black Bull. *Page 343*
57. Note on Sitting Bull's boyhood name. *Page 344*
58. Note on Indian portraits. *Page 346*

IV. CHRONOLOGY.
59. A Hunkpapa Sioux Calendar. *Page 348*

MAPS AND ILLUSTRATIONS

Sitting Bull at Fort Randall, 1882	*Frontispiece*
	FACING PAGE
Sitting Bull's Grave at Fort Yates, North Dakota	*36*
Sitting Bull's Portrait in Oils by Mrs. C. S. Weldon	*108*
Map of the Fetterman Fight near Fort Phil. Kearny, December 21, 1866	*132*
Map of Colonel Baker's Camp on the Yellowstone River, August 14, 1872	*168*
Map of the Reynolds Battle on Powder River, March 17, 1876	*178*
The Cheyenne Chief, Two Moon	*180*
Long (Tall) Mandan, Two Kettle Sioux Chief	*222*
Gall, the Hunkpapa Sioux	*226*
Chief Joseph, of the Nez Percés	*240*
Section of Sitting Bull's Camp at Fort Randall, 1882	*264*
Sitting Bull, his two Wives (Seen-by-Her-Nation and Four Times) with three of his children, at Fort Randall, 1882	*274*
Running Antelope, Hunkpapa Sioux Chief	*340*

PART I

DOCUMENTS PERTAINING TO THE GHOST
DANCE AND THE DEATH
OF SITTING BULL

I. OFFICIAL PAPERS

(a) PAPERS PREPARED BY OFFICIALS OF THE INDIAN BUREAU

No. 1. *Report of John M. Carignan (undated), referring to four letters listed below as "Exhibits A, B, C & D."*

THE GHOST DANCE TROUBLE IN 1890, ON THE STANDing Rock Reservation, started with a visit from an Indian called "Kicking Bear" from one of the lower agencies. He came to Sitting Bull's camp on the Grand River in August, for the purpose of imparting to him the new Religion or craze of the coming Messiah. It soon got rumored around among the Indians what he was there for, and as soon as Major McLaughlin (who was then agent) learned of it he detailed the captain of police and two others to go down to Sitting Bull's camp and order Kicking Bear away, this was done, but too late, as only a few days afterwards the ghost dance craze was in full blast. On September 1st I opened up school about one mile from the camp with an attendance of about 40 pupils and an enrollment of about 60 the difference in attendance from the close of school on June 30th being about 40 percent less. My attention was called to the decrease in attendance and enrollment and I done all in my power to bring the attendance up, but in spite of my efforts, the attendance kept getting smaller and smaller. Sitting Bull and many others of the prominent chiefs visited the school off and on, and at these visits I remonstrated with them, at the way in which they were going on, especially keeping their children out of school, etc., to all of which their replies was that they were keeping their children from school in order to prepare them for the coming of the Messiah. In October the attendance had fallen away to about 15 scholars, I visited the Sitting Bull camp every chance I had, to watch the Ghost Dance, and report its progress to the agent, my presence was seldom noticed, but one time I remember of being asked to remove my hat, when I got too close to the circle. Major McLaughlin made a trip down to the camp in October some time, and endeavored to dissuade them from keeping up the dance, but failed to accomplish anything, upon his return to the Agency he threatened to cut off all those who were dancing from the ration rolls, but even this failed to stop them.

In November my school attendance had got down to about 8 or 9 pupils, and the Ghost Dance was about in its prime.

I was visited by a Chicago paper reporter, by the name of Sam Clover, whom I took up to the dance and who took a kodak picture of same. The day that I took him back up to the Agency Buffalo Bill or William Cody started for Grand River, he was to have come to my school, (so I understand) and get me to go up to Sitting Bull's place with him, but when he learned that I was coming into the agency that day he struck across country to head me off and having failed in this, followed me back to the four mile creek, a little ways below the agency, and the next morning his power to visit Sitting Bull was taken away from him.

Upon my return to Grand River I found a good deal of excitement among the Indians, Sitting Bull visited me at the school, and wanted to know who the white man was that I took up to the dance and into the agency, I replied that he was a friend of mine, he also wanted to know if it was true that Buffalo Bill was at the agency,—I replied yes, and that he wanted to see him, thinking that he might go into the agency, but he said he could not get away just then, as he had to instruct his young people in their new Religion.

He asked me to intercede with the agent for them, and wanted beef and rations sent down to the school for me to issue to them, as the distance into the agency and back for rations was too great, hard on their horses, and besides kept them away from their religious duties. I promised to do what I could for them, but told them that their chances were slim for having favors granted them as long as they kept their children out of school. On November the 21st a courier from the agency delivered the following letter a copy of which marked "Exhibit A" is attached, and on November 27th another one marked "Exhibit B," I then took my mother and sister who were with me at the school into the agency, and returned alone back to the school, so as not to create suspicion in the minds of the Indians, and from that time on couriers came late and early on Dec. 14th. I wrote Major McLaughlin in a letter marked "Exhibit C," and received in return about midnight of the same day by courier, Policeman Loneman, instructions contained in "Exhibit D." Immediately upon receipt of this letter I sent Loneman a few miles further down the river to bring in Policeman Hawkman, (who was killed) Brownman and Looking Elk, and accompanied by these four, proceeded to Bull Head's house up the river about five miles from the school, and in order to reach there had to go thru Sitting Bull's camp. The night was very dark and hazy and in passing by, some one called out of one of the tents and asked who it was, I replied in Indian giving my name, I was best known as "Jack," which seemed to satisfy him. I reached Bull Head's house about 2:30 A. M., but found no one at home excepting his wife, two children and an Indian woman. They informed me that Bull Head and a small force had proceeded over to Gray Eagle's house by a roundabout way in order to be closer to Sitting Bull's at day break, and that I was to send my instructions over by courier to him there, and to use my team and wagon in taking his family in as far as Oak Creek, where he would meet me with his prisoner.

I cautioned the four policemen I had with me and told them to go on to where Bull Head was, and tell him to be sure and take a light wagon and team with him, and that had he not left word, that he did, with his wife, I would have gone over myself with my team and wagon. It seemed as tho they did not follow out the instructions, about taking a team, and when they got their prisoner, a delay was made in rigging up a horse or something to take him in, and as a consequence the camp was aroused and the fight followed, which would have ended in the total extermination of the police force had it not been for the prompt arrival of troops under command of Capt. Fechet.

No. 2. *Letter from Philip Wells to Major James Mc-
Laughlin, October 19, 1890*
Printed ruled writing paper
On back: Pine Ridge Agency, October 10, 1890
Phillip Wells.
Reports with regard to the practice of the Indians in the matter of dancing in connection with the new craze as to the coming of the New Messiah next spring.

United States Indian Service
Pine Ridge Agency, S. D.
Oct. 19th, 1890
James McLaughlin, U.S. Ind. Agt.
Standing Rock Agc. N. Dak.

Dear Major: Pardon me for the privilige I take in asking you some questions in regard to your Indians taking part in the new religious craze the Ghost Dance or what is known as the coming of Messiah next Spring. Are your Indians practicing it to such an extent that you anticipate any difficulty in supressing it, or what in your opinion would be the best means of stoping it. The reason I ask is our Indians are getting so crazy over it that it is certainly getting serious, as they are defying the Police force, and from what I can lern the Rose Bud Indians are worse than ours, and there is no telling what will grow out of it in the near future. Some time ago Col. Gallagher myself and a lot of Police went to the Place of dancing to stop it but they had stoped before we got there, but the Indians were laying in ambush for us, all armed and striped for fighting, and as we rode up they drew their guns on us, but the Col. told the Police to stand back in readiness and walked into their midst and ordered them to lay down their guns, a few of the leaders who were in sight did so, we found out before we left there that the woods was full of armed Indians. I am telling you this that you can see the magnitude the craze has taken if it will be any service to you to know. Dr. D. F. Royer our new agent took charge this week, but I think he has got an elephant on his hands, as the craze had taken such a hold on the Indians before he took charge. As yet I have all hopes he will be able to stop it without any serious trouble. If you will kindly give me your valuable opinion on the subject you will confer a great favor on me and it will be confidently kept by me, so far as getting any information from you, if you so desire it. I will at any time cheerfully give you any information on the subject you desire.

As yet we have not been paid for last quarter. Now there is no likelyhood of it before the last of this month and so far as I know there are no appointments made yet, as yet there is no certainty about my being kept on, but I think I am sollid.

Tom Reey is hanging on a balance now and is ondesided which way to fall, whether he will quit the Indian service or not as we have all been kept in unceartainty since July 1st.

The Col. will move to Shadron Neb. next week to remain there for the Winter.

Frank Young got married last Sunday to a very nice halfbreed girl of this place.

Both Tom's & my family are all well.

Give my warmest regards to Mrs. McLaughlin & children and except the same yourself.

Yours cencerly

P. F. Wells

P.S. While on my way to mails this to you I met Amos Ross a halfbreed missonery who was just from Standrock convocation. He came through Cheyenne Agency and he learned there that Mato Wanahtake[1] the Indian who is the orignation of all this trouble is going amongst your Indians to start it there if you can nab him before he can get them started you will save yourself no end to trouble. I say this because you or any one els can have no idea how bad it takes hold of the Indians as some of our best Indians are nearly crazy over it.

Yours &c.
P. F. Wells

No. 3. *"Exhibit A"—McLaughlin to Carignan, November 21, 1890*

"*Exhibit A*".

Standing Rock Agency, N. D.,
Nov. 21, 1890.
4 P. M.

John M. Carnigan, Esq.,
 Grand River, S. D.
Dear John:

I send you this (to be on the safeside) to say that a dispatch has just been received here, stating that it is reported that fighting between U. S. Troops and Indians, commenced at Rosebud Agency yesterday. I do not believe it, as neither myself nor the Commanding Officer have heard from our respective Departments. It was a private dispatch to Ft. Slocum from New York. Well, I do not want to create any suspicion in the minds of the Indians and have selected "Take the Hat" to carry this letter to you, with the impression that it contains important papers for your signature.

---

1. Mato Wanahtake, i.e., Kicking Bear, who brought the Ghost Dance to Standing Rock. See Official Papers No. 1, above.

I think it best that you come in at once, and as tomorrow is ration day it will cause no suspicion. I would have sent teams for your chief household effects and clothing, but do not deem it prudent to arouse the suspicion it would cause.

I have sent a team to Bull Head with some building material with a letter to Mr. Shields and the other workmen to come in. Should there have been any fighting at Rosebud yesterday it would be known to the Indians by courier by tomorrow night.

Very respectfully,
(Signed) Jas. McLaughlin,
Agt.

Do not speak of this report to any Indians, and be careful to do nothing that may arouse their suspicion.
J. McL.

No. 4. *"Exhibit B"—McLaughlin to Carignan, November 27, 1890. 4 p. m.*

"Exhibit B."

Standing Rock Agency, N. D.,
Nov. 27, 1890.
4 P. M.

J. M. Carnigan, Esq.,
 Grand River School, S.D.
Dear Sir:

A telegram just received states that Indians from Grand River were seen crossing Bad River, (a number of young men) en route to Pine Ridge. I do not believe it, but send the bearer to ascertain facts. I want him (or if his horse is too tired, some other policeman) to return with the news or true state of affairs at once, so that I can advise the proper authorities. I have directed him to report to Bullhead, who is specially charged to watch just such a move, and who should know if there is any truth in the report.

Everything is reported quiet or rather quieting down at the other agencies, and I do not believe any trouble will grow out of this craze if prudence is used.

A telegram says that Col. Cody (Buffalo Bill) and a special agent are in Mandan en route here, and will reach here tonight.

Write me a line and send by bearer as to what your observations have been since you returned to Grand River.

Is the Dance going on, are the number of dancers increasing or decreasing, is their enthusiasm as great, as it was and do you believe that any Indians have gone to Pine Ridge or other agencies from here?

Very respectfully,

(Signed) James McLaughlin,
Ind. Agent.

No. 5. *Carignan's Reply to McLaughlin, November 27, 1890, 10:30 p. m.*
(*Ruled letter paper*)

10:30 P. M.

Grand River
Nov. 27/90

Maj. James McLaughlin
Standing Rock Agcy.
        N. D.
Dear Sir:

I send courrier back immediately as I do not wish Indians to know of his coming down. I have been out twice in the Camps since Tuesday and find everything quieter; dancing still at Sitting Bull's, but not in such large numbers, owing to the fact that "Male Bear" has started a dance on "Little Oak Creek." At a Council held at Iron Star's house to-day, I saw the principal men of the new dance, with the exception of "Sitting Bull," if any one were to leave the reserve I am confident that some of those at Council would have been amongst them. The Indians seem to be very peaceably inclined, and I do not apprehend any trouble. I will send for "Bull Head" in the morning, and if he has any more news, I will send policeman "Looking Stag" in with it by tomorrow night.

The Indians have been told that the Soldiers are coming down here, and are badly frightened if they were assured different there would be no danger of any of them leaving. I have done all I could in telling them that the reports they have heard are all lies, and that no one would try to prevent them from dancing. I am positive that no trouble need be apprehended from Sitting Bull and his followers, unless they are forced to defend themselves and think it would be advisable to keep all strangers, other than employees, who have business amongst the Indians away from here, as Sitting Bull has lost all confidence in the whites since Mrs. Weldon has left him.

I am going up to the Agency Saturday, and will have all the information possible on the question.

Please tell my Mother & Sister that John & I are all right.

Yours very respectfully,
John M. Carignan

No. 6. *Henry Bullhead to McLaughlin, December 9, 1890*
Envelope: John Carignan's letters—relation to Sitting Bull—November, 1890
(*Small ruled note paper*) Standing Rock Agency
 N. D. 12/9/90
Maj. J. McLaughlin:
U. S. Ind. Agt.
Sir: I desire to express my judgement concerning the separate beef issues to both wel-behaved and back-ward Indians on *Grand River* respectively;—that it would be well, if the plan may be applied to allow those Indians under control of the Ghost outfit to enter *bands* of good *chiefs* to draw their beef on Grand River as may gradually change their mind into good ones and retaining the rest to come after their beef up here; for some of the Indians of unsettled mind may be cured to some extent by the application of my judgement, and the number of the backward Indians will be diminished and be won to the right path.
 I request to know as to the propability of the application of my suggestion by next ration day.
 Very Respectfully
 Henry Bull-head
 Capt. U.S. Ind. Police

No. 7. *Louis Primeau to Charles DeRockbrain, December 12, 1890*
Envelope: (Writing in pencil very blurred:
 kingi wicasakte 2
 tutunka yotunka 5
 tutunka wanpila 2)
 Matokokipapi or
By Courier Chas. De Rockbrain
White Bird. Grand River, S. Dak.

(*Also some Sioux names scribbled in pencil on back of envelope, almost illegible*)

kasinke kinyun	1	citan mato	1
sungila lutu	1	mato hinske muzu	1
Wicaru tankulu	1	atuya unkenna	1
makusan		lote yuhuyapi	1
hakikta napin	1		

(*Sioux and translation both enclosed*)
(*foolscap*)
*Translation from
the Sioux*   Standing Rock Agency, N. Dak.
                            Decr. 12th, 1890
Chas. De Rockbrain—Afraid of Bear
Dear Sir:

    Tell Afraid of Bear, (Bull Head) not to come in here. You will proceed to build the station I spoke of to you, at the same time you must watch Sitting Bull closely. We learned sufficient news to lead us to believe that he (S.B.) is going to leave the reservation. If he should you must stop him and if he does not listen to you do as you see fit, use your own discretion in the matter and it will be all right. I want you to assemble the Police force and tell them for an excuse that you want them all together to build the station which will be a good excuse to assemble them without suspicion. Bull Ghost brought a letter to me and it stated that he (S.B.) wanted to go on a visit, and that is why I want you to keep a good watch on him, and if he should insist on going you can do as you think best and it will be all right. Shave Head will meet you tomorrow. And should I think of anything else he will instruct you.

    I am your Cousin, Louis Primeau.

(*On back: Copy Letter of Louis Primeau Chief of Ind. Police under direction of James McLaughlin U.S. Ind. Agt. to Afraid of Bear and Chas. De Rockbring. Dated Dec. 12th, 1890.*)[2]

No. 8. "*Exhibit C*" — *Carignan to McLaughlin, December 14, 1890, 12:30 a. m.*
"*Exhibit C.*"

Grand River S. D.
Dec. 14, 1890.
12:30 A. M.

Major James McLaughlin
   Standing Rock Agency, N.D.
Dear Sir:

   Bull Head wishes to report what occured at Sitting Bull's camp at a council held yesterday. It seems that Sitting Bull has received a letter from the Pine Ridge outfit, asking him to come over there as God was to appear to them. Sitting Bull's people want him to go, but he has sent a letter to you asking your permission, and if you do not do it, he is going to go anyway; he has been fitting up his horses to stand a long ride and will go horseback in case he is pursued.

   Bullhead would like to arrest him at once before he has the chance of giving them the slip, as he thinks

---

2. The Indian words scribbled on the back of the envelope form a list of Indian proper names, for the most part improperly spelled. I am indebted to Mr. Frank Zahn of Fort Yates for correcting and translating the names as follows:

kingi wicasakte	(Kangi-wicasa kte)	Kills Crow Indian
tutunka yotunka	(Tatanka iyotake)	Sitting Bull
tutunka wanpila	(Tatanka-wanjila)	One Bull
kasinke kinyun	(Tasunke-kinyan)	Flying Horse
sungila lutu	(Sungila luta)	Red Fox
Wicaru tankulu	(Wicarpi-tankala)	Large Star
makusan	(Makasan)	Gray Earth
hakikta napin	(Napa)	Retreats Looking
citan mato	(Cetan-mato)	Hawk Bear
mato hinske muzu	(Maza)	Iron Bear Tusk
atuya unkenna	(Scuya-unkenne)	Reclines pretty
lote yuhuyapi	(Lote-yurugapi)	Chokes

that if he gets the start, it will be impossible to catch him. He says to send word to him by courier immediately, also to let him know what your plans are, if soldiers are to come—he says to send them by Sitting Bull's road.

He also mentions something about Shave Head coming down here, but as I am not a good enough interpreter to understand, he has said that you can use your own judgment in regard to that one thing. I understand thoroughly and that is that the poor man is eat out of house and home—he says that with councils and couriers coming to his place that even the hay he has is nearly all gone. I sympathize with him, as I am nearly in the same boat.

If you send a dispatch to Bullhead through me, please send me some envelopes, as I am entirely out can't even find one to enclose this letter.

Yours very respectfully,
John M. Carnigan.

No. 9. *"Exhibit D"—McLaughlin to Carignan, December 14, 1890, 4:30 p. m.*
"*Exhibit D.*"

Standing Rock Agency, N.D.
Dec. 14, 1890.
4:30 P. M.

J. M. Carnigan, Esq.
   Grand River, S. D.
Dear Sir:

I send a letter, by bearer of this to Bullhead, ordering him to arrest Sitting Bull to night. It must be done without fail as the Cavalry will start this evening and reach the Sitting Bull crossing of Oak Creek to-morrow morning to protect the police from that point into Post. Should by any chance Bull Head be away from

Grand River having started into agency to fix upon a plan of arrest, let Shave Head carry out the orders and arrest him as directed in the letter to Bull Head, which you will find herewith. It will hardly be necessary for all the police to come in with Sitting Bull, unless they should be opposed by all the infected Indians following them after they reach Oak Creek, a number can return and keep watch of the other Indians that none attempt to leave the reservation. Have it announced in the plainest way possible that no Indians will be disturbed and all will be treated in a kindly manner, unless they should attempt to leave the reservation.

I trust that the whole police force can be concentrated promptly.

Very respectfully,
(Signed) Jas. McLaughlin,
Ind. Agent.

P.S. Be sure to see that they have a light wagon ready to bring Bull in, so that there will be no delay by such an oversight. You had better come in for a time. If Bull Head's wagon is not convenient and they need yours I will see that you are compensated for its use.

J. McL. Agt.

No. 10. *McLaughlin to Afraid-of-Bear (Bullhead) and Shavehead, December 14, 1890*
(*Half-sheet foolscap*)
On back: "Copy Letter from James McLaughlin U.S. Ind. Agt. to Afraid of Bear and Shave Head. Dated Dec. 14th 1890."

Standing Rock Agency N. Dak.
Decr. 14th, 1890

Afraid of Bear and Shave Head.

I am in receipt of the letter you sent by courier Hawk

Man and I have come to the conclusion that the time has come to arrest Sitting Bull. I am afraid that if we should put it off any longer that he will get away on us. So to-night you will proceed to his house and arrest him before daybreak. Louie will lead the troops down, on the road you suggested, to Oak Creek crossing and stop there. I mean the Sitting Bull and Spotted Horn Bull, Crossing at Oak Creek, where I told you to build the station and they will await you there. If anything should happen you will bring the news to the troops immediately.

I am your agent
(Sgd.) James McLaughlin
who says this.

No. 11. *Report as to Ammunition in Hands of Indian Police, After the Fight on the Morning of December 15, 1890*

Number of cartridges on policemen after the fight with Sitting Bull and his followers on Grand River on the morning of December 15, 1890.

Name	Revolver	Gun
Bullhead (First Lieutenant)	30	.. (mortally wounded)
Yellow Wolf	8	1
Eagleman (Sergeant)	10	3
Red Tomahawk (Sergeant) Hat	13	8
Little Soldier	24	6
Iron Cedar	3	2
Take-the-Hat		5

Name	Revolver	Gun
Alex Middle	30	(mortally wounded)
Looking Elk	8	19
He-Alone-is-Man	1	6
Gray-Corn-Man	18	3
Running Hawk	12	4
Black Hills	16	7
Hen	8	
Bob-Tail-Bull	7	
Iron Star		
Cross Bear		
Bad Horse	8	
Paints Brown	1	
Red Bear	4	2
White Bird	23	
Pretty-Voice-Eagle	6	
High Eagle	6	
Hawk Man (No. 1) courier to troops		
Weasel Bear		
Magpie Eagle	10	
One Feather		
Black Prairie Chicken		
Good-Voice-Elk	4	
Shoots-Walking	3	
Afraid-of-Hawk	1	
Iron Thunder		
Shave Head (First Sergeant	27	39
Hawk Man (No. 2)		
Little Eagle	34	
Afraid-of-Soldiers (Warriors-Fear-Him)		

Name	Re-volver	Gun
Strong Arm (Armstrong)		(mortally wounded)
Kills-Mounted		8
Volunteers:		
Gray Eagle (Sitting Bull's brother-in-law)		4
Otter Robe		3
Young Eagle		35
Spotted Thunder		
	210	260	Totals

No. 12. *Report of Casualties of Indian Police and "Hostiles," December 15, 1890*

Casualties in the Police Force

Henry Tatankapah, (Bull Head) *1st Lieut. in Command.*
  Dangerously wounded, four wounds.
Charles Kashlay, (Shave Head) *1st Sergant.*
  Mortally wounded, since dead.
James Wambdichigalah, (Little Eagle) *4th Sergant.*
  Killed.
Alexander Hochokah, (Middle) *Private,*
  Painfully wounded.
Paul Alichitah, (Afraid of Soldier) *Private.*
  Killed.
John Armstrong, Special Police, Killed.
Hawk Man, Special Police, Killed.

Casualties in the Hostiles.

1. Sitting Bull.
2. Black Bird.

3. Catch the Bear.
4. Little Assinaboine.
5. Crow Foot (Sitting Bull's son.)
6. Spotted Horn Bull, (*A Chief*).
7. Brave Thunder, (*A Chief*).
8. Chase Wounded.

No. 13. *Pass Issued by McLaughlin, December 21, 1890.
Endorsed by Wm. D. Hodgkiss*
(*Ruled writing paper: printed:*)

United States Indian Service
Standing Rock Agency,
Decr. 21st, 1890

The bearer "Orloyeca"[3] is hereby authorized to proceed to Grand River to send his father "Fool Thunder" and "Afraid of his Track" into the Agency who are reported to be waiting for him at their homes in the Sitting Bull settlement. After starting the above named towards the Agency he will continue on to "Horpi Moza's" on the Moreau River where Sitting Bull's two sons are reported to be waiting for means of returning home and he will bring them and all others belonging to this Reservation back with him who wish to avail themselves of the opportunity.

James McLaughlin
U. S. Ind. Agt.

(*on back in pencil*)

Moreau River District

White Horse Camp, S.D.
Dec. 23d.
Yesterday "Two Crows" left with a party for Standing Rock Agency—and this A. M. "Red Thunder" left—

3. Orlogeca, i.e., Hollow; Horpi Moza (Horpi Maza), i.e., Iron Nest.

And parties are going. And after to day I do not think any of the "Indians" here referred to will be in this District.

          Wm. D. Hodgkiss
             Farmer

No. 14. *Telegram, Major McLaughlin to Commissioner of Indian Affairs, January 9, 1891*

Telegram

          Fort Yates, N. D.
           January 9, 1891

Commissioner Indian Affairs
 Washington D C

Reports of Indians leaving this Agency entirely unfounded. None have left since the Sitting Bull affair. Three hundred and seventy two (372) men, women and children now absent, of whom two hundred and twenty seven (227) are prisoners at Fort Sully and on 3rd (3rd) instant General Miles telegraphed the Post Commander here that seventy two (72) Standing Rock Indians were made prisoners at Pine Ridge Agency, which leaves only seventy three (73) unaccounted for of whom forty (40) were absent before the stampede of fifteenth (15th) ultimo * * * *

           McLaughlin
             Agent

No. 15. *Secretary of the Interior to John M. Turner, January 19, 1891*

(*Copy*)   Jan 19/91
        Department of the Interior
        Washington
        January 19, 1891

Mr. John M. Turner
The Mandan Roller Co.
Mandan, N.D.
Dear Sir:

Yours of the 15th instant has been received, in relation to Mr. James McLaughlin Indian agent at Standing Rock. There is no intention to change Agents at any of the agencies. The change at Pine Ridge was caused by very peculiar circumstances, not necessary to dwell upon. The reputation of Mr. McLaughlin stands very high in this department and I have no fear of his removal now.

Yours truly
John W. Noble
Secretary

No. 16. *Major McLaughlin to Colonel W. F. Drum, February 10, 1891*

"Standing Rock, Feby 10, 1891
  Dear Col Drum;

Replying to your note I desire to state that so far as known no other Indians than those already reported were killed in the affair at Grand River.

152 persons (49 men 47 women & 56 children) who were at first believed to have fled from the reservation came into the Agency within the first few days after the stampede of Dec 15, and 22 men 30 women & 26 children who fled to the Moreau river returned to this Agency about two week later.

No change since my report to you of Dec 27-1890

Very respectfully,
James McLaughlin
U S Ind, Agt."

(b) PAPERS PREPARED BY OFFICERS OF THE U. S. ARMY

No. 17.   *Colonel W. F. Drum's Report to Asst. Adj. Gen. Dept. of Dakota, December 17, 1890, Enclosing No. 18*

Fort Yates, North Dakota,
December 17, 1890

The Assistant Adjutant General
 Department of Dacota,
  Saint Paul, Minn.
Sir:

I have the honor to report that on Sunday the 14th inst., Agent McLaughlin received a letter from John M. Carnigan, school teacher, on Grand River, (copy enclosed marked "A") indicating that Sitting Bull was preparing to leave the reservation, and that Bull Head the Lieutenant of Police, was anxious to attempt his arrest. It was found on inquiry that there were not more than twenty lodges in the immediate vicinity of Sitting Bull's house. In accordance with telegraphic instructions of Dec. 12, 1890, and after consultation with Agent McLaughlin, it was determined to order the arrest of Sitting Bull by the Indian police, about forty of whom had already been assembled in that vicinity as a precautionary measure. The arrest was to be attempted before daylight on Monday the 15th instant, Bullhead in charge, and with strict instructions that Sitting Bull must not escape or be rescued. I then ordered Troops "F" and "G" 8th Cavalry, with one Gatling and one Hotchkiss gun, Captain E. G. Fechet 8th Cavalry commanding, to move out Sunday night in light marching order, to meet the police on their way in with Sitting

Bull, to prevent rescue on the road,—the Cavalry not to start before midnight so that an Indian runner could not give the alarm before the police had acted.

At 12:30 P. M. 15th instant, I received word from Capt. Fechet that at 7:30 A. M. he was within three miles of Sitting Bull's camp and was met by a policeman who informed him that the police and Indians were fighting; that Sitting Bull had been arrested and afterwards killed to prevent his escape. That the Cavalry would push on as rapidly as possible to the assistance of the police.

On receipt of this information and not knowing how large a force the hostiles might have, nor how long it might be necessary for the Cavalry to remain out, they having no baggage or rations, I moved out of the post for Grand River at 12:30 P. M., with 30 men of Company "H" and 37 men of Company "G" 12th Infantry, (as many men as I thought it safe to take from the post) 10 days rations, 10 days forage, and necessary camping equipage for both Cavalry and Infantry. To do this I was obliged to hire six two-horse wagons to haul forage.

On the march I received more assuring dispatches from Capt. Fechet, but thought it best to push on. Owing to the heavy loaded wagons I did not reach Oak Creek until 11:30 P. M.,—distance 22 miles.

I found the Cavalry at Oak Creek, to which point Captain Fechet had returned. Went into camp and at 10:00 o'clock P. M., next day, finding that the hostiles had scattered, and that if I moved forward to Grand River I would probably do more harm than good, I broke camp and returned with the whole force to this post.

Enclosed is Captain Fechet's report of the operations of the Cavalry. The energy displayed by Captain Fechet, and the officers and men of his command in going to the assistance of the police and in dispersing the hostiles is highly commendable. The officers present with the two companies of Infantry were:

Captain Craigie and Lieutenant Uline, Company "G" and Capt. Haskell and Lieutenant Baker, Company "H", both officers and men showed fine spirit, and if they had had an opportunity would have done good service.

The distance marched between 2:30 P. M. on the 15th and 5:00 P. M. on the 16th was 44 miles. To do this with Troops just out of Barracks, it was necessary to assist them by letting a few at a time ride in wagons. Both Cavalry and Infantry are in good condition, and ready for any future service. Too much cannot be said of the excellent conduct of the police, had they been better armed and been supplied with ammunition, I am of opinion that many more of the hostiles would have fallen.

I earnestly recommend that Congress be asked to provide for the wounded Indian Police and for the families of those who were killed. No soldier could have rendered better service and it would greatly encourage other Indians. Agent McLaughlin has rendered most valuable assistance by his advice, by furnishing information and by his able management of the police force, which is composed of picked men.

For list of killed and wounded see paper attached to Capt. Fechet's report.

Very respectfully,
Your obedient servant,
W. F. Drum,
Lieut. Colonel 12th Infantry.

No. 18. *Extract from Orders No. 274 by Colonel W. F. Drum, December 14, 1890*

Fort Yates, N.D.,
December 14, 1890.

Orders)
)
No. 274) ———Extract———

Captain E. G. Fechet, 8th Cavalry, will proceed with *Troops "F" and "G"* 8th Cavalry, the *Hotchkiss gun* and one *Gatling gun* to the crossing of *Oak Creek* by the *Sitting Bull road* for the purpose of preventing the *escape* or *rescue* of *Sitting Bull* should the *Indian Police* succeed in arresting him.

The command will move out at *12:00 o'clock midnight*, in light *marching order*, and will be supplied with *50 rounds of carbine* and *12 rounds of revolver ammunition* per man, *4000 rounds of ammunition* for *Gatling gun*, *one days cooked rations* and *one days forage*.

After receiving the prisoner, *Captain Fechet* will return with his command to this post reporting to the *Commanding Officer* on arrival.

If on arrival at *Oak Creek*, *Captain Fechet* learns that the police are fighting or need assistance, he will push on and if necessary follow *Sitting Bull* as long as possible with his supplies, keeping the *Post Commander* informed by courier of his movements.

The march will be so regulated as to reach *Oak Creek* by *6.30 o'clock, a. m.* tomorrow the 15th instant.

Should arrest be made every precaution will be taken to prevent escape or rescue.

Two Indian scouts will accompany the command.

Assistant Surgeon A. R. Chapin, Medical Department, will report to *Captain Fechet* for duty with the expedition.

First Lieutenant S. L. H. Slocum, 8th Cavalry, with Troop "F" will also report to *Captain Fechet* for orders.

Second Lieutenant H. C. Brooks, 8th Cavalry will also report to *Captain Fechet* for duty with the expedition.

One *Hospital Ambulance* with necessary supplies will accompany the expedition, the *Quartermaster* furnishing the necessary team.

By orders of
Lieut. Colonel W. F. Drum,
E. C. Brooks,
2nd Lieut. 8th Cavalry,
Post Adjutant.

No. 19. *Captain E. G. Fechet's Report to Post Adjutant, Fort Yates, Dec. 17, 1890* . . .

Fort Yates, North Dakota,
December 17, 1890.

To the
Post Adjutant,
Fort Yates, N. D.

Sir:

For the information of the Commanding Officer, I have the honor to report the operations of the Battalion of the 8th Cavalry under my command for the purpose indicated in Order No. 247, of this Post. (Copy attached marked "A")

The command consisted of Troop "F" 8th Cavalry, Lieut. Slocum and Steel and 48 enlisted men; Troop "G" 8th Cavalry, Captain Fetchet, Lieutenant E. H. Crowder and E. C. Brooks, and 51 enlisted men; Captain A. R. Chapin, Medical Officer and Acting Hospital Steward August Nicket; two Indian Scouts Smell the Bear and Iron Dog; Mr. Louis Primeau, Indian Department, Standing Rock Agency, Guide and Interpreter.

One Gatling gun was attached to "G" Troop and one breech loading steel Hotchkiss gun attached to Troop "F". There was furnished the command one four-horse spring wagon carrying one days' cooked rations and one days' grain for the whole command, and one Red Cross Ambulance.

Commanding Officers:
Captain E. G. Fechet, Commanding Battalion.
Lieut. E. H. Crowder, Commanding "G" Troop.
Lieut. S. L. H. Slocum, Commanding "F" Troop.
Lieut. E. C. Brooks, Commanding Field Artillery.

The command moved out at midnight before December 14th and by rapid marching was by daylight within three miles of Sitting Bull's camp, which is fully from 41 to 42 miles from Fort Yates. After daybreak I expected every minute to meet the Indian Police with Sitting Bull their prisoner, it having been arranged by Major McLaughlin, Indian Agent, that they should make a decent upon Sitting Bull's camp about daybreak, arresting Bull and delivering him to me for conduct to this Post.

It will be seen by reference to this first paragraph of this order that the command was to proceed only to the crossing of the Oak Creek, which was 18 miles from Bull's camp. After receiving this order, on consultation with Colonel Drum, Commanding the Post, it was decided that I should move as close to Bull's camp as possible without discovery, and there await the police. A short time after dawn a mounted man was discovered approaching rapidly. This proved to be one of the police who reported that all the other police had been killed.

The substance of his report with the additional

statement that I would move in rapidly and endeavor to relieve any of the police who might be alive I forwarded to the Commanding Officer.

The command was at once put into condition for immediate action. A light but extended line was thrown in advance, the main body disposed in two columns in column of fours, about three hundred yards apart, the Artillery between the heads of columns a few minutes after making these dispositions another of the police came in and reported that Bull's people had a number of the police penned up in his house; that they were nearly out of ammunition and could not hold much longer—the command was moved with all speed to a point on the high lands, overlooking the valley of Grand River, and immediately opposite Sitting Bull's house and the camp of the Ghost dancers, distance some 1500 yards.

A hasty examination showed a party of Indians approaching apparently 40 or 50, on a high point on our right front, some 900 yards distance; but whether a party of police and friends or Bull's people, could not be determined.

While trying to make out the position and identity of the two parties there were a few shots fired by the party on the hill and replied to from Sitting Bull's house, there was also firing from the woods beyond Bull's house, but on whom directed it was impossible to tell.

I caused a white flag to be erected on the crest where I was located, (a prearranged signal between the soldiers and the police) and directed a few shots to be fired from the Hotchkiss into the woods mentioned. In answer a white flag was displayed from Bull's house, and the Indians were seen leaving the woods going in the direction of the hills to the south, across Grand River.

The Hotchkiss gun was then turned upon the party on our right front, this with some fire from a dismounted line of "F" Troop caused them to retreat rapidly from their position up the valley of the Grand River to the North West.

Lieutenant Slocum with his troop dismounted, was ordered to advance immediately upon the house. Lieutenant Crowder with "G" Troop mounted, moved rapidly to the right along the high lands, covering the flank of the dismounted line. As the dismounted line approached the house the police came out and joined the command.

The line was advanced through the timber dislodging a few hostiles who disappeared rapidly up the river through the willows.

The line after advancing through the willows some six hundred yards, fell back to the immediate vicinity of Sitting Bull's house leaving pickets at the furthest points gained by the advance. Lieutenant Crowder in the meantime observed the Indians gathering at houses up the river about two miles from Bull's camp, moved in pursuit of them. The Indians fell back from every point upon the approach of the troops, not showing any desire to engage in hostile action against the soldiers.

All the houses for a distance of about two miles were examined and all were found deserted, but showed signs of recent occupation.

Failing to come up with the Indians in this direction "G" Troop fell back and joined the main command at Sitting Bull's lodge.

Upon arriving at this place I found evidences of a most desperate encounter between the Agency Police and Sitting Bull's followers.

In the vicinity of the house within a radius of 50

yards were found the dead bodies of 8 hostiles including Sitting Bull; two horses were also killed. Within the house there were found four dead and three wounded policemen.

It was learned through the Interpreter that the hostile Indians had carried away with them one of their dead and five or six of their wounded, making an approximate total of fifteen casualties in Sitting Bull's band.

A list of casualties by name on both sides is hereto attached marked "B."

From the best evidence obtainable I am led to believe that the police under command of Bull Head and Shave Head, about 40 strong entered Sitting Bull's camp about 5:50 A. M., on the 15th instant, for the purpose of making the arrest of Sitting Bull. Sitting Bull was taken from his house, and while the police were parleying with him, endeavoring to induce him to submit peacefully Bull Head was shot by Catch the Bear in the leg. Bull Head immediately shot and killed Sitting Bull, when the melee became general with the result heretofore given.

The fight lasted but a few moments when the police secured the house and stable adjoining, driving Sitting Bull's men from the village to cover in the adjoining woods and hills.

From these positions the fight was kept up until 7:30 A. M. when the troops came up. I learn that soon after the occupation of the house and stable by the Police, volunteers were called for to carry a report of the situation back to the approaching troops. Hawk Man offered to perform this perilous service and at the imminent risk of his life, assisted by Red Tomahawk he effected his escape, being shot through his coat and gloves while engaged in the attempt.

This was the first scout met by the command. My orders were also explicit as to the arrest of Sitting Bull but contemplated no pursuit of his band. Therefore did not feel authorized to follow the Indians up the valley, especially as I felt satisfied from the report of Lieutenant Crowder that it would only result in unnecessarily fighting peaceful Indians away from their homes and that the withdrawal of the troops, together with the messages I communicated to the Indians to the effect that the capture of Sitting Bull only was desired, would tend to reassure those who were loyally disposed towards their Agent.

Accordingly I gave orders for the command to withdraw to Oak Creek, of which the Commanding Officer of Fort Yates was informed by courier, with the request that he communicate his further orders to me at that point. Previous to leaving word was sent up and down the valley to the friendly Indians of this movement, in order that they might avail themselves of the protection of the troops in their withdrawal to the Agency, which they did in considerable numbers. All the dead Indian Police together with their wounded and the body of Sitting Bull were brought in by me.

Upon reaching Oak Creek at 6:00 P. M., I was met by a courier who informed me that the Commanding Officer at Fort Yates with two companies of Infantry and ten days supplies, would reach Oak Creek some time in the night. Upon their arrival at 12:00 o'clock, I turned over the command.

I cannot too strongly commend the splendid courage and ability which characterized the conduct of the Indian Police, commanded by Bull Head and Shave Head throughout this encounter.

The attempt to arrest Sitting Bull was so managed

as to place the responsibility for the fight that ensued upon Sitting Bull's band which began the firing.

Red Tomahawk assumed the command of the Police after both Bull Head and Shave Head had been wounded, and it was he who under circumstances requiring personal courage to the highest degree, assisted Hawk Man to effect his escape with a message to the troops.

After the fight no demoralization seemed to exist among the Police and they were ready and willing to co-operate with the troops to any extent desired. The attention of the Commanding Officer is invited to the celerity of this movement. In brief the command marched from here to Sitting Bull's camp and back to Oak Creek, in 17 hours. This with the ground covered in getting into position and the demonstration to the right by Lieutenant Crowder, made a total distance of at least 70 miles.

It must be taken into consideration that the movement back to Oak Creek, 18 miles, was made very slowly. Thus it will be seen that the march out, including the movement into position, were made at the rate of over six miles an hour. During the whole march the column moved steadily, without stretching out or closing up, a most satisfactory commentary upon the drill and discipline of the two troops composing my command.

To say less would be a want of appreciation on my part of the command under my orders.

(Signed) E. G. Fechet,
Captain 8th Cavalry,
Commanding.

*No. 20. Colonel W. F. Drum to Major McLaughlin,
February 26, 1891*
(*Small, coarse, unlined paper, perforated edge at top*)

Feb. 26/91

Dear Major:

Have you heard anything in regard to an Indian wearing a ghost shirt[4] who came near the police and troops at Sitting Bull's house on the morning of Dec. 15th and was fired at by the police. The Indian escaped without being hurt and I have heard a report to the effect that he afterwards tried to influence other Indians to join Big Foots band by saying that he had proved the virtue of the ghost shirt and that all who wore it could not be hurt. The report goes on to say that he was the same Indian who started the Wounded Knee fight in the same belief that the shirts would protect them. This sounds like fiction but if it is true might account for the desperate attempt made by the Indians at Wounded Knee.

If you have an opportunity in the next day or two please make some inquiries about it & fhly yrs.

W. F. Drum

4. THE GHOST SHIRT.—When the troops reached Grand River on December 15, 1890 they found the Indian police and Sitting Bull's people engaged in a hot fight following Sitting Bull's death. Military reports state that the friends of Sitting Bull left the valley as soon as the troops appeared, falling back from every point "upon the approach of the troops, not showing any desire to engage in hostile action against the soldiers." Only one demonstration was made after the troops entered the valley. A single warrior paraded back and forth within rifle range to show off his courage and test out the bullet-proof qualities of the sacred shirt. Through the kindness of Mr. Frank Zahn I have learned that this man was named Crow Woman (Kangi-Winyan). He rode a black horse and carried a long staff in his hand. He wore a red ghost shirt and sang the following song:

"Father, I thought you said
We were all going to live!"

Crow Woman rode so near the police that Little Soldier, a policeman, who is still living, fired at him, but missed. Crow Woman rode on toward the troops then on the hill northeast of Sitting Bull's camp. This Crow Woman was the son of Red Blanket (Sinaluta).—S. V.

(*on back in another handwriting*)
>Ft. Yates
>Feby 26/91
>Col. Drum

No. 21. *Colonel W. F. Drum to Major McLaughlin, August 20, 1891, Enclosing No. 22*
(*Small writing paper*)
>Camp near McLaughlin's Ranch
>Aug. 20th, 1891

My dear Major:

Enclosed is a letter just recd. from Capt. Lee—It speaks for itself—After reading please return it to me—I am very sorry that he was not in Washington but in case he has an opportunity I think he will do all in his power for you—I hope he is mistaken about the friendship of Army officers injuring you—I expect it might be best to treat his letter as confidential but I thought you might be on your guard about the *spy* system—Now that Stewart is free . . . .

>Very truly yours,
>(Sgd.) W. F. Drum

(*Note on back—Capt. Lee's letter returned to Col. Drum in the field, on Sept. 2/91*) (*Sgd*) McL.
Letter attached on foolscap

No. 22. *Letter from Captain Jesse M. Lee to Colonel Drum, August 20, 1891*
(*Note on back: Aug. 20/91 Copy of Capt. Jessie M. Lee's letter to Col. Drum relative to Agent McLaughlin*)
>(*Copy*)
>Chicago, Illinois
>August 20th, 1891.

My Dear Colonel Drum.
Yours of 13th inst. has just reached me here. I have just returned from Pine Ridge and Fort Niobrara where I have been looking into the Indian Soldier business. I expect to leave in a day or so for the department of Columbia, and I hope that will conclude my traveling work. I regret exceedingly to hear that any one would think of making any complaints against Major McLaughlin; and I also regret that any credence should be given to such complaints, against the best Indian agent in the service. In my official report through military channels I took occasion and pleasure to say as much. I had heard much of Major McLaughlin's good work, but when I saw with my own eyes what he had done and what he was doing I realized that "the half had not been told me." The department should hold up his hands and support him and his good wife in their grand work instead of permitting anyone to try to pull them down. If I had the opportunity of seeing commissioner Morgan and talking to him I would take special delight in informing him fully as to my high opinion of Major McLaughlin as an Indian agent and a gentleman. No greater wrong can be done to the Indian Service to the progress of the Indians than to impair in anyway the influence of such an agent as Major McLaughlin is well known to be it is nothing less than an outrage. I will say frankly that in my opinion no flimsy charges would be entertained against Major McLaughlin were it not for the fact that he is a Catholic and in harmonious relations with army officers. These are, I believe regarded as suspicious circumstances in the mind of such a man as Morgan. I would write a letter to the Commissioner Indian affairs in behalf of Major McLaughlin but I fear that anything

from me would be regarded as presumptious and might increase the prejudice. My inclination is to write to the department but my Judgment restrains me lest my commendations might do harm. Do you known that at almost every Indian agency there are some persons who make private and confidential accusations against good officials? And it seems that the Indian Bureau rather encourages such contemptible proceedings. I believe the accusations against Major McLaughlin had their origin in this way. I saw Doctor Dorchester at Fort Bennett. I think I told him my opinion of Major McLaughlin. If he visited Standing Rock he saw for himself the splendid state of agency affairs there. I hope Doctor Dorchester will do Major McLaughlin Justice. You are at liberty to read this to Major McLaughlin and can make any use of it or any part of it which either of you may deem proper. I shall probably not be in Washington for some time. Please remember me to all the officers whom I may know. With best regards to Mrs. Drum yourself and Son.

Most truly Yours,
J. M. Lee.

P. S. Remember me most kindly to Major McLaughlin. I regret very much that I did not meet Mrs. McLaughlin while there.

J. M. Lee

No. 23. *Major George P. Ahern to General ————,*
June 20, 1929

The Woodley Apartments, 1851 Columbia Road
Washington, D.C. June 20, 1929

General ———— ————,
War Department,
Washington, D.C.
Dear General:

It is with a feeling of deep regret that I find myself

COURTESY, DR CLYDE FISHER, AMERICAN MUSEUM OF NATURAL HISTORY

Sitting Bull's Grave at Fort Yates, North Dakota

unable to accept your kind invitation to meet at luncheon your Indian guest, Red Tomahawk. My reason for this action is as follows. My first station upon leaving West Point in 1882 was Fort Randall, Dakota Territory, where Sitting Bull and 154 followers were held as prisoners in a camp adjoining the post. At the request of the Commanding Officer I took charge of Sitting Bull's mail, translating his French and German letters for him.

For several months I was in daily contact with Sitting Bull, and learned to admire him for his many fine qualities. Indian chiefs from all over the Sioux Territory came to seek his advice. I was always asked by Sitting Bull to attend these conferences, and found them most interesting, as they showed the deep respect in which Sitting Bull was help by his people.

During the Indian campaign of 1890 and '91 I was in the field with my regiment in eastern Montana and was shocked to learn at that time of Sitting Bull's death. I learned of the details from several sources, all of which indicated that he was killed while unarmed and offering no resistance. It was reported that an Indian policeman by the name of Red Tomahawk was the man who shot Sitting Bull. In my search for details of this incident I find no hint at a justification for the killing of this Indian chief. It was reported that there was some shooting preceding Sitting Bull's death, but of no great importance and such as could have been easily handled by the police detachment present at the time.

Hence my inability to accept your kind invitation,

Very respectfully yours,

(Signed) George P. Ahern,
Major, U.S.A., Retired.

II. UNOFFICIAL PAPERS

(a) PAPERS PREPARED BY SIOUX INDIANS

No. 24. *White Buffaloman to Sitting Bull, November 11, 1890*

Envelope:
State's Attorney,
Stanley County,
Fort Pierre, South Dakota.

Postmark:

Fort Pierre,
Nov 11, 1890
S. Dak.

        Sitting Bull
        Standing Rock,
        Agency
        N. Dak.

In pencil:
White Buffaloman

Printed ruled writing paper.
        County of Stanley

Fort Pierre, S. D.
Nov. 11, 1890

Sitting Bull Esq.,

    I understand that my rashens are stoped, and I am now under guard by the soldiers, and that they are talking of sending me off somewhere.

They wanted me to stop the dance, and I did not do it, so I understand that is what it is all done for. Will you let me know why they are doing me this way. If you can stop the action taken against me I will take it a great favor.

      Respectfully
      White Buffaloman
      (*Nephew*)
  (*In pencil and another handwriting*)

No. 25. *Brings Plenty to Sitting Bull,* (*Undated*)
Sitting Bull   Bird Wing
      Pine Ridge Agency
      Sent throught
      He Bear

Brother I am going to write to you today. I want you to come back but you didnt. I want you to come this time. There is lots fight going on at Black Hill I am in it all of them. We Kill lots white people and take away every thing they got. We are at Pine Ridge Agency.
The Rosebud Indians are very bad. if any body comes over the hill they Kill him so they are very dangerous. the main fight is going to be in spring so I am telling you this. so Keep a gun be ready for action. What I said is truth I have told you come but you didn't while the fight is last. I had three war horses but two of them died. the one race have still alive Lower Brule Crow Creek Rosebud Chyennes and other tribes are coming to Pine Ridge Agence in the Spring, and they going have a big council. relations think about this and make some saddle and be ready we going have a big fight.
 I shake hands with you all.
      Brings Plenty
 He Bear uncle try and come back. I remember my

grandmother try and Keep a gun and to defend yoursef.
                            Brings Plenty
                            I am.

No. 26. *Gall to Major McLaughlin, November 29, 1890*
(*Long ruled writing paper*)
                            Grand River Nov. 29th, 1890
Maj. James. McLaughlin
Standing Rock Agcy. N.D.
Dear Sir:
   Gall wishes to report what he has done up to to-day. —He says he held a council at the Mouth of Little Oak Creek yesterday and asked the Indians to stop dancing and send their children to school, which they all agreed to do. Running Horse in behalf of his band upheld Gall. He says he has employed "Hawk Man" and a fellow called "Onkce Wanibli" to act as Spies, with the understanding that they were to be made policemen at once. He says he has told you often about his horses and Wagon; meaning that he wants a different outfit; he says that he has not been to Bull's Camp yet, but he says that he will go up to-day and they are dancing yet up there, he says he brought a Wagon load of children to school today.
   He says he wants to shake hands with yourself wife and family, and signs himself respectfully
                            Gall.
On back:[1] Maj. James McLaughlin, Standing Rock Agency., N. D.

   1. Here follow translations of the Sioux scribblings on the back of this letter (courtesy of Mr. Frank Zahn):
   Ta houla   Rawhide
   Snaya wakua   Rattling Charge (Snaya-wakuwa)
   Tabanka kte   This should be (Tatanka-kte) Kills Buffalo
   Toka   Enemy
   (Wambli Nonpa   Two Eagles
   (Mato Kawinge   Retreating Bear

Notes in pencil: total 7 men & 8 *women aless* Nov. 29/90

Ta houla
Snaya wakua
Tabanka kte
Toka
(Wambli Nonpa
(Mato Kawinge
Takosko kicica
(M.K. tanke ku

He ton wha cinca
Mato ho tanka"

Wanbli cinca

One Bull told Eagle Boy not to tell anything about the council to anybody.

winyan kasu wha ko ujae
Zinbkala Mato hunku
Ite oga cinca kicica
Hehan gi
Wikmuke wakua
tawici win koska kici
winyan au koksila
Igoga *from* spot.H. Bull Camp.
There may be some children with them

No. 27. *Spotted Mountain Sheep to Kills Standing,*
Dec. 7, 1890 (Translation)
(Translation)

Takosko kicica With son-in-law
(M.K. tanke ku His sister
winyan kasu wha ko ujae (Can't make out this) wrong spelling
Zinbkala Mato hunku (Should be Zintkala-mato-hunku) Mother of Bird Bear
Ite oge cinca kicica (Son of False-Face, or with the son of False-Face.)
Hehan gi This should be Pehan-gi (Yellow Crane)
Wikmuke wakua This should be Wikumne-wakuwa (Rainbow chaser)
tawici win koska kici (Can't make this out, wrong spelling)
winyan au koksila (Appearing like a young woman)
Igoga *from* spot. H. Bull Camp—(Should be Iguga, meaning nigger-head stone) from Spotted Horn Bull's Camp.
He ton wha cinca (Wrong spelling)
Mato ho tanka Loud-voiced-bear
Wanbli cinca Young Eagle

Dec 7-90

Kills Standing

My Brotherinlaw, I wish to write you a letter today. There are 20 companies of soldiers at this place. And we thought of fighting them but gave it up until spring. Then is the time we decided on fighting. There are 10100 lodges of Brules. Now my Brotherinlaw I wish to ask you for some sweetgrass, so if you can let me have it I wish you would write me a letter. That is all I have to say.

I am Spotted Mountain Sheep
or
Wecinskayapigleska

Post Mark bears date Dec. 7/90. Pine Ridge Agency, S. D. This is written to Luke Najinhkte and was intercepted at Agency Office by Chas. DeRockbrain,
J. McL.

No. 28.   "*I Saw the Ghost Dance at Standing Rock,*" *by Robert P. Higheagle*

I was home from school and Lone Man, my relative, had some business with Sitting Bull and had to see him. I went up with him. He was one of the Indian Police.

I had heard of this Ghost Dance while I was away at school. One of the school boys had run away. They were very strict about keeping the children in school but this boy was gone about a month, at the end of which time he was brought back. When he came back everybody crowded around him. He was telling some interesting stories and singing Ghost Dance songs. He also wore a bullet-proof shirt. This was in the summer, 1890. He got the crowd of boys around and they began to sing these songs. I asked him one day about this and he told me they had started this Ghost Dance and showed me the bullet-proof shirt. It was buckskin with a picture of a crescent on the front and a picture of a buffalo on the back. It meant the buffalos were coming back. That is what they were praying for. The moon meant that every time there was a new moon that was the time to pray the most.

I asked him if he thought the shirt was bullet-proof. He said he hadn't tried it. Well, we had a game among the boys called Throwing Mud. We put a piece of mud on the end of a long willow. We would throw this mud and have fights with it. Sometimes when we ran out of mud we could use our sticks to strike the opposing players.

It happened that the Blackfeet Sioux boys and Yanctonais were going to have a match. They said it was not fair to have the boy with the bullet-proof shirt on one side. Then they said, "Now, we are going to see if this shirt *is* bullet proof." This bullet-proof shirt boy didn't run away at first, but we ran after him and one big boy jumped on him and downed him. They kicked him, took off his bullet-proof shirt, etc. They made fun of it.

Later I was curious about this Ghost Dance, so I went to see. We were camping near Sitting Bull's place on Grand River and there was a dance going on in the middle of the circle. There were guards all around the camp. Anybody not wearing Indian clothes was not allowed in the camp. We took out our saddle blankets to wear, but they wouldn't let us in unless we also took off our store clothes. So we stayed back. They were dancing, holding hands. After a while one fell down and they all stopped to see what he would say. He would then tell his vision. Then they would continue dancing until some more fell down and were given a chance to tell what they had seen.

I had an uncle who was one of the main administrators of this ceremony. He came over and asked me if I wanted to join it. "Don't you want to be saved? All those who wear white men's clothes are going to die." He gave me a feather to wear and wouldn't let me in unless I would discard my civilian clothes. Lone Man had a policeman's uniform. He called Sitting Bull over and interviewed him in his log house. He had some orders from the agent, I think.

This was the only chance I had to see the Ghost Dance. I kept this feather and every now and then they told me to throw it away. Later I went away to school and left this feather at home and my brother got to believing in the Ghost Dance and sent me the feather, telling me to wear it when the time came for the Messiah to return.

Sitting Bull was all painted up when I saw him. He was dressed in his ordinary Indian way, but he wore no feather on his head. It didn't appear to me that he was the leader. He was merely a sort of advisor. He didn't wear a ghost shirt when I saw him, but wore a blanket. He was very nice and invited Lone Man and me to supper. We went into a tent alongside of his log house. He had some cattle and horses there, especially the white circus horse he had got from Buffalo Bill. He had a deep bass voice. He was very kind that day, as was his general custom. He was a little bit shorter than Black Prairie Dog, but heavier set, about the size of Gray Whirlwind. He welcomed children to his home at any time but did not give them presents or anything like that. He was always very kind. He dressed very much like other Indians, but had to live up to his office of chief by painting his face, etc. and had to be kind to everybody.

No. 29.

THE ARREST AND KILLING OF SITTING BULL

Told by John Loneman, one of the Indian Police ordered to arrest the Chief. Translated and Recorded by his relative, Robert P. Higheagle.

One morning, the 14th day of December, 1890, while I was busily engaged in mending my police saddle at my home on the Grand River, about 36 miles south of Standing Rock Agency, Policeman Charles Afraid of Hawk of Wakpala District came to me with the message that all of the members of the entire Reservation Indian Police had been ordered to report immediately, to the Lieut. Henry Bullhead's place, about three miles south of Bullhead Sub-Issue-Station. This place was about 30 miles up the River, west from my home, and about 40 miles southwest of the Standing Rock Agency. Afraid of Hawk was sent to notify me in person.

I asked him what was up. "Oh," he said, "I have a hunch that we are going to be ordered to arrest Sitting Bull and his ghost-dancers, which I am very sorry to say." "That is just what I had expected all the time—something unpleasant would be the outcome of this Messiah Craze," I said to him.

I invited him to dinner—fed his horse—he was on horseback and I got ready. I had an excellent saddle horse—an iron gray gelding—in the best condition for service. I had him shod all around on all fours with "Neverslip" horseshoes. I named him Wacinyanpi—Trusty for he had proven himself a thoroughly reliable horse. My wife hearing the news became rather nervous and excited for she seemed to realize that there was a serious trouble coming.

Dinner being over, I bade my wife and children good bye and we left for Bullhead's place. On the way up we notified several police—Bad Horse, Armstrong, Little Eagle, Wakutemani, Brownman, Hawkman and Good Voice Elk and others so that, by the time we arrived at Bullhead place there were about 12 of us from our way and the rest of the 37 were all from different districts in the reservation. Of course, we had quite a lot to say on the way among ourselves knowing full well that we were called to take a final action to suppress this ghost dance which was becoming a menace to the Tribe. I'm simply expressing my viewpoint as one who had reformed, from all heathenish, hostile and barbarous ways, formerly one of the loyal followers of Chief Sitting Bull. But ever since I was about ten years of age and was one of the most active members in the Band for I had participated in good many buffalo hunts and fought under Sitting Bull against different Tribes but the most important fight I took part in was the Custer Fight. After this fight I still went with Sitting Bull's Band to Canada and after being in Wood Mountains two years I returned with the first bunch of Sitting Bull's followers who were shipped down by steamboat from Fort Keogh to Standing Rock Agency. We were not taken as prisoners of war—we came in at our accord after the Great White Father stripped us of all our ponies, weapons of war and in some cases, valuable belongings such as robes, elk teeth and other relics of our by-gone days. Even after Sitting Bull was returned to Standing Rock Reservation, I remained in his camp near the Agency, where I tamed down somewhat, received my share of annuities and rations as provided under former treaties and started building a permanent log cabin for my family as well as shelter for my oxen and a few ponies.

I also started a little garden where I took particular pains to raise corn and some vegatables. Major McLaughlin, then Indian Agent took a liking in my efforts trying the new way of living and at once appointed me assistant boss-farmer—a position I held for two years. I took a claim where I have been living ever since when the Hostile Camp broke up and moved out to different parts of Grand River to establish for themselves permanent homes. I was promoted to the position of private Indian police—a work which, they say, I was well-fitted for on account of my past career with the Hunkpapa Band. I merely say this because I was at one time one of the strong supporters of the Chief but did not join him with his Messiah Craze. I had adopted new ways and had discarded all superstitions and other old time customs and practices.

It was about 6 or 7 o'clock in the evening when we reached our destination. White Bird and Red Bear—Police privates, were assigned to take care of the saddle horses belonging to the Indian Police. These two were my relatives so felt quite at home with them. Lieut. Bullhead was likewise a relative to me and needless to say anything of his ever warm reception for me in his home. While we were all assembling two members of the Force from what is now known as Kenil District arrived. They were Shavehead and High Eagle. Lieut. Bullhead went out to meet them. There Bullhead and High Eagle were standing with hands clasped and lockarms. Bullhead said: "So, brother, you are going to be with me again." High Eagle replied, "Wherever you go—I shall always follow you even unto death." Bullhead said "Good."

It was a well-known fact that these two comrades had been pals from childhood up "sharing each others sorrow, sharing each others joy."

After our supper, when all had arrived, Lieut. Bullhead called a meeting and they all got together on the very spot where Sitting Bull was born many years before. Bullhead said: "Friends and relatives, I am sure you are all overanxious to know why you had been called here this evening and am quite positive that every one knows and expects that sooner or later we would be called to this serious order. I have this communication from Major McLaughlin, which will be read to you by our friend Charles DeRockbraine who is serving as assistant farmer and interpreter in this District." Here Charley, popularly knows as Chaska among the Indians, came forward and read the order in Sioux language so that everyone understood what the order was about. I do not think any of the Indian Police, present, could read or write in English or Dakota language. We all felt sad to think that our Chief with his followers had disobeyed orders—due to outside influences, and that drastic measures had to be resorted to in order to bring them to discipline. Personally, I expected a big trouble ahead for during the time this ghost dance was indulged in, several times have the leaders made threats, that if the policemen tried to interfere with the matter, they would get the worst of it for the ghost-dancers were well-equipped with "ogle wakan"—medicine shirts, which were supposed to be bullet-proof, and for the further fact, several attempts were made by different officers of the Police Force had attempted to break up the camp in a peaceable way, but failed.

During the month of August, when the ghost dance was in full blast, I became curious to know, the trust of this thing that has set my people "crazy." I in company with my brother, White Horse, made a special trip to witness the performance.

Having spent nearly all day, during which I had a chance to have a personal interview with the Chief and having satisfied myself of his deepest and sincerest interest with the ghost dance and as I have always been on the best terms with him and did not care to embarrass him in any way, I refrained from mentioning or asking any questions about the matter. I decided then and there, that if this thing was allowed to continue, some serious trouble would eventually be the outcome of it.

The order being for us to act about daybreak and as the night was rather long, we tried to pass the intervening time in telling war stories. The Indian Police who were on this campaign were a class of Dakotas who had enviable achievements and attainments and who on account of having highest estimation in the minds of government officials, missionaries, traders, as well as possessing good influence in their respective communities.

Daybreak was drawing near and Lieut. Bullhead asked that we offer up a prayer before starting out and without waiting or calling upon anyone else, led us in prayer. After this order was issued to saddle up our horses. When everyone was ready we took our places by two and at the command "hopo" we started.

We had to go through rough places and the roads were slippery. As we went through the Grand River bottoms as seemed as if the owls were hooting at us and the coyotes were howling all around us that one of the police remarked that the owls and the coyotes were giving us a warning—"so beware" he said.

Before we started, Bullhead assigned Red Bear and White Bird to have the favorite white horse of Sitting Bull's, (which was always kept in the shed or in the corral at nights) caught and saddled up and be in readiness for the Chief to ride to the Agency upon his arrest. The rest of the force were ordered to station themselves all around Sitting Bull's cabin for the purpose of keeping order while the officers went into the cabin and cause the arrest. Bullhead said to me "now you used to belong to this outfit and was always on the good side of the Chief. I wish you would use your influence to keep order among the leaders who are going to become hostile."

We rode in a dogtrot gait till we got about a mile from the camp, then we galloped along and when we were about a quarter of a mile, we rode up as if we attacked the camp. Upon our arrival at Sitting Bull's cabin, we quickly dismounted and while the officers went inside we all scattered round the cabin. I followed the police officers and as per orders, I took my place at the door. It was still dark and everybody was asleep and only dogs which were quite numerous, greeted us upon our arrival and no doubt by their greetings had aroused and awaken the ghost dancers.

Bullhead, followed by Red Tomahawk and Shavehead, knocked at the door and the Chief answered "How, timahel hiyu wo," "all right come in." The door was opened and Bullhead said "I come after you to take you to the Agency. You are under arrest." Sitting Bull said, "How," "Let me put on my clothes and go with you." He told one of his wives to get his clothes which was complied with. After he was dressed, arose to go and ordered his son to saddle up his horse. The police told him that it was already outside waiting for him. When Sitting Bull started to go with the police that, according to the custom of Indian wives and other women relatives, instead of bidding him good bye, the way it was done by the civilized people, one of Sitting Bull's wives burst into a loud cry which drew attention. No sooner had this started, when several leaders were rapidly making their way toward Sitting Bull's cabin making all sorts of complaints about the actions of the Indian police. Mato wawoyuspa, the Bear that Catches, particularly came up close saying "Now, here are the 'ceska maza'—'metal breasts.' (Meaning police badges) just as we had expected all the time. You think you are going to take him. You shall not do it." Addressing the leaders. "Come on now, let us protect our Chief." Just about this time, Crow Foot got up, moved by the wailing of his mother and the complaining remarks of Bear that Catches, said to Sitting Bull: "Well —You always called yourself a brave chief. Now you are allowing yourself to be taken by the Ceska maza." Sitting Bull then changed his mind and in response to Crow Foot's remark said, "Ho ca mni kte sni yelo." "Then I will not go." By this time the ghost dancers were trying to get close to the Chief in every possible manner, trying to protect him and the police did their best, begging in their way, not to cause any trouble but they would not listen, instead they said "You shall not take away our Chief."

Lieut. Bullhead said to the Chief: "Come, now, do not listen to any one." I said to Sitting Bull in an imploring way: "Uncle, nobody is going to harm you. The Agent wants to see you and then you are to come back,—so please do not let others lead you into any trouble." But the Chief mind was made up not to go so the three head officers laid their hands on him. Lieut. Bullhead got a hold on the Chief's right arm, Shavehead on the left arm and Red Tomahawk back of the Chief—pulling him outside. By this time the whole camp was in commotion—women and children crying while the men gathered all round us—said everything mean imaginable but had not done anything to hurt us. The police tried to keep order but was useless—it was like trying to extinguish a treacherous prairie fire. Bear that Catches in the heat of the excitement, pulled out a gun, from under his blanket, and fired into Lieut. Bullhead and wounded him. Seeing that one of my dearest relatives and my superior, shot, I ran up toward where they were holding the Chief, when Bear that Catches raised his gun—pointed and fired at me, but it snapped. Being so close to him I scuffled with him and without any great effort overcame him, jerked the gun away from his hands and with the butt of the gun, I struck him somewhere and laid him out. It was about this moment that Lieut. Bullhead fired into Sitting Bull while still holding him and Red Tomahawk followed with another shot which finished the Chief.

The rest of the police now seeing nothing else for them to do but to defend themselves became engaged in a bitter encounter with the ghost dancers. It was day-break and the ghost dancers fled to the timber and some already started running away into the breaks south of the Grand River. The police took refuge behind the sheds and corrals adjoining the Chiefs residence, knocked the chinks out, firing in the direction of the fleeing ghost dancers. One of our police was lying on the ground behind a shed when some ghost dancer shot him in the head and killed him instantly. This was my brother-in-law John Strong Arms, who came with me from our camp.

Finally, there was no more firing and we proceeded gathering up our dead and the wounded.

Hawkman, another relative of mine, a cousin, who hailed from same camp I came from, was sent to carry the news of the fight to the Military Forces. We brought them to the cabin and cared for them. While we were doing this, my friend, Running Hawk, said to the police: "Say, my friends, it seems there is something moving behind the curtain in the corner of the cabin." The cabin, instead of being plastered, the walls were covered with strips of sheeting, sewed together and tacked on the walls making quite a bright appearance within. All eyes were directed to the corner mentioned and without waiting for any orders I raised the curtain. There stood Crow Foot and as soon as he was exposed to view, he cried out, "My uncles, do not kill me. I do not wish to die." The police asked the officers, what to do. Lieut. Bullhead, seeing what was up, said, "Do what you like with him. He is one of them that has caused this trouble." I do not remember who really fired the shot that killed Crow Foot—several fired at once.

It was about this time that the soldiers appeared on the top of high hills toward the Agency. According to the instructions received we were expecting them but they did not show up in our critical moment. Maybe it was just as well they did not for they would have made things worse as heretofore they generally did this. Immediately they fired a cannon toward where we were. Being ordered to display a "flag of truce" I tore off a piece of the white curtain, tied it on a long pole, ran out where they could see me, thinking they would cease firing but all was of no avail. They continued firing and the cannon balls came very close to where I was that at times I dodged. Finally, they stopped firing and made a bee-line toward us. They arrived and upon learning what had happened the officer ranking highest proceeded to where Sitting Bull's corpse was and with a (branch/brush) took the third *coup* and said: "Sitting Bull—big chief, you brought this disaster upon yourself and your people." Louis Primeau was interpreting.

The soldiers having dismounted rushed to the camp —ransacking anything worth keeping. Red Tomahawk took charge of the police force and after everything was prepared to take the dead and the wounded Indian police as well as Sitting Bull's corpse, discharged us from this campaign, and having complimented us for doing our duty as we did, ask us to attend the funeral of our comrades, killed in the fight. Strong Arm, Hawkman, Little Eagle and Akicita were killed. Bullhead, Shavehead and Middle were wounded seriously. Seven ghost-dancers besides Sitting Bull were killed on the Sitting Bull's side.

About this time, some of the relatives of the police killed arrived and such lamenting over the dead was seldom known in the history of my race. Taking a last look on my dead friends and relatives, I, in company with Charles Afraid of Hawk, started for home. On the way, we past several deserted homes of the ghost dancers and felt sorry that such a big mistake was made by listening to outsiders who generally cause us nothing but trouble.

I reached home and before our reunion I asked my wife, brothers, sisters and mother to prepare a sweat bath for me, that I may cleanse myself for participating in a bloody fight with my fellow men. After doing this, new or clean clothes were brought to me and the clothes I wore at the fight were burned up. I then, was reunited with my family. God spared my life for their sake.

The next day I took my family into the Agency. I reported to Major McLaughlin. He laid his hand on my shoulders, shook hands with me and said: "He alone is a Man, I feel proud of you for the very brave way you have carried out your part in the fight with the Ghost Dancers." I was not very brave right at that moment. His comment nearly set me a crying.

No. 30. *"Note on Crowfoot" by Robert P. Higheagle*

Sitting Bull seemed to be fond of Crow Foot, his son. He seemed to listen to him a great deal. Crow Foot was not like the rest of the boys. He did not get out and mingle with the boys and play their games. He grew old too early. He was more with the old men and joined their conversations. For this reason boys did not care much for him. He was strong and healthy.

He was instructed to act as he did, I think. Many times the old men would talk to him, the old-timers and followers of Sitting Bull. I often heard them preaching to him and giving him advice to be like his father. He should be a help to the tribe and not go out like other Indian boys, but should stay home and get older men's ideas and follow the footsteps of his father. The old men were training him for chieftainship.

His father and mother also gave him advice. His mother was a woman who could not say very much. Her influence is felt on account of her good disposition and patience. That is, every woman would not have had so much patience with the number of visitors who came to the lodge every day as she had. Many people came every day because it was the chief's place and according to the old custom the chief was supposed to have an open lodge for anybody. The younger wife was also a woman of quiet disposition. I never heard of any of the Mrs. Weldon scandal stories. These are just invented stories. The younger wife was more inclined to be jolly than her sister, the older wife. Standing Holy, Sitting Bull's daughter, was like her mother. She was quiet.

It was my relative Loneman told me that it was Crowfoot who urged his father Sitting Bull to resist the Indian Policeman the day the chief was killed. You will find that story in Major McLaughlin's book, also. Loneman was one of the Policemen sent to arrest Sitting Bull. It was like Crowfoot to do that.

No. 31. *Grass and Gall to Major McLaughlin, December 15, 1890*

Ruled writing paper.
On back—Dec. 15, 1890—Chief Gall & Grass

        Standing Rock Agency, N. Dak.
      Dec. 15, 1890

Dear Major Jas. McLaughlin, we heard something about the soldiers But we haven't heard how we going to do about it. We'll camp all together here at Oak Creek But if any Gost-Indian come this way for run off please let us know what we going to do about it, and if you heard something bad about the Gost; Please send us about ten guns of coarse we don't want to run off: we stay in our places for hold our school Boys & Girls teachers. We want heard them things if any Gost-Indian come this way what we going to do about it.

Please send us 10 guns & send a note & tell us what we going to do. We camp here all together.
                    Yours respectfully
                         Chief John Grass
                         Chief Gall Pizi

No. 32. *Little Soldier to Major McLaughlin, December 31, 1890*
(*On back: Little Soldier Dec. 31/90*)
Ruled writing paper,
           United States Indian Service
                                        printed at top.
                    Standing Rock Agency,
                         Dec. 31, 1890
Maj. James McLaughlin,
    Dear Father:
        I wish to tell you something, I wish to tell something from very heart. I followed S Bulls advice and he ran me over a bank, but that is old now. My Uncle Gray Eagle has been giving me good advice for several days. The Great Spirit the Great Father and the agent there were his subjects to give me good advice. From this on, I will always look to you. I want to work and be able to buy horses. One Bull and I together own very near 100 head of cattle, with these I will become rich and look to the future. So Father my heart is good to think I will be able to follow my own judgment and be happy. On account of this I would like to know what you have decided doing with our horses. I will live to follow the good advice of you and Gray Eagle. That is all I have to say and I shake hands with you, with a good heart.
                    I am,
                                        Little Soldier

No. 33. *One Bull to Major McLaughlin (by Carignan),
January 6, 1891*

(*Ruled writing paper, letterhead as follows:*)

H. F. Douglas,	Douglas & Co.,	Douglas & Mead,
Post Trader,	Winona,	Glendive,
Fort Yates,	North Dakota.	Montana.
North Dakota		

Standing Rock Agcy.
Jan 6th, 1891

Maj. James McLaughlin.

Dear Sir:

"One Bull" would like to know what your intentions are in regards to him:—

He says he thinks you would like to do something to help him, but that it would cause dissatisfaction among certain parties who are down on him.

He also wished to say that he is, and always was well disposed towards you, but that his Uncle Sitting Bull, was the cause of his disgrace, and he would like to raise himself in the estimation of everybody, but does not know how to go at it. He thinks if you were to make him chief of Bull's Band that his influence would be of some benefit to you, and he would do all in his power to obey, and make his followers obey you.—In any case he would like to do some work, of any kind, and he cannot rest easy untill he has proven that he is a good man.

Yours very respectfully,

J. M. Carignan

(*On back: One Bull Jany, 6/91*)

No. 34. *Laurence Industrious to One Bull, March 4, 1891*
(*Long ruled notebook paper*)

      Pine Ridge Agency, S. D.
       March 4, / 91

I received your letter yesterday in which you ask me two questions. I am able to answer one. Kicking Bear and Short Bull each accompanied by 10 followers were taken east by Miles to remain there 6 years, the object of taking them east is to show the Ghost Dance and its effect if any. I understand they have danced and the general opinion of the whites is that the dance was harmless and would not have any bad effect and that a great many lives had been lost for nothing, and these people will be returned to their agencies early next spring. Taku-ta in sni is the only name I know outside of the two leaders—you ask me how the people here are. I must say that the present condition of the Indians is very hard, you see they never expected to return to the Agencies again as they had made up their minds to fight the whites as long as they lasted and consequently burned up their former homes killed all their cattle and burned all the hay they had, and now that peace has been restored they are suffering very much, to add to the misery, the snow is very deep. To see the Indian camped as in early life does one good they are camped in the Bad Lands. It would make you feel good to see them. It is possible that they will give Kicking Bear his dance back to him again. Bear this in mind. Keep your ears open this way I say this to you on the quiet. My heart Shakes hands with you Couzin.
    It is me.
      Laurence Industrious
      Blihica

(*on back*)
Copy of letter of March 4/91. From Laurence Industrious, Pine Ridge Agency to One Bull, Standing Rock Agency, Rcod March 20/91.)

No. 35. *Many Eagles to His Sister, March 5, 1891*
(*Ruled letter paper, medium size*)

       Pine Ridge Agency, March 5/91
My Sister we have always lived in tribulation, still you remembered me even though I have left you. it gives me great pleasure to receive a letter from you as it is just as if I had seen you. In addition to answering your letter I would like to inform you of something. It is in regard to the dance which created a commotion up there. it is the truth and will surely come to pass that is why the whites are so anxious to put it out. The nation are still in expectation. Now you must use every effort to come in possession of some Eagle's-down, and have them in readiness.[2] From the time the grass starts you must be on the lookout and when a thunder storm comes up you must attach them to your hair. Take care that you heed what I say. These five camps of Ogalallas who have inlisted in the U.S. Army. It is a plot amongst the people, for the sole purpose of arming themselves. Try to get arrows, at least. That is all I have to say.
      I am Many Eagles.
(*On back—Many Eagles From Pine Ridge Agency, Received March 15/91*)

  2. The Ghost Dance doctrine taught that when the Messiah came, the unbelievers would be submerged under a flood of new earth, or turned into dogs or fishes, while the faithful Ghost Dancers would be raised above the deluge by the eagle-down plumes which they wore in their hair.—S.V.

(b) PAPERS PREPARED BY WHITE CITIZENS

No. 36. *Mary Collins Tells of the Dances of the Sioux and the Influence Held by Sitting Bull*

A Short Autobiography

If I were to tell how I happened to become a missionary to the Indians and start at the beginning I should go back 300 years for I have several ancestors who were interpreters and missionaries to them. Thomas Stanton, one of my ancestors, was appointed by the King as interpreter in the Picquot war. Another ancestor was appointed by the King and sent to Harvard to study to be a minister to the Picquot Indians, learning their language and becoming a missionary to them. When I came out here in 1875 to Oahe I came in contact with the Indians for the first time in my life and I found that there was something in me that seemed to respond to the Indian and that I had ability to learn their language and even when I could not understand them when they were speaking I intuitively knew what they meant, then 'I decided that there must be something in ancestry which accounted for my liking for and ease in comprehending them. I studied their language and customs for ten years and was asked to start a school and enter into the educational work but I was not fitted for that, my desire was for the pioneer work so I chose that rather than the school work. I went to Standing Rock in 1885 when Sitting Bull's people were not civilized; they did not appear in the dress of later days but were wild and crude in all their ways. Before I went to them I had acquired some knowledge of medicine and had quite a little faculty for nursing and caring for sick people so that when I came to the Indians they welcomed me warmly as a "medicine woman." Sitting Bull lived ten miles from where I was and of course he was the head chief of the Indians. He was very much opposed to the Indians becoming civilized and so he came to see me probably to discover what my intentions were. He was very glad to find that I was a medicine woman and tried to have me agree that I would not have the Indians leave their old ways of living but that I should teach them to read and to care for them when they were ill; he urged most strongly however that they must not be persuaded to abandon their dances. This of course I wouldn't consent to do. The Indians proved anxious to learn tho and I started a little school and taught them to read. Ten or twelve young men Indians were especially bright and interested and we formed a little society; I entertained them at my house where they studied and became Christians. At this time the Indians seemed to have arrived at a period that was very favorable for this sort of work; they appeared to be just ready for something of that sort and received it heartily.

Antelope, one of the head chiefs, at about this time came to me and complained that these twelve young' men had not been attending their dances. He and Sitting Bull were very willing that I should teach them but they insisted that I should try and make the young men return to the usual custom of assisting in these dances which they held at all times.

I explained to him that I couldn't do this for him; that the dances were not what the good Indians should attend. Sitting Bull came to my house and rode up to the fence and called "Wenonah, Wenonah." I heard him but did not answer. (The Indians had given me the name "Wenonah," which means Princess when I first came to them and which I appreciated because it was a mark of honor. The oldest daughter of a high chief is called Wenonah and the oldest son Chasca which means princess and prince, respectively.) Again he called me and still I did not answer. Then he swung off his horse and came to my door. Again he called me and then came in. I saw him and spoke to him. He was a little bit angry and said, "Wenonah, I called and called you, did you not hear me?" "Yes, Sitting Bull, I heard you." "Why, then, didn't you answer me or come out to see what I wanted?" and I answered, "Sitting Bull, ladies never go out to the fence to speak to gentlemen, gentlemen always come in to speak to ladies." He looked down and replied, "Oh, I didn't know that."

The next time he came with 12 Indian chiefs from different parts of the reservation and I hadn't chairs enough to go around in my little house so he sat on one of the chairs and the remaining chiefs sat around in a circle. Then Sitting Bull took out his pipe of peace and offered it to the Indians to smoke. "Brother Sitting Bull," I said, (for he always called me sister) "I never have any smoking in my house so you will have to wait until after our conversation is over before you smoke that you may so do outside," and he put away his peace pipe.

During his counsel we talked of many things and Sitting Bull discovered that I was thoroughly enlightened concerning all their relations with the Government. This fact much delighted him and his chiefs. I talked over situations with them and told them the straight facts, not omitting details that were unfavorable to the Indians, for you know many, if not all, of the white people who talked to them told them only the favorable sides and left the disagreeable things out, which of course makes it much harder for the Indian in his unenlightened life to know just what his desires are concerning the government questions.

My counsel with the Indians was very satisfactory and I learned many things about Sitting Bull's individuality. He had some very indefinable power which could not be resisted by his own people or even others who came in contact with him. When I become a more thorough student of psychology I shall understand him better, but even with that knowledge I did have I comprehended more easily the character of the Indian Chief who was always so tender, gracious and invariably sweet.

About this time the people were much concerned about the dry year; there had been no rain for months. The Indians went to Ft. Yates for their rations and one day at this period, they were gathered together, Sitting Bull announced that it would rain. He took a buffalo skin, waved it around in the air, made some signs, placed it upon the ground and—IT RAINED. Not immediately of course, but in a day or two. I had some practice myself in discovering signs of rain but on this occasion I was not prepared from the looks of the weather to agree with the prophet Sitting Bull. He saw, tho, by some means unknown to the rest of us that it *was* liable to rain. This is only one incident which shows *why* people had such faith in him. His knowledge of the elements was very accurate and he was always shrewd enough to make advantageous use of these things to better his own power and influence. He understood the grass signs and could tell by observing it closely what sort of a winter we would have, whether it would be mild or severe. I remember particularly that during the winter of the Ghost dance he prophesied that the winter would be mild and said, "Yes, my people, you can dance all the winter this year, the sun will shine warmly and the weather will be fair." He told by the growing of the grass as to whether the snow would be deep or not.

At the time of the Ghost Dance Sitting Bull had a three days dance and notified all the people of the ceremony to occur. The dance became almost like the Sun dance and was continued from evening until morning and from dawn till night. The people gathered from everywhere for the dance. Thousands came to participate. Then it began to be talked about in the papers and created trouble at Standing Rock. When the Indians went for their rations each time to Ft. Yates the soldiers were all drawn up with great display and a cannon was hauled out and target practice was carried on. All this was intended to intimidate the Indians. All these details tended to excite Sitting Bull and his people. As the excitement grew, the dance became wilder and more excited. People gathered by the thousands and the dance became more and more like the sun dance which was forbidden by the government. To make the illusions more complete and to verify the dreams which Sitting Bull had in relation to this time couriers would come in on the gallop and address different persons and say, "I saw your father out in the White mountains, risen from the dead," and to others, "I saw your son, etc." Sitting Bull was endeavoring to make the people believe that he was a Christian and believed in the Christ as they did; consequently that a resurrection would come, not in the future for the Indians, but NOW and that the Indians, their ancestors were all risen from the death;

all the buffalo, deer and their best dogs were also again alive and that everyone now would live happily for ever and ever and ever as in the older days before the advent of the white people into their country. These couriers would shout that they had conversed with the different ancestors, sons, chiefs, etc. and the people were worked up to a state of wild excitement.

He told them that The Christ had come for the Indians but not for the white people; that the Indians would all rise from the dead but that the white people would not and that soon all the land would again be as in the time of their fathers. The Indians which had joined the Congregational faith were not so much influenced but many of the Roman Catholics were enthusiastic over the dances, and Sitting Bull, because he knew just enough about the Bible to speak with some authority, and because of the faith the people had in him from the other things he had fortold them which had come to pass, relied upon his word. It soon became evident that something serious would result from these dances if they were not stopped. At two villages in particular there were 'prayer trees' erected, at Little Oak Village and at the Village of Flying Bye. Mr. Reed, who was in charge of some of the Indians, erected a log house and held services for the people. At this time the excitement was so intense that all times of the day and night the Indians were coming to tell me of different things that were going on here or there or to warn me of their dances and the like. I could not even sleep with my clothes off at night for the reason that they came at any time to see me. I called one of my helpers, Mr. Grindstone, and said to him, "You go to the village of Little Oak and I will go to Flying Bye where these two main prayer trees are to be held and we will see if we can break up the meetings." Mr. Grindstone was a little old man but possessed a great deal of character. He went, according to my suggestion to the village of Little Oak. There he saw the prayer tree and hundreds, even thousands of people around it. This tree was filled with rags which represented the prayers of the people. Sitting Bull and the chiefs preached to the people and told them that if they did not believe all that they told them and if they did not dance with the rest that they would either turn into a dog or that the earth would open up and swallow them. At this time Mr. Grindstone shouted, "I don't believe it." The people stared, not knowing what would happen. Again he repeated, "I don't believe it. You see that the earth hasn't swallowed me and I am still on two legs." Then the Indians *laughed*. The crisis had passed and they all turned and went home. The laugh had saved them.

Now that the Ghost dance proceedings had gone so far the government deemed it wise to order all the white people into the garrison. All the white persons practically were gathered in except the Farm School people. I had gone to the garrison a day or so previous and when the government decided to order the people to come there they would not let me go out again. Word came that night that the Indians had come down from the reservation and that there was going to be a battle. They, (the Indians) had heard that I, too, had gone to the garrison and they said "If Wenonah too has gone to the garrison then even she has deserted us and there will be war." I wanted very much to leave the garrison and go back to my house and thus let the Indians still have their faith in my loyalty to them at least for I was not afraid of them. Colonel McLaughlin and Colonel Drum, who were in charge of the garrison, plainly saw the situation and asked me if I cared to go out and I told them that I did. Consequently they allowed me to go and as I rode over the prairie over each little butte I could see an Indian looking at us. As they discovered it was 'Wenonah' they spoke my name and dropped out of sight; we were not molested once. They were all delighted to think that I had returned to them. This occasion happened sometime in October or possibly in November and I was detained at the grarrison but a short time.

On the Sunday following I went to see Sitting Bull and found thousands of people gathered there. I held services with Mr. Grindstone and to this day I never hear 'Nearer My God To Thee' but I think of that dreadful time. Our converts sang the song in a wild rough way and the music, screams, and shouting of the awful dance were mingled with our voices until you could scarcely hear anything. The incident was one which would never occur again in a life time and would surely never be forgotten. After our services I went to the Holy tent of Sitting Bull, and asked admittance. He sent out word that he could not see me at that time. I replied that I wished most earnestly to talk with him and after a while he sent out a message that he would speak with me. He directed that I must pass to the left and not step on certain places. I went in and sat down as he told me and he continued performing other ceremonies. At length I explained to him that he must scatter the people who had gathered here in such a throng for this dance. I said ,"Sitting Bull, you know you do not believe these things that you are telling your people, you know that the Indians have not risen from the death out in the White mountains and that the buffalo and deer and your favorite hunting dogs are not alive again; you know that you are deceiving your people who have always trusted you. The law orders you to go to Ft. Yates and you must obey. You must go and talk with the officials there and tell them that you will have this dance cease. Otherwise the soldiers will come and kill all of your people. Your best warriors and men will be shot and the families will go unprovided for, and you, Sitting Bull, will be responsible for this terrible calamity. You must send the people home." Here I mentioned the names of the leading chiefs and pictured to him how they would be killed without hesitation by the soldiers and their families would die of starvation.

After this I went out from the tent and looked at the people screaming, dancing, and widly waving their arms in the air. One man whom I knew well fell upon the ground affecting that he was unconscious. I went up to him and said, "Louis, get up, you are not unconscious, you are not ill; get up and help me to send these people home." Louis rose and looked about him. All the people saw him obey me and of course lost their faith in the dance. Many of them turned to go home tho some still stayed. I think we met at least a mile of wagons filled with Indians returning to their homes. At least many of them were convinced that it was useless to dance and that what Sitting Bull had told them was false. Many were sent from the dance and others returned before entering it at all. This was the last occasion I had to see the people before the awful tragedy occurred which ended Sitting Bull's life. I think I was the last white person whom they saw before that time. Colonel McLaughlin and others were there shortly before but not at so late a date and when so many hundreds of people were gathered together when the dance was at its height.

If Sitting Bull had been left to himself, without interference of the white people, in this dance proceedings with what knowledge he had of the Bible it is not certain just what would have happened. He tried many times to compromise with me in so far that I would agree to teach his people, for which he would be very thankful, and that I must induce them to go to the dances as they had always done. These two things could not be done tho for the people whom we had converted believed that there would be a resurrection day and that the Christ would come sometime but that it would be in the future while Sitting Bull, with his winning personality and gracious presence was not to be resisted with his theory that the Christ had come for the Indians now and that they alone would rise. He made them believe, so far as he could, that the whites never would be resurrected and that if the Indians were brot to life that of necessity the animals would have to be also for without them they could not live for there would not be sufficient food for them and all their ancestors. He told them that they would soon see their friends and there would be plenty to eat for everyone and that all the Indians would hereafter live in eternal joy, and that they would go back to their old way of living.

Then Buffalo Bill came out after Sitting Bull, sent by the government. Of course others who had not seen all the circumstances did not realize the situation. Buffalo Bill was so drunk that he could not even express what he wanted to do. Col. McLaughlin and Col. Drum gave him a squad of soldiers and he started out to find Sitting Bull. Col. McLaughlin, knowing the Indians and their ideas, sent a messenger to warn Buffalo Bill that Sitting Bull was coming to Ft. Yates by another road. Buffalo Bill immediately turned back. This was only a ruse to dissuade Buffalo Bill from capturing Sitting Bull but he was ignorant of the fact and returned. That gave Col. Drum time to get Buffalo Bill sent away. When the battle took place the Indians said that Sitting Bull had found that the policemen were coming for him and that he had ordered his horses to go with them that he might talk with them. As he mounted his horses one of his enemies cried out, "He is running away." Then they killed him. They stoned him and pounded him until he was horribly mangled into a jelly.

After this I told the Indians that if any of them wished to go to the Fort that they must carry a white flag. This would be the sign of truce and the soldiers would not harm them. Col. McLaughlin told me afterward that when the Indians went to the garrison that they each carried a white flag and whenever they met a soldier they raised and muttered, 'Wenonah,' 'Wenonah.' He said he never saw so many Indians belonging to one woman before.

If Sitting Bull had not been defeated in his attempt to make the Indians believe all that he did he probably would have ended as many other noted Indians have ended. In the first place his chieftancy was not inherited and that alone made the people look down upon him. Gaul inherited his position and that made him respected. Sitting Bull had been raised to the position of chief because of bravery and good deeds. It would seem that this would cause the Indians to love and respect him but, while they obeyed him because he was their chief thru bravery, they did not at any time consider that he was anything but a common Indian. Gaul was a very different man. He was haughty and held himself aloof from the people. His character was stronger than Sitting Bull's but he never was as pleasant to meet and he lacked the winning personality which the latter possessed. Antelope who was one of the chiefs in Sitting Bull's time always boasted that he never fought the white people. Gaul was a relative of Black Moon who was also of the line of hereditary chiefs.

John Grass as a civilized Indian was not a strong character. He could make wonderful and stirring speeches; . . . . In the treaty of '89 John Grass made a strong plea for the government and was among the first to sign it and the Indians had confidence in him and followed him and after everything was over they saw that he was presented with a frame house and other fine things. . . . . He was a member of the Episcopal church and he thot they did not give as much as he thot he should have and sent for me. He was, at this time afraid of Gaul. It was said that Gaul had threatened to kill him. Grass gave out word that he was ill and did not leave his house for weeks and later sent for me to come to him. I went to him and he wished me to ask him to join our church. Wauketemone, our minister, who was an Indian and a chief by inheritance, also wished me to ask Grass to join us but I told him that if we did then when the other white people found it out and the Indians too, that they would think that Grass was a peculiar man to wish to leave one church to join another for no very good reason, and that I should not ask him for the white people would then be against him. John Grass told the Catholic people the same story he told me and they asked him to join their church. The

Catholics had a great meeting at his house and he joined the Catholic faith.

No. 37. *Grait Manitoo to Sitting Bull, November 19, 1890*

Envelope:
    Mr. Sitting Bull
    Standing Rock Da.
                      Postmark blurred
    In care of Mr. McGlochin Nov. 19, 1889
    Agent.

Ruled Writing paper
                      Mount Tacoma Wash.

    Sitting Bull dear friend—I send you kind greeting I have decreed you will be successful in your raid I am the grait manitoo. I would like to see you personly but I can not Come any lower then I am you Start in potter co Take Seavn dogs Starve Them 3 days feed them the hearts of Seavn Jack Rabbits Steep the hearts in oil of vitrel and carseen Let your dogs of war loos Scalp 10 percent A minute Every Chicken thief every Shack robber every oats Stealer every water thief Do not miss the long Traced puslits they will steal the gee string of your old Squaw when the blisard is blowing at forty miles an hour Make drums of thare cantamnated skins Make tobacco bags of thare rotton bladders Leave thare ribs stuck to thare backbones as I want to fry Rattle Snakes in them For the condemned Soles of the condemned Soles of decotareno
                      In Hadies
                      Your grait Manitoo

No. 38. *V. E. Parr to Major McLaughlin, November 21, 1890*

(*Half-sheet of ruled writing paper*):

LaGrace Nov. 21/1890.
James A. McLaughlin Indian Agt.
Dear Sir:

Inclosed we hand you petition asking that the Indians be not allowed to come on this side of the river. Our people are greatly afraid and some are leaving the country for fear of them.

Hoping you will give this matter your attention we remain

Yours Truly

V. E. Parr

On back: La Grace Nov. 21, 1890
  V. E. Parr
Encloses petition of citizens asking that Indians be not allowed to cross the Missouri.
Letter in reply Nov. 25/90
Standing Rock Agency (stamped)
Recd. Nov. 25/1890

No. 39. *Agent McLaughlin's Work* (*News Clipping*), *November 22, 1890*

Clipping enclosed:

AGENT M'LAUGHLIN'S WORK

Sitting Bull's Dances Stopped and His Followers Being Won Over.

Standing Rock Agency, N. D., Nov. 22—Major McLaughlin's visit to Sitting Bull's camp last Sunday has the effect of stopping for a time at least the ghost dances held in connection with the Messiah craze. McLaughlin received a letter from Bull yesterday and says he has taken his friends' advice and stopped the dances. He regards McLaughlin as the best friend he ever had and when he follows his advice he never makes a mistake. Bull's child is very sick or he would come to the agency to draw rations. He hopes to see his friend, McLaughlin, as soon as the child recovers. Bull's followers are growing less all the time and that discourages the old chief.

The agent thinks there is no probability of trouble at present and may not be this winter or spring. He is working hard with a corps of able assistants and makes strong arguments about the craze, talks to them, convinces them there is no reason for their belief. The rest of the band, about 100, he can draw away from Bull by argument. The agent is very successful in his method of winning Indians away from the craze.

People on the east side of the river are fleeing for their lives, and no man in pursuit. The excitement is all unwarranted.

Reports of a massacre forty miles south of the agency are believed to be unfounded. Lieutenant Crowder and men with an abundance of ammunition and rations for six days cross the river early tomorrow morning to make a tour of the country said to be infested by Indians. The agent refused to deliver rations to squaws unless the bucks were along.
Nov. 22, '90.

No. 40. *Abstract of Petition From La Grace, S.D., December 2, 1890*

Dec. 2/90
La Grace, S. D.

Petition signed by six citizens of La Grace asking that Indians be allowed to cross the river at that point for trading: "The Indians are always well-behaved & only evil disposed persons could have any reason to complain."

No. 41. *Some Man in Georgia to Sitting Bull, December 8, 1890*

Envelope:
Mr. Sitting Bull,   Postmark:
Chief Sioux Indians   Augusta Ga.
Pine Ridge Agency Standing Rock   Dec. 8 90
South Dakota

(*Half sheet foolscap*)

Augusta Ga.
Dec. 8, 1890.

 Sitting Bull, old boy, of course you are aware of the newspaper noteriety you have gained through your cussedness, and the uneasy feeling you have caused as an agitator—a worse "tater" could not be found.

 Now, I will proceed to express the object of this letter, which is to inform you that if the Military Authorities do not punish or cause the troops of the Regular army to quench your bloodthirstiness, there are 20 or 30 of us Georgian "Corn-Crackers" who will go up there & do you up in a brown rag. We mean business, & dont you "fordoubt" it.

 I tell you this as a friend & hope you will accept it as advice, for I dont want to see you hurt, and "I would hate to have to go up there to hurt you myself."

 You have danced a long jig now. You had better let somebody else have a chance.

 I will close now by telling you that if we hear any more of this monkey business, we are coming and the first thing we do will be to cut your right leg off & beat your brains (or horse sense) out with the bloody end of it.

Hoping these few lines will be a valuable warning to you, I await results of my effort to save you & your tribe from being wiped from the face of the earth like hogs with the measles. If there is any more moon-light hops, you will be swept away like the chaff before a jimmykane.

With due respect, I am, A preventor of cruelty to (you) animals.

P.S.—If you have time "when you have time" I would be glad to hear from you by letter. Give my love to Misses Sitting Bull & all the other cows.

No. 42. *J. A. McDougal to Major McLaughlin, December 31, 1890*

(*Printed ruled stationery.*)

                                                    Dec 31/90
            McDougal & Gunn
                Dealers in
                Hardware.
                    Mandan N. D., Dec. 31, 1890
                        Jas McLaughlin

Dear Sir As a friend and acquaintance I write you this letter.

We have strong partizans here and I would advise you to fortify yourself. As from what I overheard that steps would be taken to have you relieved of the Agency office you so abely filled.

They say here that you and Aungles has run matters at the Rock to suit your-selves.

It may not amount to anything but the feeling and —————— is right here and the Senatorial Contest may develope it &c. politisins will paw the cur in Bismark Soon—And in their sudden anger may include a fight on your case.

This is intended to be kept private and if it will benefit you any I shall be pleased—Your friend

J. A. McDougal.

No. 43. *H. R. Lyon to Major McLaughlin, January 6, 1891*

(*Ruled stationery—small paper*)
Letterhead First National Bank.

Mandan, N. Dak. Jan 6, 1891

Maj. James McLaughlin
Standing Rock Agency,
N. Dak.
My dear Major:

Regarding your trouble with General Miles if you will kindly tell me where I can write to do the most good I will send as strong a letter as I can write or do anything you may suggest to strengthen your position. I will gladly do it. With all due deference to Genl. Miles we regard ourselves as better judges at some matters than he is.

Yours very sincerely
H. R. Lyon

No. 44. *John M. Turner to Major McLaughlin, January 8, 1891*

First Natl. Bank (*letterhead*.)

Mandan, N. Dak., Jany 8th, 1891

Major James McLaughlin
U.S. Indian Agent
Standing Rock
Dear Major:

I note a little unpleasantness all around. Have no

doubt you are well fortified but if I can do anything, see anybody or write to any official or individual or in any way assist you I will be only too happy to respond to your request or suggestion in my most substantial manner. Trust it will all blow over.

John M. Turner

No. 45. *Newspaper Clipping, "Chattanooga Times," January 11, 1891*

HISTORY OF SITTING BULL
by
Bird M. Robinson, formerly secretary to Major James McLaughlin—(*Chattanooga* [Tenn.] *Times,* Jan. 11, 1891)

Sitting Bull, or "Tatankaiyotaka," was killed on the morning of December 14, 1890, by Bull Head, Lieutenant, and Shave Head, Sergeant, of the Indian Police of Standing Rock Agency, N. D. This is very generally known, and there is universal satisfaction over the fact. But especially is his death gratifying to those parties in charge of Indian affairs. This satisfaction does not arise from the fear of any great danger impending from him, but because he was an arrogant, obstinate, conceited.

No. 46. *John M. Turner to Major McLaughlin, January 13, 1891*

Printed letterhead Mandan Roller Mill Co.

Mandan, North Dakota, Jany 13/91

My Dear Major

Yours of the 11th inst. at hand and fully noted—I have this day written a letter to the Sec'y of the Interior expressing my views in the matter—Copy enclosed—I trust your sense of security may not be dispelled

Sincerely
J. M. Turner

No. 47. *John M. Turner to the Hon. Secretary of the Interior, January 13, 1891*

Jany 13th

Hon. Secretary of the Interior
   Washington, D. C.
  Sir:

   At the request of a large number of citizens of this city I have the honor to address you in the interest of Mr. James McLaughlin, Indian Agent at Fort Yates and to assure you of the confidence the people have in him and in his ability to control his Indians—The citizens are indignant that a General of the Army should request his removal upon the most superficial examination of prejudiced testimony. We are here with our wives and children and have great faith in any statement made by McLaughlin, as he has always been fair and truthful to his Indians and has their confidence.

Respectfully yours,
John M. Turner.

No. 48. *Arthur W. Tinker to Major McLaughlin, February 20, 1891*

(*Envelope:*)   (*In one corner in pencil:*)
  Major James McLaughlin,
    U. S. Indian Agent,   Inspector Tinker
    Standing Rock Agency,
    Fort Yates, North D.

(*Writing paper, printed at top:*)
Department of the Interior
Washington.

20th February, 1891

My dear McLaughlin,

I have seen your protest, and it is good. Don't allow any one to step on you without a "push in the face." I am of the opinion you are all right. Our Secretary is a dandy, and will try and care for his own. I leave here this P. M. at eleven for Indian Territory with a bag full of old battles. What a time some poor fellow will have when I get at him. I have watched you all through the late *tryal* to make large men, and think you got there all the time. I was just one day late to see the delegation from Standing Rock. Am sorry.

Give my regards to Douglass and all my friends.

Remember me kindly to your family. I hope to see you again in the near future.

Your friend,
Arthur W. Tinker.

To James McLaughlin.

No. 49.

DR. V. T. McGILLYCUDDY ON THE GHOST DANCE

It was a pitiable, disgraceful affair forced on Indians and whites alike by politics, graft and bad management.

I was in the field all that winter from November until February, as Asst. Adj. Gen. representing Gov. Mellette of Dakota with Indians, Troops, and settlers. . . .

Well, I had a devil of a time myself that winter. I was a "free lance" going and coming among Indians, Troops, and Settlers, the Indians friendly and hostile were all my friends, as were the troops, but necessarily I felt it in the air so to speak that I was more or less a "Persona non grata." I knew the past too well, and sized up existing conditions too well, and Washington and the Harrison administration knew it.

First thing, as a matter of form, I presented my credentials, as Asst. Adj. Gen., and Colonel on the Governor's Staff of the Sovereign State of Dakota, to Gen. John R. Brooke, U.S.A., who as Commanding officer of the Department of the Platte was sent in there with a thousand men, to protect Agent Royer at Pine Ridge, but I was all alone and had no army with me, did not even have my gorgeous colonel's uniform, and when I requested from the General permission to investigate matters, the old chap looked rather cross-eyed at me, and granted the permission, with the request that I would advise him of the result, etc.

The next day, Red Cloud and the other chiefs took me out to the "hostile" village or camp in the Bad Lands, and Red Cloud addressed the council, telling them that I was "Little Beard" who had been their agent winters ago, when I was a boy, which he did not like, and also that I had come from the army which he did not like, that he and I had quarreled a great deal, and that in those days I did many things as a boy, as *he* thought, just to show my power and authority, but my answer to that was it was for their good and some day they would see it.

Then Red Cloud stated, "I see it now, and if we had in those days listened to him we would not have this trouble now."

Then the old chief turned to me with the following words:

"Little Beard, we have not behaved half as badly as we did in your day, but you never sent for troops. Why have these soldiers been brought here, coming in the night with their big guns? It looks as if they have come to fight, and if it is so, we must fight, but we are tired of war, and we think of our women and children, and our property, our homes, our little farms, and our cattle we are raising. Can you not send these soldiers away, and if you will, we give you twenty-five of our young men you can take as hostages, and everything will be settled in one sleep."

My reply had to be, "My friends, I am no longer your agent, and I have no power here, I only represent the Governor, but I will take your words to the soldier chief at the Agency."

That night I went over the conditions with Gen. Brooks, and in a very pompous manner he remarked, "Do you think that you could settle this matter?" My reply was, "Yes, I think so. Take the troops over the Nebraska line, and trouble will end."

He replied in a sarcastic manner, "You have an exalted opinion of your influence over these people."

I then turned loose as follows, "Possibly, General, but I know these people. I have known them more years than you have days; ten of the best years of my life have been spent among them. They have my confidence, and vice versa. It is now November, a cold Winter is coming; this is not the time Indians go on the warpath.

"I took charge of these people in 1879, I organized the Indian Police, had the troops removed, and for seven years we were without troops, sometimes in harder propositions than we have today, and I won out; these

Indians are not fools. I cannot but regard it as a mistake to have run troops in here in a religious excitement, but you are here, and your presence will have to be justified, and it will be, because you are going to have the biggest racket you ever had on your hands."

He went up in the air, and had I not been there representing the Governor I think I would have been removed from the reservation.

The next night The Hereditary Chief, "Man Afraid" came to my cabin, with these words, "Father, fourteen winters have passed since the Custer Massacre. The children of those days are our warriors now. They do not know the power of the white man, as we older people do, and they think that they can hold their own. The troops came here, Sitting Bull in the North at once sent his runners through to us to stir our young men up, and unless the soldiers are taken away, we will not be able to hold our young men."

A few days later, Special Indian Agent Cooper, who had been sent out from the Indian Office in Washington to investigate conditions, came to me and announced, "Major, I have instructions from the Indian Office to investigate you on charges," and after argument showed me a copy of a telegram from Agent Royer to the Indian Commissioner, reading as follows, "McGillycuddy is here abusing the administration, inciting the Indians to disturbance, and doing me dirt and I want him removed."

Major Cooper was at a loss what to do. So, to expedite matters, I opened up on the Indian Office by wire through the Governor, and insisted on an immediate investigation, as it was a charge that, if true, should warrant my being led out and shot, but I heard nothing more about it.

The end of December came and with it the "Battle of Wounded Knee."

Riding in from the battle that day, to the agency, I was intercepted by a party of blanket Indians on a cross road in a wagon, and one of them accosted me in these words, "Little Beard, eleven years ago we made an agreement and promise with you that if we would give you fifty of our young men to act as police, you would have the white soldiers taken away, the police would control, and we would have a home government. We kept our promise, and you kept yours."

Then he threw his blanket off, and showed me a bullet hole through the left arm, received that day and from which the blood was trickling, remarking, "I was one of your police. Who brought back the soldiers, and what were they brought for?"

Very reluctantly I had to reply, "I am sorry, my friend, but I am no longer your agent." . . . . .

What was back of the Ghost Dance so far as Pine Ridge was concerned?

A shortage in the beef ration, resulting hunger, and a hard winter.

The Government Indian beef contract, provided that "all beef received under this contract shall be what is known as Northern Wintered Beef, i.e., fed for not less than two winters preceding delivery, on Northern Ranges." For experience had shown that the shrinkage on "through Texas beef," by reason of the severity of the Dakota winters, would amount to about 40% to 50%.

In this connection it should be remembered that hides, horns, hoofs, and bones do not shrink, but the shrinkage comes out of the edible portion of the animal.

In the previous October 5,000 head of beef had been received under the contract to be herded for issue and food during the winter.

In January following the Battle of Wounded Knee, I examined the Agency Beef Herd, remaining out of that 5,000 head, and found that the animals were all "through Texas Beef" carrying nothing but the Texas brands, and no Northern Ranch brands, hence the shrinkage and resulting hunger.

About that time Harries, correspondent for the *Washington Star*, happened along, and interviewed me, and he referred later in his paper to the Texas Beef matter, and that *did* get me into trouble.

Late in January, the "War" being over, I returned to my home in the Black Hills.

Along came an official letter from Pres. Harrison's Indian Commissioner Morgan, an ex-Baptist preacher, calling my attention to the interview in the *Washington Star*, and remarking "Your attention is called to the fact that during your incumbency as Indian Agent at Pine Ridge, many grave charges were made against you, and it is not to be presumed that with your memory of those charges, you will now make statements that you can not substantiate; hence you are called upon for an explanation."

I replied that I had a very vivid recollection of those old charges, as I had been tried before Cleveland's Secretary of the Interior Lamar on the same, but not convicted; but in that connection I failed to see how those old charges had anything to do with his feeding the Indians "through Texas beef" in violation of the contract, and I would look further into the matter and advise him."

I was at that time consulting surgeon for the Union

Pacific Railroad, so I got access to their books, and traced the 5,000 head of beef from the time the same was loaded on to the cars at Clayton and Amarillo Stations, Texas, the prior August, until received at Pine Ridge, and so informed the Commissioner.

Naturally I became a "persona non grata," to politicians, contractors, and others, both Republican and Democratic.

Late in November, when the storm was brewing, I induced my old friend Little Wound, a leading War Chief, to call on Gen. Brooke and Agent Royer, at the Agency Office, to talk over matters.

Gen. Brooke asked Little Wound if he was a Ghost Dancer. His reply was: "No, my friend, over sixty winters have passed over me and I am too old for dancing, but now that you have asked me that question I will tell you what I know and have heard about the Messiah and the Ghost Dance.

"There have lived among my people for many winters the holy men or missionaries whom the Great Father has sent to us to teach us your religion, and how much better it is than ours. They bring with them the holy book, the Bible, from that book they tell us wonderful stories, they tell us of the man who went into the den of wild animals, and was not harmed because his Great Spirit protected him.

"They tell us of the men who went into the fiery furnace, hot enough to melt bullets, but their hair was not even singed.

"Then they tell us a wonderful story, of how many ages ago the white men's brains got to whirling, they lost their ears, they would listen no more to the Great Spirit, and they strayed off on the wrong road, and finally the Great Spirit sent his Son on earth to save them.

"He lived with those white men for over thirty winters, and worked hard to get you back on the road, but you denied Him, and you finally nailed Him up on a great wooden cross, tortured, and killed Him. He was known as the Messiah, and when He was dying on the cross, it was promised that He would come again some time to try and save the people. These things the missionaries tell us.

"About two moons ago there came to us from the far North, from the Yellowstone country, a young Cheyenne, named Porcupine, with a strange story. He had a vision—in it he was told to go to a large lake, in the Northwest (Walkers Lake, Nevada,) and there he would meet the Messiah.

"He told me that the Messiah was a tall white man with golden hair and whiskers, and blue eyes, a well-spoken man, and he said, "Porcupine, I am the Messiah; my father the Great Spirit, has sent Me a second time to try and save the people, but when I was here before, they denied Me and killed Me. When the Spring time comes with the green grass, I am going to visit the different Indian people, and the whites.

"But this time I have arranged a certain dance and signs, and in my travels if I am so received I will stop with them and try and help them. If I am not received in these signs, I will pass them by.

"Now Porcupine, I will give you these signs and this dance, and you go ahead of Me and teach them to your people."

Said Little Wound: "Now whether Porcupine really saw the Messiah, or only had a pleasant dream, I do not know. I got my people together and said, 'My friends, if this is a good thing we should have it; if it is not, it will fall to the earth itself. So you better learn this dance, so if the Messiah does come he will not pass us by, but will help us to get back our hunting grounds and buffalo.' "

Then the old chief turned to me with these words, "My friend Little Beard, if the Messiah is *not* coming, and by his coming he will again make us a strong people and enable us to hold our own in this land given us as a home by the Great Spirit, and the white man is not afraid of that, *why* have these soldiers been brought here to stop the dance?"

I could not but remark to Gen. Brooke as follows, "Little Wound's remark, 'if this is a good thing we should have it, if it is not, it will fall to earth itself,' is the key to the whole situation. It means that they will dance through the winter. The green grass comes, with it no Messiah, and the thing ends.

"If I were agent here, I would let them dance themselves out. What right have we to dictate to them on a religious belief founded on the teaching of the religion of the white man? If the Seventh Day Adventists get up on the roof of their houses, arrayed in their ascension robes, to meet the "second coming," the U.S. Army is not rushed into their field."

Yours truly,
V. T. McGillycuddy.

P.S. Go into the highways and the byways, and spread the gospel, smite the heathen, despoil them of their lands.

I remember the remark of my old friend Mark Twain, in talking with him on the Indian question:

"Our Pilgrim Fathers were a Godly people, when they landed that day on Plymouth Rock, from off the

Mayflower, they fell upon their kness, they thanked Almighty God for the many blessings he had vouchsafed them that day, in enabling them to reach the land of liberty and free thought.

"Later on they fell upon the aborigines."

P.P.S. Additional from Chief Little Wound: "I try hard to see goodness in the White Man's religion, and why he killed the Messiah, for if our Great Spirit, Wakan Tonka, the Great Mystery, were to send his Son on earth to help us, we would feel honored, build a great house for him, and try and keep him with us forever."

No. 50. *C. N. Herreid on Sitting Bull* (*Newspaper Clipping*), *September 13, 1891*

(*Newspaper clipping—Name not given.*)

SITTING BULL

When the news was telegraphed from the Standing Rock agency last winter that the great warrior and chieftain, Sitting Bull, was dead, I instinctively exclaimed, he has been murdered! I was then nearly two thousand miles from the wigwam where the famous chief of the Sioux nation met death at the hands of the Indian police. A few days ago I visited Ft. Yates and there, unsolicited, heard expressed the deliberate judgment of men who were familiar with all the circumstances, that the killing of Sitting Bull was nothing more or less than cold blooded, premeditated murder. Not satisfied with the life of the old patriarch himself, we were told that his son, a mere youth, was aroused from his innocent slumbers in his aged father's tepee, dragged from his bed and shot dead while the agonizing cries of his mother and sister were piercing the silent night air imploring mercy from the judgment seat of the Great Spirit. We were also told that the feeling of disgust among the Indians for a government that tolerates such atrocities is universal and enduring.

Blinded by prejudice, intensified by perjured reports, the popular feeling against this remarkable red man was that of intense hatred. In striking contrast let me quote the testimony of W. H. H. Murray of New York:

Sitting Bull was the George Washington of the Sioux nation. Too intelligent to be hood winked and too honest to be corrupted by the influences that have been at work among the unlettered wards of our government, he stood firmly for the rights of his people. For a generation he had seen his people driven from the ancient possessions of their fathers, their morals corrupted by the vices of the white men, the race withering before the hardships of hunger and cold and disease. He was a standing protest against the barbarity so often practiced upon his people under cover of protecting and civilizing the Indian. He was a stumbling block in the way of the schemer and the despoiler of Indian virtue.

And so he was slaughtered triumphantly, by his own fireside in his old age, among those who relied upon him, and loved him while his voice was for peace, by members of his own tribe wearing the uniform of our own government.

When the future historian writes the history of the red man of the forest and the prairie the name of our great departed Sioux chief will appear among such noble characters as Massasoit, Uncas, Pontiac and Tecumseh. He was shot and buried, not like a great chief but like a dog, but let those who scoff remember that

"In that deep grave, without a name,
 Whence his uncoffined clay
 Shall break again—O wondrous thought!

Before the judgment-day
And stand with glory wrapped around."
Sept. 13, 1891.

C. N. Herreid.

(c) PAPERS PREPARED BY MRS. CATHERINE S. WELDON, AND OTHERS REGARDING HER.

No. 51. *W. J. Godfrey to Major Roberts, July 11, 1889*
Ruled writing paper.
Sioux, Nbr. 7/11 1889
Maj. Roberts,
Sioux Commission, Standing Rock Agency, D. T.
Dr. Sir:
I herewith inclose you a fair specimen of a letter from a female crank; and if it but provokes a smile, after perusal, its mission will have been accomplished.
Very truly yours,
(Sgd.) W. J. Godfrey.

No. 52. *Mrs. Weldon to Chief Red Cloud, July 3, 1889*
Yankton Indian Agency
July 3rd, 1889.
Chief Red Cloud,
Last spring I received an invitation from Dr. Bland in Washington, to come and meet you there. I am a member of the N.I.D.A. & he wished me to go and talk the Sioux question over with you and the other members. I was ill & could not go at the time. I had long ago contemplated a visit to Dakota, to visit some Indian friends. Some are at Cannon Ball now, some at Standing

Rock and some at the Yankton Agency. I was glad to get away from the busy world to breathe air of Dakota once more & to see the faces I liked to look upon. I arrived at the cannon Ball river and visited some friends 8 miles south of it. Sitting Bull was almost dyeing at the time & was reported even dead. He recovered and when he heard I had come sent a messenger with a letter. This letter was entrusted to the Agents son & ———, a Photographer of Bismarck. I heard of this letter 2 weeks later from Sitting Bull himself: *but I had never received it.*

Sitting Bull sent another messenger whose message was delivered 5 days later than it should have been. A third messenger came with the news that the old chief wished to speak to me but was too weak to ride up. Up to this time I had been ignorant as to whether he was alive or dead & much worried about him. The Agent had come up & seemed very friendly & commenced at once to talk of Sitting Bull although no one had mentioned the chiefs name. Said he was a coward, a selfish man, on ones friend, of no importance & a heavy burden on the younger men who were more progressive. He also spoke of Dr. Bland & said that he had no foot hold or influence whatever at Standing Rock. I did not answer, & I do not *know* whether he was aware that I am a member, but I think he is else he would not have spoken of the N.I.D.Asso. I saw Sitting Bull at Yates; he had come up 40 miles, ill as he was to meet me. He was glad to see me for he had many things to tell me. He has become a member of the N.I.D. Association, also Thunder Hawk, Hohecikana, Bears Rib, Wakinyanduta, Circling Bear, Matowaoynpa, Ceya Apapi (Strike Kettle) Black Shield, Wasicun Maza Wizi Hansku & Tasmka Duta. Many more would have joined but I had no time, nor chance to see them, but Sitting Bull said he knew they would join, but he wanted their own word for it.

It had been my intention to travel through the Indian country on the journey to the Yankton Agency & I told Sitting Bull of my intentions. He said that if I was satisfied and he was strong enough he would escort me to Cheyenne himself. The wagon was comfortable & members of his family would be in attendance. I accepted gratefully & he gave orders to have things in readiness. A relative of Sitting Bull, Mrs. Van Solen, suggested that we had better go for a pass for Sitting Bull as he could not cross the border without one. I reluctantly consented & asked the Agent for it telling him how kindly Sitting Bull had offered to escort me. He refused the pass & said that of all men Sitting Bull could not be absent from the Reservation as the Commissioners were expected & refused me the pass through the Indian country. I asked him if he was afraid of a woman & of a womans influence & threatened to report him at Washington. High words passed between us both & I rose indignantly & left the office. I dispatched a messenger to S Bull's camp with orders not to get ready for the journey. He came down then some how & I explained to him. He was very angry & indignant. Next morning he went to the Agent's office but did not see him, instead he spoke to Louis *Farrabault*, who walked him to the Guard House; hinted at the penitentiary & said he was intending to carry me off. The old chief was so much surprised and pained that his heart ached when he heard these vile insinuations. He told Farrabault how he looked upon me as upon his own daughter and would have shielded & protected me from all harm. I felt much disappointed & pained & resolved to leave Yates at once. Sitting Bull was so kind as to drive me down to the river as I wanted to cross over to Winona. His polite attentions & friendly words were heard & seen & straightway a romantic story was printed in the Sioux City Journal of July 2nd. A story full of the vilest falsehoods, stating that I had told Sheriff McGee of Emmons County that I purposely came from New York to marry Sitting Bull, that the Agent tried to prevent a meeting, but that Sitting Bull succeeded in seeing me. I never saw nor spoke to this man to my knowledge, in fact do not know who he is & he dares to circulate such atrocious untruths. All this is the Agents work. He fears Sitting Bull's influence among his people and therefore pretends to his face that not politics were his motives for refusing the pass, but my welfare & he took this opportunity to humble the old chief & make his heart more than sad.

In order to lessen my influence as a member of the N.I.D.A. he makes me ridiculous by having the story printed, in which it is stated that I should have said that I came all the way from N. York to marry Sitting Bull. Red Cloud, is there no protection for defenceless women?

Have the Dakotas ceased to shield their trusted friends. If a white person becomes the true friend of a Dakota must he battle with all the world? Last Summer I kept Sitting Bull informed of all the movements of the Commissioners, supplied him with maps and price lists of land, because I did not want the Dakotas cheated.

The Agent fears my presence & did all he can to destroy me.

     (Sgd.) C. Weldon
      Yankton Agency
        S. Dak.

I forgot to mention that Sitting Bull would have

liked to see you & that he says he will never sign nor will his followers, but that he is afraid some of the other chiefs may sign in order to become popular.

No. 53. *News Story About Mrs. Weldon and Sitting Bull (Undated)*
(*Newspaper clipping—Name of paper not given, No. 4,574.*)

. . . . .He has been a disturbing element here since his return from confinement as a military prisoner in the spring of 1883; but he has been growing gradually worse the past year, which is partly to be accounted for by the presence of a lady from Brooklyn, N. Y. named Mrs. C. Weldon, who came here in June, 1889, announcing herself as a member of Dr. Bland's society, the Indian Defense Association, and opposed to the Indians ratifying the act of March 2, 1889. While here she bestowed numerous presents upon Sitting Bull considerable being money, which had a demoralizing effect upon him, inflating him with his importance.

"After her departure she kept up a correspondence with Sitting Bull until early last spring, when she again returned and located on the north bank of Cannon Ball River just outside of this reservation, and about twenty-five miles north of the agency. Sitting Bull has been a frequent visitor to her house, and he has grown more insolent and worthless with every visit he has made there, her lavish expenditure of money and other gifts upon him, enabling him to give frequent feasts and hold councils, thus perpetuating the old-time customs among the Indians and engrafting with their superstitious nature this additional absurdity of the 'new Messiah' and 'return of the ghosts,' and in this coming Sitting Bull, whose former influence being so undermined and tenure so uncertain, asserts himself as 'high priest.' "

No. 54. *News Clipping on Mrs. Weldon and Sitting Bull, "Bismarck Daily Tribune," July 2, 1889*

SHE LOVES SITTING BULL
A new Jersey Widow falls victim to
Sitting Bull's Charms.

A sensation is reported from the Standing Rock Agency, the chief participants being Mrs. C. Wilder, of Newark, New Jersey, and Sitting Bull, the notorious old chief. Sitting Bull has many admirers and among them is numbered Mrs. Wilder. During Bull's recent illness she visited him at his camp, and when he recovered sufficiently to travel she made arrangements with him to convey her in his wagon from Standing Rock to the Rosebud Agency. It is against the rules to leave their reservation without permission. A person to whom Mrs. Wilder told of her contract with Sitting Bull suggested that she had better see Agent McLaughlin. She acted upon the suggestion and the Major informed her that he could not permit Sitting Bull to go about from one agency to another and positively refused to have the wily old chief accompany her to Rosebud.

No sooner had the agent refused than Mrs. Wilder flew into a rage, and declared her intention to see her political friends in Washington and secure Major McLaughlin's removal. Those who came from Standing Rock state that she used the most scathing and abusive language to the Major and accused him of using the Indians as prisoners. So abusive and threatening was her language that the agent politely ordered her to leave the reservation.

Mrs. Wilder is a widow and is visiting the reservation. She is a great admirer of Sitting Bull, and it is gossip among the people in the vicinity of the Agency that she is actually in love with the cunning old warrior.

Agent McLaughlin's position in the matter is unquestionably right, especially at this time, as Sitting Bull would surely prove a disturbing element at the lower Agencies during the conference of the Commission of the question of opening the reservation to settlement.

(From the *Bismarck Daily Tribune*, Tuesday, July 2, 1889, Page 3, column 4.)

No. 55. *Mrs. Weldon to Major McLaughlin, April 5, 1890*

Brooklyn, April 5th 1890

Maj. Mc Laughlin
Dear Sir:

You will doubtless be surprised to receive a letter from me after our not very amicable conversations regarding my intended journey to Cheyenne.[3] And indeed it is with reluctance that I humble myself to address you, knowing that you cannot feel friendly disposed towards me. I do so however out of love for my Indian friends and because you are probably the only person who can furnish me with some necessary information and possible permission. Even enemies can act magnanimous towards each other, and I hope you will extend to me the courtesy of a gentleman to a lady, and answer my questions with a frank yes or no. It had been my intention for years to spend the remainder of my life in Dakota among or near my Indian friends. Twice I

---

3. Mrs. Weldon here refers to her proposed trip to the Cheyenne River Reservation with Sitting Bull and his family, in order to heckle the Commissioners then trying to buy Sioux lands at that Agency. McLaughlin, as narrated in her previous letter, would not give the chief a pass to leave Standing Rock. Sitting Bull obediently remained at home.

have been there and returned disappointed. Especially last summer, when the most insulting libels were printed in a Bismarck and Sioux City Journal, and which[4] were copied by nearly all eastern papers and given to the public with variations. I am not of a revengeful disposition but I sincerely hope that the instigator of those falsehoods[5] will meet with the reward he so richly merits. It is such a brave noble deed for a strong powerful man (created to protect woman) to trample upon, to annihilate woman. But I must beg pardon for digressing from the original subject. After last summer's disappointment had grown less keen I promised my Indian friends to return to them. It had been my intention to take a claim on the "New Land" ceded by the majority of Indians last year, to build a house upon it, and have certain days set apart for Ind. women and girls to come to me for instruction in useful domestic accomplishments. My Indian friends however wish me to live upon the reservation and were willing to put up a house for me. They thought it would be alright. I however did not think it would be alright and declined to live upon the reservation; but would buy of the land ceded. As the opening of the reservation seems doubtful at present, I would risk all I possessed if I took a claim built a house bought stock and then—fail. I probably would not be able to dispose of first class paintings or plush lambrequins or be able to teach modern languages on the prairies. I would like to live on the reservation perhaps a little while, until I looked about me, and selected land provided it can be bought. I suppose there will be no timber-culture claims. I would like to keep my prom-

4. See above for these press clippings.
5. In her letter to Chief Red Cloud included here, Mrs. Weldon blames McLaughlin for these newspaper stories. Apparently, she still held him to blame at the time she wrote this letter.

ises to my old Indian friends. I have never broken one to them, in my knowledge. I will not go to Dakota however without positively knowing that there will be no unpleasantness nor opposition about the matter; and that if I put my foot upon the reservation it will be with your full consent. I suppose it is needless to state that I have no intention to become either Sitting Bull's wife or a squaw, as the sagacious newspapers editors surmised. I honor and respect S. Bull as if he was my own father and nothing can ever shake my faith in his good qualities and what I can do to make him famous I will certainly do and I will succeed, but I regret that at the present time he is so universally misjudged:—I would be under great obligations to you if you could conquer your dislike for me sufficiently to answer me regarding my intended removal to Dakota and possible short stay at the reservation if you approve or disapprove. It is a hazardous undertaking, and my boy is not quite fourteen years old; consequently but of little protection. Yet I would like to live in Dakota and imagine that I can be happy no where else.

Hoping for an early answer I am yours respectfully
(Sgd.) Mrs. C. Weldon
16 Liberty Street
Brooklyn
New York.

No. 56. *Mrs. Weldon to Major McLaughlin (undated)*
Envelope: Maj. McLaughlin to Mr. Goudreau
Mrs. Weldon (*written in pencil on the end*)

Notes written on old calendar memorandums: (small slips of ruled paper—dated at top in print.)
Wednesday, June 15, 1881

Maj. McLaughlin—
Sir:

Have pity on our Uncpapas & Sitting Bull. The poor man's brain is dizzy & he knows not w........ (*the letter breaks off in the middle of the word.*)

Monday, June 13, 1881.[6]
Maj. McLaughlin
Sir:

Please have pity on the Uncpapas & Sitting Bull, who has been under the evil influence of Mato Wanah Taka.[7] Have pity on him & do not send the police or Soldiers & I will induce him to come to you of his own accord. (*On back dated Sunday, June 12, 1881, but evidently a continuation*) S. Bull will surely accompany me to the agency: but please do not detain him his brain has suffered; but his heart is good. He will be all right now that Mata Wanah Taka has gone. (*Sheet dated Wednesday, June 8, 1881.*) My heart is almost breaking when I see the work of years undone by that vile imposter. I will stay here of my own accord for several days & see what my influence can do.

C. Weldon

(*On another sheet dated Saturday June 11, 1881, but still seems to be a continuation.*)

Miss Carrigan came for me but I thought best to stay. S. Bull said after she had gone that I ought to have gone with her. He was willing.

C. Weldon

6. The dates of these papers (1881) are not, of course, the date of writing (1890) but merely the dates printed on the old calendar memorandum pad on which Mrs. Weldon wrote—probably not having any proper letter paper at hand.—S.V.

7. i.e., Kicking Bear.

No. 57. *Mrs. Weldon to Major McLaughlin, October 24, 1890*
(*Small size plain white letter paper*)

                              Cannon Ball Oct. 24—90
Major McLaughlin
Dear Sir:

Will you be so kind as to give the pocketbook which I sent to you by Miss Carrigan to Mr. Robt. Goudreau(?) All was quiet at the Grand River on the 22nd when I left there; I think that all the disturbance was occasioned by the visitors from other tribes, *who* influence on the Sioux is most pernicious. By attacking and defeating "Mato Wanahtka," I have turned my former Uncpapa friends into enemies, & Some feel very bitter towards me. Even Sitting Bull's faith in me is shaken, & he imagines that I seek his destruction, in spite of all the proofs of friendship which I have given him for many years. In fact His brain is so confused that he does not know friend from foe. Circling Bear's influence over him is malignant & he has done his best to convince Sitting Bull that I am his Enemy, as well as that of Mato Wanahtaka. The latter is a nephew of Sitting Bull. This false prophet & cheat claims to have spoken to "Christ" who is again upon the earth and who has come to help the Indians defeat the whites. I believe that the Mormons are at the bottom of it all & misuse the credulity of the Indians for their own purposes. I have every reason to believe that 5 tribes are ready to fight. It is heart-rending to see how zealous they are in their faith of this false Christ, & reject the true Christ about whom I spoke to all the Indians explaining our faith. They believe that some terrible fate will overtake me for my sacrilegious utterances against their Christ. Poor mis-guided beings, so earnestly desiring to seek God, groping blindly for the true light & not finding it. If I had known what obstinate minds I had to contend with, I would not have undertaken this mission to enlighten & instruct them. It was money, health & heart thrown away.

I am very Respectfully,
C. Weldon

No. 58. *Mrs. Weldon to Sitting Bull, November 20, 1890*
(*Envelope—mourning*)   *Postmark:*
                                  Kansas City, Mo.
                                  Nov. 20, 90

Chief Sitting Bull
Standing Rock Agency
North Dakota.
(*In pencil: Found in Sitting Bulls house after his arrest and death—handed me by Indian police. J. McL.*
Mrs. Weldon)

Black-bordered writing paper.
                     Kansas City, Nov. 20th, 1890
Chief Sitting Bull,
My friend,
    My boy, my Christie, died on the Missouri River Steamer "Chaska." He stepped on a nail while we were at Mrs. Parkins; the foot got better; but on the boat he got cold in it & spasms & lockjaw set in & he died, suffering the most terrible pains. We could not land, the boat stuck on a sand-bar opposite Pierre, and when the boat could land, and the Doctors were sent for, it was too late. He did not like to die, but clung to life & to me; for day & night. I could not leave his side & held his hands until he died. I took his body on shore & left the boat at Pierre. Put him in a coffin & an extra

box & took him with me to this place, Kansas City. Last Monday the 17th we buried him here. All this extra expense has made me *poor*. You know that I told you I was no longer rich. Now I have nothing more to live for. Away from the Dakotas, my boy gone forever, what is there left for me? Unfortunately I cannot die, it seems to me that nothing will, or can kill me, and I would be so glad to go where the rest have gone. If I only knew where my boys spirit is. I never can dream of him since he has died, & before that I dreamt of him always. I sent White Eagle to you with a message before I left the Cannon Ball. I wrote you a letter too before I went & gave it to Miss Louise Primeau. Go and get it, or send for it. I do not want it lost. I also sent you a note from the boat, when we stopped at Yates landing, by a Yankton Sioux. The papers are full about the Indians, and that they may make war upon the white people. I have nothing more to say and advise that what I always said. I always advised you & your people for their own good and the day will surely come when you all will know it. War can do no good, only hasten your destruction. Oh, my friend, and my Uncpapas, you are deceived by your prophets, and I fear some bad white men who are leading you into endless troubles. I said enough when I was among you, you ought to remember my words. If I spoke harsh to you sometimes, forgive me; a true friends warning is not always pleasant to hear. I meant it for the best.

Plenty of soldiers surround you now, on all sides; Should the Indians make trouble, it will be bad for them. Be reasonable, & take care!

Remember my boy! He was the only son of your best friend; Mourn for him. Tell Hoheci-Kana, my brother, & all my friends. And if your prayers to the Great

Spirit are heard, pray to him to give me a speedy death, that my heart may find peace.

Toka heya mani win [i.e., *Woman Walking Ahead*. S.V.].

C. Weldon

No. 59. *Mrs. Weldon to Sitting Bull, November 23, 1890*
Envelope: Sitting Bull
  Please forward.

Black-bordered writing paper.
          Kansas City Nov. 23rd 1890
  Sitting Bull,
Once my best friend, what now? I send you an article cut from the papers it surprised me very much. I wrote to you informing you of the death of my boy. I addressed the letter directly to you. Did you get it? Since my boy is dead it seems that I have turned to stone. I could not weep until today when I went to Church; then the ice around my heart seemed to give way & I feel more human. When he first died I was strongly tempted to kill myself; so that my heart might find peace; but then I thought of my niece & nephew & how such an act would disgrace them; and our religion teaches me that anyone who would do such a thing would not meet their friends again in heaven. My boy has been taken from me here, I would not want to be separated from him in the next world. Then when I read in the papers that there would probably be a fight between the soldiers and the Indians, I thought I would return to you so that I could be killed also & with the Indians; but when my brain grew more quiet, I thought I would become a sister, and devote the remainder of my life to God alone, & to the memory of the dead who have gone before me. God took my boy from me, be-

cause I did not deserve to have him. I gave my heart & soul to you & to the Dakotas, & their welfare alone was my care; & my poor boy was motherless. Had I taken better care of him, he would be with me still & we could be happy; instead of that black despair has seized my heart, & it never can find peace again, until I close my eyes in death. If God only will be merciful to me I hope it will be soon. I cannot see the green grass here, nor the sunshine without a heartache, for my boy in his grave cannot see them. I have spoken to a priest here I want to join some order. He advised me to do nothing rash, because I might regret it. While I am under the influence of this passionate grief I might conclude to do that which I would not do, were my grief less; but day by day I feel more determined to renounce the world. What right have I to enjoy what my boy cannot have, what he can not see? I always had a heart for all unhappy people & tried to help & comfort them; but now it seems I am dead to all on Earth & only everlasting sleep I want. I wrote to Washington and stated how very small the Indians rations are. Your wife showed me what she received & I wrote everything to Washington, also that the Uncpapas do not get clothing. The major in his report to the Ind. Com. Morgan made many false statements about me & you. I send you the paper. He knew that he was lying about me while he wrote it. Will God ever punish him for his doubledealing.

    I wish you would try to live an honest, noble life, & do what is right in the eyes of God, & let your heart be true to those who deserve it, that when death comes to both of us we may not be eternally separated, but meet again in a better world. I have made great sacrifices for you and your people, & you & they have stolen my heart and soul away from my own relatives, & made their hearts bad with grief & jealousy. Should you and the Dakotas lightly forget "Tokaheya mani win" then all my years of love have been in vain. I send my farewell to you all & to my brother "hohecikana." [*Little Assiniboine. S.V.*]. I know he will grieve for my loss.

C. Weldon

No. 60. *Mrs. Weldon to Sitting Bull, December 1, 1890*
Envelope: Postmark:
                                              Kansas City
                                              Dec. 1 90
Sitting Bull
Standing Rock Agency
North Dakota   Please notify......(*paper torn*) &
                    give to him or member of his
                    family.

Small writing paper.   Kansas City, Dec. 1st 1890
    Sitting Bull,
    My friend,
  I do not know if this letter will ever reach you, but I am going to send it all the same, and trust to goodluck. I am so unhappy since my only child is dead, that I have no words to express my grief. You will understand me better than anyone else for the death of your own daughter left a wound in your heart never to be healed. If you want to learn the particulars of Christies death Louise Primeau will tell you all about it. If he had died on the Cannon Ball I should be more content; for then I would have buried him there & remained near my Indians, which would have been some comfort to me. Now I am far from all my Dakota friends, & from you, and my only child gone too. Nothing left to me.

This city is a horrible one. If my nephew & niece would not have returned here from Europe I never would have come here. It was the very worst thing I ever have done in all my life, & which will probably destroy me utterly. If I had only returned to Brooklyn or New York as I had intended last September & October, all would have been well & my dear boy might still live. When I think of it I become almost insane. There is no one here who sympathizes with the Indians; people take no interest in them. This is a very poor place & there is no business doing here. One could starve here. The papers make many unpleasant statements about you, & call you many bad names. My friends in the East send me the "Herald." That paper always speaks well of the Indians & you & me—instructs the public why the Indians want to fight because they are starving & because the Gov't does not fulfill the treaties. My dear friend, I am quite sure that you, do not believe in this false report about the "Son of God" who is to help the Indians. You know that I always warned you not to be deceived. I very much fear that some bad white people are at the bottom of it all. I wish that "Mato Wanah'-taka" would have come forward like a man when I was staying at your house so that I could have talked to him & convinced him of the truth of what I said. I fear that my poor Indians must suffer for opposing the Gov't. & fear for you. All the Mandan, Bismark, Chicago & St. Paul papers have been making statements about me which are quite false. Because I am your friend they denounce me, & even lay the blame for the Ghost Dance & the threatened outbreak at my door; & you know best that I opposed the dance, & always counciled against war, & opposition against the Gov't. I had not slept for months while in Dakota fearing this;

COURTESY, U. S. SIGNAL CORPS

Sitting Bull's Portrait in Oils by Mrs. C. S. Weldon

for I knew the minds of your people; but I always hoped you would keep your people in check; you had assured me that for my sake you would not fight against the white people any more. How I do regret having left Dakota; I might have prevented much unpleasantness had I remained with you. Since Christies death all has gone wrong with me. It is as if an Angel had left my side. And I feel like a poor Eagle shot in the wings not wounded enough to die & too helpless to fly. You know how many goods I had with me at the Cannon Ball. When I got off the boat at Pierre, with the dead body of my boy, I took but a small trunk with me containing some travelling clothes. I could not look after much baggage, so I let that follow me as freight. All my silver, & you know how much I had; all my valuable books & paintings, including your two portraits are with it. My clothes, beds, carpets & artist materials in fact all I possess. Our letters & all valuable documents. I arrived here on the 16th Nov. Now we have the 1st of Dec. & my goods are not here and noone knows anything of them. Captain Talbot of the Steamer "Chaska" "Abner O'Neil" promised to put my goods on shore at Sioux City & then send them by mail to Kansas City. I had paid for the freight until Sioux City; from there it was to come C. O. D. all the freight officers here have telegraphed to Sioux City, but no one knows anything at all about my goods. You can imagine how I feel. If I should lose my goods I would be poorer than any poor Indian. If I had not always helped others as I have done, I would not feel so bad; but as long as I can remember, I have done all to help others, whites & Indians, & gave my time & my money, & now when I am childless & helpless people seem to take advantage of it. If the Captain would have acted right I would have my goods long ago. All my beautiful Indian trinkets are with them & Circling Bears painted robe. I have nothing of value with me at all. I wish you would write to me. Dr. Bland & his wife wrote to me when they learn of Christies death & their letter did more towards softening my heart than anything else could have done. It is such a comfort to hear from one's friends when our hearts are bad & hopeless from grief. I have received letters from Mrs. V. Solen Parkins & Mr. Parkins & all my Eastern friends & Christies death has caused more grief among them than I ever imagined it would, for he was but a child. He suffered terribly & his dying groans are still in my ears & I will hear them while I live. If his body & I were only in Dakota I would be more content. I hate to have him lie here. Although there is always sunshine here & the grass green like in the Spring, I hate this city. The sky is black with the smoke from the factories & one can hardly look across the Missouri. Remember me to all our friends & if you see White Eagle, too, & Hohicikana my brother, & if your heart has not turned from me because I am a white woman, write to me as you have always done. It will be some comfort to me in my great troubles. I never gave you cause to be displeased with me in any way. If I spoke against the dances & war it was because I am your true friend, have seen more of the world & knew what the result would be. A true friend will warn, & point out the dangers. Did you let me ride my wild horse when I wanted to? No. You forcibly detained me for my own good. Oh, my friend, may the Good God who used to watch over both of us, open your eyes to the truth.

Address. C. Weldon

Care F. Schleicher, 1106 Baltimore Ave.
R. 406 Kansas Cy. Mo.

No. 61. *Mrs. Weldon's Address to the Indians—"My Dakotas," (Undated)*

My Dakotas:

When I visited you last I was ill in body and mind and I could not speak to you then as I will now. My brain is clear now, although my heart is very heavy. Everyone tells me that the Uncpapas love me dearly. I believe it, and thank you all. Because I love you. I have come to speak to you, once more. I do not want any Uncpapas deceived and you are deceived, and those who deceive you are leading you astray, leading you into trouble, out of which you cannot come out again. I have heard of Mato Wanahtaka and that the Son of God should come to help the Indians. The white people should be driven out and the Indians again regain their power & all their land & all the dead should come back to life & be with their friends again. It is not true. Your dead friends will not come back. Save your money & take care of the living. Do not make clothes for the dead, but give it to the living who need it more. The white people and those who do not believe in Mato Wanahtaka will not be turned into fishes or anything else. It is false. I, your friend tell you so. I love you more dearly than my life & to prove it I will meet Mato Wanahtaka & tell him that he is either insane, crazy, or that he deceives you. They say that wo does not believe in him, he strikes dead with the power given him by God. It is false. He may have some power, but it is the power that each one of you can have if he will have it. What makes the telegraph wires speak? It is the same power of the lightning. The power that is in the air which is in each man, only he knows it not. It is in Each mans brain, in Each man's blood if he will only knew how to use it. The white people long have used it. It is nothing *wakan*, nothing holy. It is quite natural. Let me prove it to you. Look at this Magnet. A piece of steel so bent that it can attract—Do not fear, it is not holy, can do you no harm. Now I have brought you a box in which the same power is confined. The white people use it to cure the sick: for Rheumatism & many other diseases. It removes pain, & gives strength. In the hands of a villain it might kill, & lately the white people do not have murderers anymore, but kill them by this same power. It is not holy, it is quite natural—& that power is in Each one of you. Mato Wanahtaka may know it and may use it to gain power over you to make you the slaves of his will; his strong will & you are the weak fools to believe him. There are plenty of white men who have the knowledge of making people sleep for a while then waking them up again. They appear dead & come to life again. It is the same power which is in Each one of you, if you only knew how to use it— It is the power of a strong mind, over a weak mind. Now about the coming of the Son of God to help the Indians. About 2 years ago a medicine man of the Susuni (Shoshones) who lived not very far from the Custer Battle ground, & Cati SO 'Ka Wakpe, he said a God would come who would destroy the white people & put the Indians in power again & (restore) give back to them all their lands, their game & all they had before. This Medicine Man of the Susuni preached this to his tribe & they believed him. The the Arapahoes of the North, on the other end of the Big Horn Valley, believed his preaching, then the Crows (Kangi) then the Cheyennes on the Tongue River; at last it reached the Sioux, & now a man at Wakpe Wasti[8] Mato Wanahtaka[9] tells it & that the dead will come to life again to help the rest. So the poor Indians save their money and make clothes for the dead who are expected to come back to them, & secretly they go down to the Wakpe Waste Mah pi Ya sa duta tipi to visit their dead relatives & Consult Mato Wanahtaka. Now my friends, listen, Do not be blinded & deluded (cheated) Mato Wanahtaka has no more power than any one of you & your dead wives, sisters, brothers, fathers, mothers & grandparents, your dead children will never come back to you & you will never see them again, unless *perhaps* when you die and go to the next world. Perhaps you will see them again! In this world *Never!* Many Indians already have gone to the Northwest & to the Southwest to see & meet their dead. Now I tell you & I know it that they have not met their dead. Their brain is sick with dreams & they are cheated into believing that which is not true. I who love you dearly, who have made greater sacrifices for you than any of you think of, tell you this because I do not want any Dakotas cheated by evil people who doubtless have their motive for leading you into trouble. It may be that Mato Wanahtaka himself is deceived by others. I will hope so. I should hate to believe that one Dakota would deceive another Dakota. I rather think that he is the tool & dupe of white people. I even think that the Mormons, who live in Utah, where the Safa Wicasta Oyate (utah) live are those who started it, & also one white man who calls himself the Son of God. I have spoken to Sitting Bull about him & warned him not to be deceived.

8. i.e., Good (Cheyenne) River.
9. i.e., Kicking Bear.

I will tell you what I know of him. A German (Iasica) came across the Ocean (Miniwanca akasam) He went West, I think it was Illinois. After a while he preached that he was the Son of God, Christ who had come again upon the world to help people. He showed the marks on his hands & feet where he had been put upon the Cross. Many people believed in him. Some gave him lands, some houses, some farms & some money. He is rich. Women left their husbands, children their parents to follow him. He preaches what Christ did preach so many believed in him & they all say that he is a good living man. He was born in Germany & studied to become a priest, but did not follow his profession, but came to this country & passes himself off for the Son of God. Some say that he is either insane or a great cheat. This spring the papers were full about him & some gave his picture which I saw. I think that after being exposed he possibly has few followers among the white people now, & is trying his wiles (cheating) upon the Indians. He might even color his face & body, & stain his hair in order to pass himself off for an Indian. For a while his headquarters were in Illinois not very far from Chicago—I suppose he travels around, perhaps among Indian tribes, & he certainly does a great deal of *mischief in deceiving the Indians*. The true Son of God was crucified & went to Heaven nearly 2 thousand years ago. (Waniyetu Keklopa Winge nonpa Ketama). He will not come again until the End of the World (perhaps?) If the true Son of God was upon this Earth I would go from one end to the other to meet him & worship him. Not because I am a pious woman, but because I have not been true to him, not worshipped him, not obeyed him. To be forgiven by him & to look upon his face I would go all over the world. But he is in Heaven & only there will all good people meet him. There is no Son of God in shape of man upon this world *now* to help either white people or Indians The true Son of God told all the people to avoid war & blood-shed to be mild & gentle & loving to one another & to forgive wrongs. That God would avenge all wrongs & to him should man leave it. Anyone who preaches of wars, of destruction & death could not be Christ, the Son of God. Christ when he was upon the Earth healed people & made the dead live again. (cured) He never destroyed those who did not believe in him. He gave life *to all and death to none.* It is my firm belief that this deceiver, this German (with the Mormons) perhaps is using the belief of the Christians & corrupting it to deceive the Indians, with the help of other Indians who are either themselves deceived or are paid for deceiving the rest. I am willing to meet this false prophet at any time, to face him, & I am not afraid of his power.

End

No. 62. *Miscellaneous Notes in Sioux and English in Mrs. Weldon's Handwriting, Found in Sitting Bull's Cabin After His Death*[10]

Have the Dakotas heard of the White people of the West who have many wives? Do you not think that they might want to use the Dakotas as tools for their own purposes? & when the Dakotas have helped them & done their duty, they will then throuw them away again & perhaps fight them.

10. Obviously, Mrs. Weldon was not yet master of the Sioux tongue. Many of her notes are illegible and unintelligible. The following items may be made out:

    ma cuitan (Macuwita)—I am chilly.
    eya Tka . .They said
    Pte san mani Wicasa—White buffalo walking man
    Wakpe waste he tipi tawa—Lodge of Pretty Creek

The reference to Chaska was her reply to Sitting Bull when he asked her to marry him, and reminded her that Chaska (another Sioux) had married a white woman.

S. Bulls heart, secret, not open like to a friend, but secret, like to an Enemy. I am like an open book to him & have been all these years, & not one thought of my mind has been secret to him.

If Mato Wanahtaka is sent by the true God, then may he strike me dead. If he preaches false & deceives then May the true God expose & confound him.

---

ma cuitan—I am cold, chilly
eya tka—he or she said

---

tokeca, tehan wanica inkle wacui

Kappea-/memorandum of what to say to S. B. Hectaku Ohan Wakau Warica—Wo winihan
    wonderful—Wanica   Owewakan—a lie

Tokeca Occiya Kin kte. I will tell you about it presently.

Niye it Kokim Wan—To meet you I come.

Impahent Wacan 'tanka, inah 'ne

You had no business to tell me of Chaska. Is that the Reward for so many years of faithful friendship which I have proved to you?

[*The following are the Sioux notes on the back of a page noted above*]
    Mato Wanah'taka. Heuta Wakpam ne. Totantka Tatanka Isipi

Pte san mani—Wicasta—
———————

Cuive ku sold Sister—Wacin ga nuns
                            Insane
Gnas 'kinyan—craza tempass ame
———————
        anka
Gacanca naic auka—trot x nau aka
                  gallop
Main's—walk
———————

Yanayan—to cheat
Owa Kanka—also cheat
———————

Eyi Jate—forked tongue
Leji nonpa—double meaning
Bury—Wicahapi (grave) on the Earth
Mato Wa nah' taka Mins conjos wicaster
Wakpe Waste he tipi tawa
Ici mani—travel around, visit
He ska—takn he? (White Butte's)
  I think myself just as great as Sitting Bull & my Hankake have been much greater.

PART II

INFORMATION WITH REGARD TO SIOUX INDIAN HISTORY, COMPILED FROM STATEMENTS OF INDIAN AND WHITE EYE-WITNESSES

PREFATORY NOTE
PART II

Inasmuch as the second part of this book presents information gathered largely from Indian eye-witnesses to the events narrated, it seems proper here to give the reader some account of how this information was collected.

I spent five years in research while preparing to write my biography of Sitting Bull. During that time I interviewed more than one hundred old Indians who had known him personally. My study was pursued not merely among the members of Sitting Bull's own family, band, tribe and nation, but among all other Indian nations with which he had contact both in this country and in Canada.

Research in Canada is a simple matter if one is armed with proper credentials from the Commissioner of Indian Affairs. The Indians in Western Canada, at any rate, regard the officials of the Dominion with confidence and respect. One has only to enter a camp of strange Indians there, find some young man who understands English, present one's credentials, and the trick is done. The young man will assemble the chiefs and elders of the village, exhibit one's papers, and declare impressively, "He has authority." The old men will then drop whatever they are doing and devote themselves to answering the questions of the investigator. No time need be wasted in making personal friends or in awaiting the slow growth of confidence.

In the States one finds a very different situation. The Indians here, as a result of their treatment by officials of the U. S. Government and by white citizens, are distrustful, suspicious, unfriendly, and reticent. As a result it is almost an axiom that a stranger among them will be met with silence and distrust or offered misinformation. Indians do not like strangers and prefer to have nothing to do with then. They are a sensitive, soft-spoken, well-mannered folk who intensely dislike the back-slapping, hand-shaking type of man. If they can get rid of him in no other way, they will do so by talking, and have their revenge by misleading their questioner. It is therefore necessary to have an introduction from some old friend in whom they have complete confidence. This is the first step and opens the door.

The introduction, however, is no more than an introduction, and time is required for the Indian to form his own opinion of his new acquaintance and to decide whether or not he is worthy of confidence. Indians know that they have been much misrepresented and misunderstood by white men. They have the sensitiveness of a conquered people, and are unwilling to lend themselves to any enterprise which may result in a caricature of their nation. Every white man is judged by his conduct and must pass the test for himself. If the Indian finds the white man deceitful, he can hardly be expected to be honest himself where so much is at stake. It is therefore essential that an investigator among the Indians be absolutely a man of his word in dealing with them and make no promises which are not fulfilled to the letter. The Plains Indian is objective in his thinking, and any statement not literally true is, in his eyes, a lie. Even the most casual weather forecast, for example, must be prefixed by a "maybeso"; for, if the promise of rain is not fulfilled, the Indian may feel that the man who made the forecast has deceived him. As Buffalo Bill stated in a press interview, "The whole secret of treating with Indians is to be honest with them and do as you agree." After I have spent some weeks in an Indian camp my wife complains that I am unendurable; she cannot get me to make a definite statement about anything not absolutely certain!

Old time Indians are themselves men of their word. For fully thirty years, I have been more or less intimate with Plains Indians. During all that time I have never known an old Indian to fail to keep his promise or to miss an appointment with me. I have lived in their camps for weeks at a time, and have left my property stacked on the prairie there day and night during my absence, and never once had anything stolen from me. I say, without hesitation, that I have never visited a white community, in Europe or in the States, where such high standards of honesty obtain. The problem therefore is primarily one of gaining the confidence of the men whom one wishes to question. Once that is done, everything else follows.

Of course one must take into consideration the standards of Indians, their scorn of any man who has not gone to war, and their veneration for the old. A young man is not regarded with much respect by Indians, particularly those older than himself. Indeed, the veneration for the old among Indians is such that it is almost impossible for a young man to bring himself to contradict or argue with an older man. Fortunately for me,

I had been an army officer, and had a sufficient number of gray hairs to inspire respect.

As Frederick Remington has well said: "There is a dignity about the social intercourse of old Indians which reminds one of a stroll through a winter forest." The Indian fought and worked for glory, not for wealth or power. Prestige was his goal. No one who fails to bear this in mind can possibly succeed in holding the confidence of old-time Sioux and Cheyennes. Ridicule is the most intolerable of insults to them, and anyone who approaches them with condescension might just as well remain at home. However, no one who knows them well and can appreciate their qualities will be inclined to regard them with any such feeling. The more one knows of them the more one will like and respect them, for, as a Jesuit Father put it long ago, "they are all gentlemen"—proud, courteous, and hospitable to an unbelievable degree, in spite of their poverty. I do not think that one can find in the civilized world, men with a higher sense of honor, or men who more consistently live up to their code. Within the limits of their interests they are intelligent, and some of them have very keen minds indeed.

Because of their objective way of thinking and their fear of ridicule in case they make a misstatement, many of them have excellent memories, such as one finds among illiterates everywhere. Very few of these old-timers can be induced to repeat hearsay; I have often been compelled to drive half a day to visit some eye-witness to an event with which my first informant was perfectly familiar, but of which he would not speak because he had no first-hand knowledge. And in all matters of warfare, old warriors generally insist on having two Indian witnesses present to attest their statements, so that, if the white man should misquote them, their reputation for veracity in the tribe will not suffer.

It is therefore essential that some arrangements be made in advance for interviews, so that all statements may be made seriously and before proper witnesses. One cannot expect a chief to unburden himself on such vital matters in casual conversation at a chance meeting. One cannot hurry an Indian.

I will now give some account of my ordinary procedure in obtaining the statements of old Indians as to their tribal history. Let us assume that I have already been introduced by someone in whom they have confidence, that I have been known to them long enough to demonstrate my sincerity and seriousness, and that they have agreed to make statements on the matters under discussion. I then ask the old man to choose an interpreter in whom he has confidence. I have found that this is a vital matter. If the investigator comes to an old Indian with an interpreter engaged in advance, the matter will not run so smoothly. It may be that the interpreter belongs to a band or a family for which the old man has scant respect, or with which he or his relatives have at some time had a disagreement. In that case the old man is likely to feel a reluctance to talk, and the interpreter, wishing to earn his pay, will press him and so make things worse than they were. There is much rivalry between bands and tribes and families, and in some cases hard feeling. It is therefore best to let the old man choose his interpreter, and to pay the interpreter handsomely, so that all parties will enter upon the work with the utmost good feeling.

There is another advantage in letting the old man choose his interpreter; namely, that he is likely to choose a man past middle life who understands the old-time Sioux speech much better than a school-boy or a younger man can possibly do. Though the vocabulary of modern Sioux does not differ greatly from that of the older men, the meanings attached to words nowadays often are quite different from those understood by older men. Of course it may happen that the old chief, not knowing any English, will select an interpreter with an imperfect command of that language, but this disadvantage may easily be overcome if one privately engages a more competent interpreter to drop in and listen to the talk in progress. Though this privately engaged interpreter will say nothing during the talks, he will observe any errors and afterward inform the investigator as to points which should be corrected or cleared up. This adds somewhat to the expense of investigation, but is far preferable to forcing the old man to work with an interpreter whom he does not like and trust. If, for any reason, the old man becomes dissatisfied with the interpreter, the interpreter must go. It is obviously important that the old man should feel perfectly at ease during the discussions.

Of course, under the conditions of Indian social life, any man who wishes feels free to drop in and listen, and when an important chief is talking, his cabin will probably be crowded with listeners, some of whom took part in the events he is narrating. If these men are reputable and important they may sometimes offer suggestions and additions to the story. But the investigator should not question them himself; he should leave such matters to the main informant. Indians are sensitive, and do not like interruptions or corrections. Moreover, one may be sure that, if any error *is* made, those who know of it will be certain to come around later and offer their suggestions on the matter.

Because of this insistence upon personal dignity among old Indians one must take great care to begin one's investigation in any given camp with the most important warrior or chief there present. For, if one begins by questioning some unimportant or inferior man, the big chiefs may very likely refuse to talk, on the plea that they do not like to contradict statements of other warriors. In short, a considerable understanding of the rating of various chiefs and warriors is an essential preliminary to any real success in research. When the big chief has spoken, one may then turn to others for corroboration and additional data; but such research, as a rule, must be conducted with one man at a time.

I have made it a rule not to pay for information, thus putting a premium upon talk. But whenever I feel that the informant is growing weary I generally arrange to make him some present which will put him in good spirits again. For example, if I find that he is in debt at the trader's for some elk skins, I drop in and settle the debt. Not infrequently I have already sent the family a box of gifts during the winter before my summer's research begins. I have found the chiefs anything but greedy, but their wives sometimes make trouble by complaining that the interpreter is getting more money than their lord and master. A few presents at such a crisis generally put things straight. I make it a rule to carry with me strings of scarlet beads, red combs, butcher knives, and other things desired by Indian women and children, and whenever a relative of the informant or interpreter drops in to greet me, I secure their good will by small presents of this sort. Indians of good family attach little importance to the value of a gift.

I also make it a rule to offer my informants tobacco when I make a request for information. This is an old Indian custom, and if they accept the tobacco I know that my request will be granted. The burning of one's tobacco constitutes a pledge. Also while the talks are going on, I keep a supply of pipe tobacco handy, from which all visitors may help themselves while in the room.

I have found it best not to attempt to record the talks myself, but to bring with me some quiet, unobtrusive amanuensis to do this. Such an assistant need not be a stenographer, since he should be able to record in long hand one sentence at a time as it is translated. Of course a stenographer is preferable. During the talks I keep a pad in my lap on which to note any matters that may require clearing up afterward. This is preferable to interrupting a story or attempting to direct the talk too closely. For very often the white man's sense of values is quite different from that of the Indian, and it is much wiser to let the old man tell the story in his own way and thus get the Indian emphasis where it belongs. In fact, some of my most valuable data has come to light in a digression which I had not the knowledge to ask for. Afterward, when the story is complete, there is time for bringing up these matters for further discussion and thus get all the details clearly set forth.

Some old men resent interruptions and must be allowed to tell their story through to the end, and occasionally one finds an informant who will not submit to direct questioning at all. In such cases one must be thankful for what one can get and push the investigation further in other quarters. On the other hand, I have found informants who would cheerfully endure cross-examination for hours on end. These of course, are the most fruitful. Of them all, Chief White Bull is the most obliging in this respect.

It is useful, of course, to have some knowledge of the language spoken by the informant. However, it is rarely possible to dispense with an interpreter and most unwise to attempt to use the language in the interpreter's presence, since in that way a careless interpreter will soon become aware of one's deficiencies in the use of the Indian tongue. If, however, one uses one's knowledge of the language only in checking the interpreter and in calling his attention to misstatements or omissions, the effect is much better, since the interpreter is impressed by one's knowledge and therefore becomes more careful. When I feel that the interpreter is tiring or becoming careless, I have made it a rule to ask him to record the informant's words in the Indian language verbatim and afterward write out a translation. I always require the Indian text for all speeches, prayers, songs, and other statements of historical importance. Also because of the poor translations of Indian names current, I insist on the Sioux version of proper names with literal translations.

I have carefully avoided any emphasis upon racial differences or of differences of custom as between myself and my informants. When I visit them, I wear the sort of clothes they are accustomed to, sit upon the ground, and take care to observe the niceties of Indian courtesy so far as I understand them. Matters of precedence in seating old warriors cannot be overlooked, and the smoking of an Indian pipe is also an affair of some importance.

In questioning Indians I have carefully refrained from asking leading questions or from giving them any indication of what answers I might expect. Each day I suggest in advance the general subject for the next day's discussion, and in this way prepare the mind of the informant for the talk to come. In such instances it is interesting to observe the old men preparing for the talk to come. Thus, before the narration of the Custer Fight, Chief White Bull could be heard in his cabin beating the tom-tom and singing a war-song. Though, as I say, I have made it a rule not to pay directly for information, I attempt to make everyone feel that I respect the old men, by gifts, by my manner, and by making a speech whenever a dance or any public ceremony offers an opportunity to declare my purpose. And of course I make it a rule to feed informants and their families who come any distance from home to meet me. This kind of research is expensive, but the expense is far outweighed by the pleasure one has in the intimate association with these grand old men.

One word more. Owing to the fact that my data has sometimes had to be combined in this book with information obtained from official records, and because old Indians narrate their stories in the pantomime of the sign language as well as with the spoken word, I have preferred to use the third person here in many instances. This has enabled me to present the whole story, with every detail in its proper place. To omit information conveyed by the sign talk would be to leave out half the story. However, I believe that I have given the matter as the Indian sees it, and while no man can fully understand another, or another race, I have done my best to present the Indians' history from the Indians' point of view. I feel that to do less would be a betrayal of their confidence in me.

STANLEY VESTAL

I. INDIAN WARFARE

(a) NOTES ON THE SIOUX WARS WITH WHITE TROOPS AND TRIBAL ENEMIES

No. 1.

AN OFFICER'S TRIBUTE TO THE PLAINS INDIANS

I desire to give a tribute to the fighting Indians of the plains. They would fight until convinced they were beaten, then they would withdraw. The Indian might fight today, tomorrow he might surrender. Then, if pressed by interest or desire, or hunger, he might enlist as a scout. He would not enlist for more than three months. During that time he was always to be depended upon in every way. But the day after his enlistment expired, look out for him. Many enlisted time after time, for three months each time, and I never knew of a single case of treachery while an Indian was serving his enlistment. These remarks apply to all the tribes comprising the Sioux nation, to the Cheyennes, and the Arapahoes, to the Creeks, the Crows, the Blackfeet, to all the plains Indians; but not to the Apaches.

Regarding the fighting ability of the Indian, I'll quote a remark of Benteen: ".... Indians; good shots; good riders, and the best fighters the sun ever shone on."

(*signed*) W. H. C. Bowen,
Col. U. S. A., retired
Late 2nd Lieut. 5th Infantry
(Miles' regiment)

No. 2.
COMPARATIVE CASUALTIES AS BETWEEN UNITED STATES TROOPS AND INDIANS DURING THE SIOUX CAMPAIGNS, 1865 TO 1876.

"Even honest men seldom tell the truth." This axiom of the trained historian is nowhere better vindicated than in official reports, and of all official reports, military communiqués hold the palm for misinformation. Of those prepared by commanders of United States troops the very flower and perfection of misinformation is to be found in the reports of engagements with hostile Indians on the plains of the West. If all the Indians killed on paper in those wars could be laid end to end, they would extend from the House of Ananias to the Castle of Baron Munchausen. Their number considerably exceeds the total male population of the bands at war, as estimated by Indian agents at the time—and certainly theirs was no underestimate. Agents, as a rule, could be trusted to pad their guesswork census, for agents who made any real money at their job in those days had to make it by appropriating government annuities for which there were no Indian consumers.

Of course, there were excellent reasons and causes for these exaggerated reports of Indian losses in battle. It was the custom of Indian warriors to carry off their dead as well as their wounded whenever it was humanly possible. Officers, finding no dead Indians on the field after the fight, had to guess at enemy losses, and a good round figure was always on the safe side. There was no chance that the Sioux would publish a correction in the newspapers or give their story the lie. Moreover an officer who made too narrow an estimate of enemy

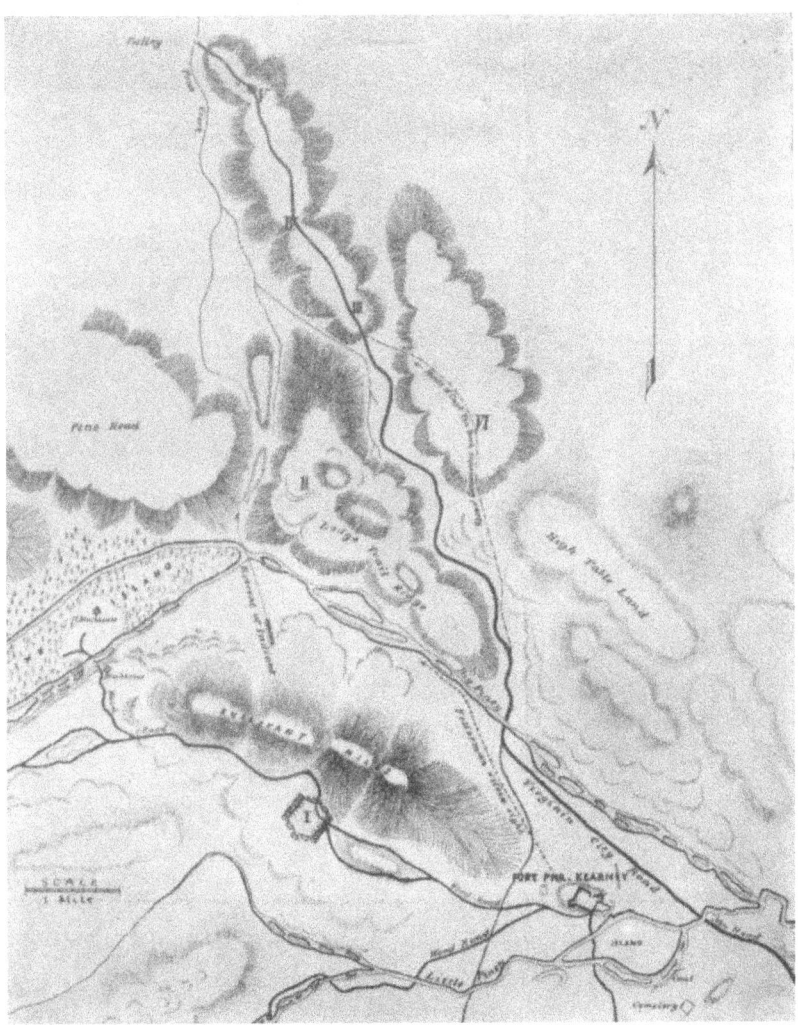

Map of the Fetterman Fight near Fort Phil. Kearny, December 21, 1866

    I. Train corralled on appearance of Indians
    II. Last view of Fetterman
    III. Bodies of Fetterman, Brown and most of the killed
    IV. Body of Lieutenant Grummond
    V. Most distant bodies
    VI. Last view of Ten Eyck's supporting party

losses would have become unpopular with his men—to say nothing of his superiors. The army employed against the Sioux had been created for the Civil War, and in a civil war an army is simply a political party on the warpath. Officers in those days might hopefully aspire to the highest offices in the gift of the voters. Under such conditions political influence was deeply felt. Moreover the taxpayers in the East, who paid for Indian wars, did so very unwillingly. Congress was constantly complaining of the cost of Indian wars, grumbled at paying a million dollars a head for dead Indians, and the army had to show results or suffer a cut in appropriations. Moreover, it must be remembered that very often a large proportion of the enlisted men in those Indian battles were rookies (owing to the unconscionable number of desertions in those days), and it is the nature of a rookie to see dead men double. The soldiers were also in mortal terror of being captured and tortured by the Redskins, and were perfectly well aware that, on occasion, American officers had abandoned their dead and wounded or marched away without ever finding out what had become of a missing detachment. The Reynolds Fight and Custer's Battle on the Washita are cases in point. Besides, when one considers what an Indian fight was like—the surprise attack in overwhelming numbers, the yelling and confusion, the hideously painted, naked warriors, the fright of the white man's horses at the smell of the Indians, the swift charges and shifting movements of that wild cavalry, and the way the warrior had of suddenly dropping to one side of his racing pony to shield himself from bullets, it is hardly surprising that even honest and unimaginative soldiers saw more dead Indians than actually bit the dust. What with the dust and the smoke of their own guns the soldiers could hardly see anything clearly, and so when the fight was over and they found no dead Indians they rubbed their eyes and swore they *must* have killed a hundred.

The Custer Fight was once the happy hunting ground of the romantic yarn-spinners, but so much careful research has been done on that affair that the romancers have had to be careful lately. The Wagon Box Fight, August 2, 1867, is now the shining example of valorous carnage, when the trusty rifle belched death like a machine gun and Redskins fell by hundreds. The site of this famous scrap lies just off the highway between Buffalo and Sheridan, Wyoming, at the foot of the Big Horn Mountains. Where the road turns off the highway just there a huge billboard informs the credulous tourist that fifteen hundred Indians fell that day before the rifles of that gallant company of thirty men.

Of course, even an uninstructed tourist is likely to gag at such figures. To anyone who knows something of Indians and Indian warfare the exaggeration is so grotesque that it is even laughable. The soldiers did not kill fifteen hundred Indians (including women and children) during all the wars with the Sioux. It is possible that some of the white survivors of the Wagon Box Fight may have believed that yarn, but nobody else can. The historians of the West have been nothing if not patriotic, but it may be doubted whether a patriotic historian is an historian at all.

Heretofore no figures have been tabulated to show comparative losses of white troops and Indians in the principal engagements of the Sioux campaigns. I offer the following.

The figures here given for white troops (including civilians with them) are taken from the official reports;

officers can generally be trusted to be accurate in their report of losses in their own commands. The figures here given for Indian losses were supplied by eye-witnesses and participants of the several battles, who—in every case—were asked not only for the number of Indians killed and wounded, but for their *names* as well. The conferences with these eye-witnesses were held at times and places far apart, and through different interpreters. Some of these figures were committed to writing by Indians as early as 1880.

I believe that anyone familiar with old-time Indians will prefer their version of a fight to that of other eye-witnesses. The Indian was by nature and training a very close observer, objective and unimaginative as few white men can be. Moreover, the Indian was a veteran who went on the warpath several times each year from early adolescence until he became too old to fight. He was therefore no rookie seeing things that never happened, and he was not in terror of being tortured or abandoned by his friends when wounded on the field of battle. He was therefore cooler and more experienced, as a rule, than his white opponents, more especially as he was so well mounted that he could outride the soldiers and therefore fought them only when and where he wished. Moreover, the warrior dreamed, thought and talked of nothing but loot and glory. War was his absorbing sport. His rating in the tribe depended upon his proven exploits in battle and he took good care to claim all honors to which he was entitled, and to demolish any false claims advanced by his comrades. Therefore in any kind of a fracas he had all the keen, clear-eyed alertness of a professional sportsman. And as long as he lived, whenever he had an opportunity, he recounted his exploits in battle publicly and in the presence of his rivals. Any leading warrior could rattle off the rating and exploits of every one of his comrades as easily as a baseball fan could give you the batting averages of his favorite players. The figures given here are from the lips of such old warriors.

The only vagueness in these figures lies in the number of wounded and in the number of Indians engaged in the fights. As the Indian had no disciplined organizations of troops and no roll call, but fought as an individual who took part or looked on at will, it is impossible to determine to a man just how many were engaged in any but the smaller affairs. There is a similar uncertainty as to the exact number of Indians wounded. But there is *no* vagueness as to the number of dead. I consider the figures given for Indian dead in the following table quite as accurate as the figures given by officers for white soldiers killed.

Name of Battle	Approximate No. Indians engaged	No. white men engaged	Killed Indians	Killed Whites	Wounded Indians	Wounded Whites
1. Pumpkin Buttes. August, 1865.	56	7	0	3	0	1
2. Fetterman "Massacre." Dec. 21, 1866.	2000	81	14	81	3	0
3. Wagon Box Fight. August 2, 1867.	1000	32	6	6	6	0
4. Baker Fight. August 14, 1872.	500	400	1	1	6	4
5. Reynolds Fight. March 17, 1876.	200	400	1	4	1	6
6. Battle of the Rosebud. June 17, 1876.	1000	1300	11	10	5	21
7. Reno in the Big Horn Bottoms. June 25, 1876.	1000	150?	8	32	2	7
8. Custer Fight on the bluffs. June 25, 1876.	1500	204	16	204	?	0
9. Reno besieged on bluffs. June 25-26, 1876.	1000	381	2	18	1	45 plus
10. Slim Buttes. September 9, 1876.	1000	2000	10	3	2	14
11. Otis & Sitting Bull. Oct. 15-16, 1876.	300	196	1	1	2	3
12. Miles & Sitting Bull. October 21, 1876.	800	398	0	0	0	0
Totals	10,356	5,249	69	383	28	102

These figures for twelve major conflicts of the Sioux campaigns indicate that the Indians, like Napoleon, fought as a rule only when they had the advantage of numbers. They fought two to one. On the other hand the white troops were always better armed and had more ammunition. The Indians never had more than half enough guns to go round and no cannon whatever. *Yet these figures show that the Sioux killed about five times as many soldiers as he lost Indians killed, and wounded approximately four times as many soldiers as he had wounded.* These figures show therefore that the Indian, Sioux or Cheyenne, was approximately four or five times as effective as the white soldier in these campaigns. It is interesting to compare this table of losses as between white troops and Sioux Indians with the following table showing losses as between Sioux and enemy Indian tribes in intertribal wars.

Name of Battle	Approximate No. Sioux engaged	Approximate No. Enemies engaged	Killed Sioux	Killed Enemy	Wounded Sioux	Wounded Enemy
1. Captive Butte. 1857.	100	10	..	10	..	..
2. Thirty Crows Killed. 1869-70.	100	30	14	30	18	..
3. Flathead fight. 1871.	425	250?	5	30	10	..?
4. Slota (French Breeds) Fight. 1873.	88	180?	8	1?	1	..?
5. Sitting Bull's Death Fight. 1890.	160?	(Police) 43	8	(Police) 6	..	(Police) 1
Totals	873	513	35	77	29	1

Here the odds in favor of the Sioux are not so great, being less than two to one. The armaments of the opposed forces are approximately equal. On the other hand, in three of the fights listed, (Nos. 1, 2, and 4) the enemy fought throughout from cover. I have included the fight in which Sitting Bull was killed by the Indian Police because it clinches the claim made here that the Sioux fought harder than their enemies, and therefore would do great damage when matched with their own people. The disparity of Sioux to enemy wounded is not so great as it may appear, since the Sioux have no way of making sure how many enemies they wounded. *But it is clear that they inflicted two deaths for every one they suffered from enemy Indians.*

From these figures (allowing for some approximation and inaccuracies) it is clear that the Sioux (and the Cheyennes, their allies) were excellent fighters—twice as effective as their Indian enemies (who were similarly armed), and about five times as effective as the better armed troops in the use of deadly weapons.

Now, nothing is more noticeable in the reports for those years of the Commissioner of Indian Affairs and the Secretary of War than the constantly recurring expressions of contempt by Indians (of *all* Plains tribes) for the white soldiers. And I have yet to find an old experienced Indian warrior (of *any* Plains tribe) who did not take it for granted as an obvious fact that the Indians were vastly superior to the whites as soldiers. This opinion was shared by practically all experienced officers who had fought Indians—as may be seen from their own published statements.[1] The Indian scouts who served with the troops are emphatic in their support of this opinion. They hastily abandoned Crook and Custer when they saw that the troops "could not protect them."

The fact is that the Sioux warrior had many advantages over the white trooper. He was far more mobile and could travel with his family, living on the country, at the rate of fifty miles a day. A horseman almost from

---

1. Consult P. E. Byrne, *Soldiers of the Plains*, N. Y. 1926. Also *The Arikara Narrative of the Campaign Against Hostile Dakotas, June, 1876*, in North Dakota Historical Collections, Vol. 6. For the opinion of the Royal Northwest Mounted Police, see John F. Finerty, *Warpath and Bivouac*, Chicago, 1890. All are to the same effect.

birth and usually well supplied with horse flesh, he knew his country like a map, was a natural born scout, and was familiar with every stream and butte. He was skilled in the use of arms from boyhood and made his living shooting running animals from the saddle, whereas the trooper, as General George Crook reports (see Annual Report, Secretary of War, 1876), could hit nothing from the saddle and could seldom hit an Indian on horseback even when standing on the ground. The Indian warrior, moreover, was uniformly sober, courageous, devoted to the friends with whom he rode and fought, and inspired by an almost insane love of military glory.

He was besides, altogether hardier and more athletic than his white opponent. It was a rare thing for a white trooper to kill an Indian warrior in single hand-to-hand combat. Even nowadays an altogether disproportionate number of big-time athletes are Indians. In those days the Indian warrior endured as a matter of course hardships (fatigue, exposure, famine, wounds) which would have disabled or killed most white soldiers. For example, at eighty-six, Chief White Bull has lost but one tooth, and rides as well now as most middle-aged cowmen.

Of course, the Indian was unable to see the importance of following up a victory. If he had understood this, and if wild game had remained abundant on the Plains, it seems unlikely that the small army then in the field could ever have conquered the Sioux, unless with the aid of other Indians.

Of course, the American patriot, justly proud of our soldiers' valor, and reading only the newspapers and official reports, had little idea how seldom victory crowned our banners. He supposed the troopers were licking the cussed Injun every day. But of the twelve major enagements listed above, only one (the last) was followed by precipitate flight on the part of the redskins. Of the others, two (Nos. 2 and 8) were disasters involving complete annihilation of the white troops; three (Nos. 3, 9 and 10) might have been disasters but for the timely arrival of a relief column; two (Nos. 1 and 7) resulted in utter rout of the troops; three (Nos. 4, 5 and 6) were defeats followed by retreats in good order on the part of the troops; while No. 11 was brought to an end by a parley and the distribution of presents to the Indians. These figures tell their own story.

Unquestionably, the American soldier deserved credit for his valor. But valor is only a part of soldiering, and was no exclusive possession of the white man. Officers who served in those campaigns knew all this well enough, and in their memoirs may be found plenty of confirmation of the Sioux Indian's high opinion of himself.

For example, Custer: "no race of men, not even the famous Cossacks, could display more wonderful feats of horsemanship". . . . . General Frederick W. Benteen: "Good shots, good riders, the best fighters the sun ever shone on" . . . . . General Charles King: "foemen far more to be dreaded than any European cavalry" . . . . .Major Walsh (of the Royal Northwest Mounted Police): "superior to the best English regiments" . . . . . General Anson Mills: "the Indians proved then and there that they were the best cavalry on earth. . . .their like will never be seen again. Our friendlies were worthless against them." Finally, if these authorities leave the patriot unconvinced as to Indian superiority, let him turn to George Washington's report, made after the debacle under General Braddock: "Indians are the only match for Indians."

Chief White Bull is in perfect agreement with the Father of his (present) Country. Indeed, the Chief assured me that it was the Sioux boys in the A.E.F. who won the war in France. As his interpreter put it, "He say it sure must of been them Sioux boys won the war. He say he know damn well no white soldiers could of done it."

No. 3.
NOTE ON THE WAYS OF WARRIORS

Chief White Bull says that when on the warpath, the Sioux and Cheyennes sometimes tried to divine the future and find out what was going to happen in the fight ahead. They would kill a badger, place it on its back, cut it open and remove the entrails, allowing the blood to collect in the cavity formed by the ribs. When this blood had stood awhile it formed a smooth red mirror. One by one the warriors would look into this mirror to read their fates.

There were three signs to be noted: (1) If a man saw himself in the mirror with gray hair, he knew that he would live to be an old man, that he would not be killed. (2) If he saw himself bloody, with his hair gone, he believed he would be scalped. (3) If his face looked long and black in the mirror, he thought that he was doomed to die of sickness.

If a man saw he was to be killed, he might turn back from that warpath without disgrace. Nobody could be expected to commit suicide. Even so, such a man expected to be killed within one year. White Bull says he himself would never look into the badger blood. "Generally," he says, "a Sioux warrior depended upon his dreams upon the warpath for warnings. A man who had bad dreams would get up and wail. His comrades would then get up and ask what was the matter. If his dream was bad they would send him back."

No. 4.
SITTING BULL AS A MEDICINE MAN

When I began my research upon the history of the Sioux and Sitting Bull, I at first proceeded on the assumption that the accepted story as to the nature of his influence upon his people was correct. That legend was to the effect that he was a medicine man and not a leader of warriors. I therefore questioned every informant with regard to Sitting Bull's activities as a medicine man. Of course I was aware that no specialization of an exclusive kind existed among the Prairie Sioux, and that every man in the tribe aspired to have divine assistance and to gain supernatural power, either through visions or by purchase from dreamers. But I was much disappointed in not finding Sitting Bull rated as a great medicine man, priest, or doctor. The Indians insisted that he was primarily a warrior and a war-chief, and constantly brought forward the names of other Indians whom they regarded as the great doctors and shamans.

In fact I could find no one who believed Sitting Bull was a doctor at all, though he did carry a sort of first-aid kit on the warpath, containing standard remedies for wounds. His father supplied these remedies, since his father was a doctor.

Sitting Bull was, however, a man of unusual mental capacity, and undoubtedly had certain powers of prophecy. So many instances of his ability and performance have been told me by men of unquestioned integrity who were eye-witnesses, that only a confirmed skeptic could refuse to accept them as substantially true.

Apart from participation in the Sun Dance and in the dances of warrior societies, Sitting Bull does not appear to have been very fond of ceremonies or to have engaged in the usual practices of dreamers and shamans. Once in a long while he would go up on a hilltop to fast and pray, and the Indians say that his prayers were strong and that he got what he prayed for. He prayed before the Custer Fight, in Canada during the famine, and in 1875 near the White Buttes on the Little Missouri. These three occasions are the only ones remembered, though they are remembered vividly by his friends and relatives. He never made the Spirit-keeping ceremony, though he lost some children during his lifetime. No one can recall his ever making the Calumet Dance or Alowanpi Ceremony. But like other Indians he was in the habit of receiving communications from animals, particularly birds.

Sitting Bull, in other words, was an all-around man. His chief concerns were war and hunting, and he lived in such hectic times that he could not have accomplished what he did both as an individual warrior and as a chief had he been the shrinking dreamer he has been represented. In fact it was his practical nature which made him so anxious to utilize his psychic powers and to obtain supernatural assistance in his enterprises. It is noteworthy that his two nephews, One Bull and White Bull, both revere him as the type of excellence. For One Bull is a man of a thoughtful and withdrawn type, much concerned with dreams and ceremonies. White Bull, his brother, is entirely a man of the world and a man of action, to whom a vision is merely a tool or a sanction.

If both these men regard their uncle as superior to them in these two respects, he must have been a well-rounded personality. I accept the Sioux opinion that Sitting Bull was primarily a war-chief and a fighter, equal to, if not superior to, other Sioux as hunter and warrior. But for those who cling to the legend of the medicine man, I have gathered here all that is worth recording of his prophecies and charms.

About the year 1872, Sitting Bull acquired a powerful war-medicine (*wo-ta-we*). It was granted to him in a vision. It was a charm to control the weather, and he constantly carried it with him on the warpath. This talisman, now in my keeping, is evidently the celebrated "buffalo robe," mentioned in the history books, with which Sitting Bull is said to have raised the storm during the Ghost Dance in 1890. He used it often to great advantage: it was one of his most cherished possessions.

It consists of a yard of unbleached muslin thirty inches wide, dyed a deep orange yellow. In each corner is painted a conventional green dragonfly—the symbol of swiftness and agility in escaping enemies. In the middle of the cloth, between two horizontal black lines representing heaven and earth, stands an elk eight inches tall. The elk is outlined in green, with red spots on the body. Both elk and dragonflies face the beholder's left.

Wrapped in this cloth is also a bit of calamus root, and the tail of a white-tail deer mounted on a short stick, with a string attached with which to fasten it to the painted cloth. The deer-tail contains the power of the fleet animal it was taken from, and adds to the speed of the charm. With these objects there is a pair of inch-wide wristlets of buffalo hide with the brown wool left on, having thongs for tying them around the wrists. These wristlets were evidently cut from a painted buffalo robe, for there are traces of the robe design on the flesh-side of the skin, in red, yellow, and blue.

When Sitting Bull wished to use this charm, he usually went to some lonely hilltop and made a sacrifice, either by cutting himself and letting some blood flow, or by hanging a piece of scarlet cloth to the top of a stick planted in the ground. Then he tied on the wristlets, fastened the deer-tail to the top (middle) of the medicine-cloth, and sang the song taught him by the visionary elk:

> I have a good friend above;
> I have a good friend above;
> I have an elk-friend above;
> On earth I speak for a nation.

This song is apparently a reminder to the god who promised aid in the vision, and a prayer for help for the Sioux nation.

After singing this song, Sitting Bull took hold of the cloth by its upper corners, and holding it spread out, struck the ground with it four times. In his vision, he had been promised that this would make the wind blow. The harder he struck the ground, the harder it would blow.

If, on the other hand, he wished to make it rain, he had only to chew a small bit of the calamus root and sputter the saliva upon the cloth, at the same time waving it in the air.

This talisman was powerful. Chief One Bull saw it used twice. Once, in the Big Bend country, on the Yellowstone River, in '78, the Crows surrounded a small party of Hunkpapa. It was a tight corner. But the chief got out this cloth, sang his song, struck the earth very hard, four times; such a terrible windstorm followed that the Crows on the prairie could not stand it and went away.

Another time, that same year, ten Sioux went on the warpath. The Crows chased them into some willow brush on Arrow (Pryor) Creek. It was during a severe drouth, and the willows were dry as a bone, so dry they were brittle. All around the willows, in the creek bottom, the grass was long—long enough to hide a man standing up. The Crows could not get at the Sioux, so they set fire to the grass. It was not windy, but the grass burned fiercely, snapping and roaring, getting nearer and nearer the cornered Sioux, coming from all sides. The whole bottom was filled with crackling flame, and the ten Sioux were choking in the smoke. They thought their time had come.

But the chief got out his medicine-cloth, sang his song, spat on the cloth and waved it hard through the smoky air. Right away, the smoke hanging above the Sioux turned to clouds. From these clouds rain fell, putting out the fire. All the Sioux were saved.

Sitting Bull kept this talisman wrapped in a dark green cloth, and carried it to war on his shoulder in a taper cylindrical case of raw-hide, fifteen inches long, painted with geometric designs in red, yellow, and blue.

Sitting Bull's power over the weather was well known to the Indians in the old days and many stories are current illustrating it. Chief White Bull, whom I consider a thoroughly reliable informant, was an eye-witness of one such surprising feat. During a Sun Dance, the weather was very hot and dry, and the spectators as well as the dancers suffered great discomfort because of the heat. During an intermission in the dancing,

Sitting Bull walked out into the enclosure in high good-humor and announced with a smile that he would bring a rain to refresh the people. At that time the sky was cloudless, but within a few minutes a small rain cloud appeared and passed over the dance lodge. A shower fell so that the Indians had to scuttle to shelter, protecting themselves under the brush shelters and under their buffalo robes. When the shower had passed, the people were astonished to find that Sitting Bull, standing in the open, was dry and that the ground immediately around him for a distance of about a yard was also unwet by the rain. White Bull did not see Sitting Bull use his medicine-bundle on this occasion. It may be that the chief had done so in private earlier in the day.

It was evidently by means of this charm that Sitting Bull was able to make such astonishing weather forecasts in the last years of his life. His prophecies at that time were well attested by white persons who made immediate record of them. Thus in August, 1889, just after the breaking up of the Great Sioux Reservation, Sitting Bull announced to the Indians at Standing Rock Agency that a bad year was ahead, that the sun would burn everything up and that no crops could be raised. It was to be a year-long drouth. From the day of his prophecy, August, 1889, no rain fell there until June, 1890, and very little snow—as may readily be learned from the official reports of the Indian Agent at Standing Rock. This drouth sent the settlers back to the East from the new state of North Dakota; Bismarck, the capital city, dwindled to about five hundred souls.

In June, 1890, after this terrible drouth, and while the sun, in a cloudless sky, was still blistering the prairie, Sitting Bull publicly announced to the assembled Indians at the agency one ration-day that it would rain, that he would make it rain; and to the astonishment of the whites who scoffed at him, heavy rains fell within two days. Mary Collins, the missionary, bears witness to this. She heard his words and saw the rain fall.

Again during the winter of 1890, when the officials of the Indian Bureau confidently reported that the winter snows would put a stop to the Ghost Dancing, Sitting Bull laughed at them, no doubt believing that he could blow the clouds away. He publicly announced to his people that they could dance all winter, that the weather would be mild, with little snow. Both missionaries and officials bear witness to this forecast and its exact fulfillment.

Major McLaughlin, in his book, *My Friend the Indian*, page 232, records another incident showing Sitting Bull's confidence in his alliance with the gods of the storm. Here follows the Indian version of the same story: In the Spring of 1887, Sitting Bull was presiding over the issue of some beef to his band when Shell King accused him of unfairness in dividing the meat. Twice, he said, he had had to take a fore quarter as his share, and now his hind quarter was lean. Shell King was very angry, mad enough to kill. He jerked out his butcher knife and rushed at Sitting Bull. But Sitting Bull caught up his small stone-headed war-club, and Shell King, who knew how skillful the chief was in throwing it, stopped short and said no more. Black Claw (or Black-Finger-Nail), an Indian policeman who was present, arrested them both and haled them before the agency Court of Indian Offences.

Chief John Grass, Crazy Walking, and Bullhead were the judges. Following the novel regulation then in force at Standing Rock, they confiscated the arms of both Indians. Shell King gave up his knife; Sitting Bull his pogamoggan; thus the fine was paid. McLaughlin, in his report of this affair, rather gives himself away. He had all along been saying that Sitting Bull had no influence. Yet here he boasts that his Court is "no respecter of persons, having recently had the conceited and obstinate Sitting Bull before them for assault." (*Commissioner of Indian Affairs*, '87, p. 52-3). Apparently, Sitting Bull was not too conceited and obstinate to submit with a good grace to the Indian Court and the Police. At times Red Cloud was thrown into the guard-house: Sitting Bull never. Are we to suppose this due to McLaughlin's forbearance, or to Sitting Bull's influence, or to the fact that he was guilty of no offence?

Though acquitted, Sitting Bull was no longer friendly with Shell King after this affair, and Shell King, though one of the Silent Eaters, allied himself with the Indians of the agency faction from then on. Shell King and his friends were resentful, but Sitting Bull was not afraid. One day in the agent's office he upbraided Shell King, saying he was a traitor to his people. Shell King, backed by the agent and other Indians of his faction, did not back down this time. He talked back to the chief, blamed him for all the hardships and misfortunes of his people. "The days of your power are over," said he. "From now on the Sioux will do as they please and pay no attention to you."

Sitting Bull replied, "You may talk that way now, but you will see. You will be punished for defying my authority."

Ten days later Shell King and one of his sons were struck by lightning and killed, and as McLaughlin has recorded, this event "had a tremendous effect in restoring the waning power of the old medicine-chief, to whose influence it was credited." After that Indians were careful not to cross him. It is not known whether or not Sitting Bull used his medicine-bundle to cause the storm which killed Shell King.

After Sitting Bull's death, Chief One Bull, his nephew, kept the medicine-bundle containing the weather charm until the summer of 1930. Then one day, when I was visiting him on Grand River, he told me about it and showed it to me. Of course I was anxious to possess such a remarkable relic of the man whose history I was studying and offered to purchase it from the chief. One Bull was reluctant to part with it, as it was known to be a powerful war-charm.

His reasons are typical of the attitude of old warriors of the Sioux today. During my research I have found them, one and all, very curious as to why the soldiers came against them in the old days. Few of them have any idea why they were attacked by the white troops and naturally see no reason why such unexpected (and to them unjustifiable) attacks should not be repeated now. Numbers of the old warriors still keep up the taboos of their war days and keep a horse saddled all day long in case the soldiers should attack them.

One Bull, however, said that if his children were willing to part with the medicine-bundle he would not stand in their way. Said he, "My friend, I am an old man. It doesn't matter what becomes of me. If my children are willing, you may have it. But for my part, I hate to give it up. My friend, this is the only protection we have against the soldiers' airplanes."

Sitting Bull at one time possessed some sacred stones, and a number of stories are told how he divined the future, found lost objects, solved crimes, by means of them. Such feats are, however, too common among the

Sioux to be worth recounting here. The reader will find a discussion of the sacred stones in Miss Frances Densmore's *Teton Sioux Music*, Bulletin 61, Bureau of American Ethnology.

More remarkable prophecies on the warpath made by the chief in the presence of multitudes will be found recounted in my *Sitting Bull*, chapters XVII and XXI. The most remarkable of these is that in which he prophesied the destruction of General Custer's command, ten days before it happened. This prophecy is well known both to the Sioux and Cheyennes, hundreds of whom heard it made. It is mentioned in George Bird Grinnell's book *The Fighting Cheyennes*.

One of Sitting Bull's prophecies was made during the last year of his life. He had been warned that his enemies would destroy him, and foretold what would happen after his death. Said he, "My people, forty years after my death, you will be torn asunder, you will be all confused and at a loss, broken into factions, quarreling with one another. You will not know which way to turn. The white men will cause all this trouble." Standing Rock Indians believe that this prophecy was fulfilled in the factional strife and bitterness engendered during the recent Senatorial investigation.

Sitting Bull seldom went astray in prophecies concerning Indians alone. But in the affairs of white men he was sometimes deceived. One day he came to Jack Carignan on Grand River and said, "A small bird warned me that there will be a shortage of beef in the next issue down here."

Jack Carignan, who was in charge of the beef issue, replied, "Well, if a little bird told you that, it lied to you. Wait and see."

Sure enough, at the next issue there was plenty of

beef, in fact a few quarters extra. Sitting Bull had to admit that this time he had been misled by his friends the Bird People. But such a mistake seldom happened, they say—and then only when white men were involved.

How are we to account for these things? Perhaps one may hazard a guess that Sitting Bull, being entirely Indian in his thought and outlook, was able to understand and see into the nature of things further than white men can. Because the civilization of the American Indian was a unit, all of a piece, geared to the world in which he lived. For perhaps ten thousand years it had been growing up all by itself, without much contact with or influence by outside races and cultures.

The white men, on the contrary, possess a civilization of shreds and patches. Their hybrid European culture is made up of odds and ends, and no man can possibly make a workable synthesis of all these diverse materials. We go clothed in the contents of a rag-bag mentally.

The machine age has not developed the mind which can function through it. Our civilization fits us like an out-size suit of armor. We live like a crab in a sea-shell. And so we do not believe in the prophecies of our leading men in finance, in politics, in business. And if we do believe, we generally live to regret it.

Sitting Bull's prophecies therefore strain our faith. But perhaps it is not true to say that prophecies are out of date, but only prophets. That is one thing which cannot be supplied by mass production.

No. 5.
NOTE ON SITTING BULL'S SHIELD

Sitting Bull's father, Jumping Bull, made four shields, all alike. One of them belonged to Jumping

Bull's youngest brother, Looks-for-Home. After he was killed in the winter of 1869-70 in the battle When-Thirty-Crows-Were-Killed, White Bull's grandmother kept it. She allowed White Bull to take it to war on one occasion. When he returned, Swift Dog received it. The second shield was given to Runs-Fearless, the third to Follows-the-Girls, the fourth to Sitting Bull. This is the shield shown in the well-known drawings made of Sitting Bull's exploits.

With the shield Sitting Bull was given a lance. To make this lance his father cut a straight ash stick two fingers thick and as tall as a tall man can reach up. To one end of this stick he fitted a notched iron blade one span long, and sharp. To the other end he attached a lustrous feather from the tail of a golden eagle—a white feather with a black tip—so that it dangled and fluttered loosely. Having thus made the weapon, he handed it to his wife, who covered the entire shaft with blue and white beads. She then gave it to her son, Sitting Bull.

This lance was always one of his favorite weapons, for he was a man of powerful shoulders and arms. In the archives of the Bureau of American Ethnology at Washington, D.C., there is a series of pictographs representing forty of Sitting Bull's war deeds, made by his uncle, Four Horns. This lance appears in eleven of the forty drawings. Old men remember it well.

The next thing was the shield.

Jumping Bull went out and shot an old buffalo bull. From the carcase he took the skin of the neck, where the hide was thickest. Then he dug a round hole, just the size of the shield he wished to make, and into this round hole he put stones heated red hot in the fire. Over the top of this hole full of hot stones he spread the rawhide, and occasionally threw a little water in upon the stones. Before long the intense heat had shrunk the rawhide until it was thick as a man's finger, tough, and hard to pierce.

Jumping Bull then took a limber stick and made a hoop about eighteen inches across—the same size as the shield he was going to make. Laying this hoop upon the tough rawhide, he trimmed it off to fit the hoop. He then had a rawhide disk the size of the hoop. Over this disk he stretched a cover of white deerskin cut round like the rawhide, but larger. The edge of this deerskin was perforated by small slits all around. Through these slits he passed a draw-string, drew it tight, and tied it on the back of the shield. This drew the edges of the deerskin over on the back of the shield all around, leaving the front smooth and white and ready for painting.

On this white surface Jumping Bull painted a design which had been revealed to him in a vision. All around the edge of the shield he painted the rainbow. Within this circular rainbow the surface of the shield was bluegreen. On this blue-green field he painted what was apparently a dark bird with wings displayed. Because the bird's breast is against the shield, and therefore invisible, there is some uncertainty as to what bird was intended. It might be one of three, old men say: one which lives in hollow trees and has a white breast; one which lives in holes on the banks of the river, a greenish-black bird with red or orange breast; or a dark green bird with speckled breast. In any case it has a split tail, and is one of those birds which dart rapidly up and down, here and there, and are very hard to hit. These are the opinions of men who have seen the shield.

Chief One Bull, however, who grew up in Sitting Bull's tipi, and himself carried this shield in the Custer fight, thinks that this "bird" really represented the figure of a man-like being who appeared in Jumping Bull's vision—a being with a dark brown body and many wing feathers growing from his extended arms. The split tail of the "bird" was the man-like being's legs, it is believed.

The blue color on the shield represented the sky; the figure was that of the Man-from-above, and the feathers on his arms showed that he dwelt above. The rainbow was there all around, because when a rainbow appears, the rain stops quick. So, when a man is being shot at, this shield would be a protection, having the rainbow on it. The hair on the head of the figure (the Creator) meant power, and the two yellow plumes on his head stood for the lightning.

When the painting was finished, Jumping Bull tied four eagle-tail feathers to the edge of the shield at equal distances apart. Each feather had a tiny bundle of medicine attached. The four sides of the shield stood for the four directions: north, east, south, west. The eagle feather was a badge of honor: it stood for success. Thus, the four feathers tied to the four sides of the shield meant that the man who carried it would be successful everywhere.

Having put a carrying-strap on the shield, and made a case for it, Jumping Bull gave it to his son, telling him to carry it upon the left shoulder and arm, and teaching him the regulations and taboos which belonged to it.

The man who carries this shield must keep it close by him, must let no woman touch it. He cannot eat from a dish touched by any woman but his mother or his wife, and when he is away from home, he must prepare his own food. Certain parts of certain animals he cannot eat at all. Above all, he dare not tell a lie or think wrong thoughts. For, if he does, the shield will fail him; he will be killed or wounded in his next fight. These were the instructions given to young Sitting Bull with his shield.

Before a fight, he was told, he must paint his face with a gray line running across his forehead and extending down each temple to the cheek-bone, where it ended in a fork. His hair must be worn in a knot like a horn on his forehead, and tied up with rawhide. Beginning at the eyes, the cheeks, neck, and legs of his war-horse must also be painted with zig-zag lines to give it the swiftness of lightning. And before entering a battle, he must strip the case from his shield and sing the song given to Jumping Bull in his vision.

The song was brief and to the point. The first line was repeated four times, the others once only. The word *wakan* (pronounced wah-kahn) means holy, lucky, or successful: there is no exact English equivalent. These are the words of the song:

Friend, you are *wakan* in four directions;
You say there is no other one *wakan*;
Friend, you are *wakan* in four directions.

Sitting Bull was shot through this shield in a single combat with a Crow chief in 1856. The bullet lamed his left foot. He is said to have kept this shield long after his surrender. One Bull says he understood that Mr. William McNider bought it, but Mr. McNider states that he never saw any such shield.

No. 6. *George Bird Grinnell on Torture in Indian Warfare*

May 6, 1929

Mr. W. S. Campbell,
University of Oklahoma,

Norman, Oklahoma.

Dear Mr. Campbell:

Your letter of April 27th has just reached me. I suspect that the fear felt and expressed by white men who took part in the wars with the Western Plains Indians were no more than survivals of the old time belief that Indians always tortured captives.

The books tell us that the Indians of the East did this, but in my opinion those of the plains practically never did anything of the kind. I feel confident that they never made a practice of it. Of course, a group of Indians, if they were particularly angry at a man, or a small group of men, might in this way satisfy their feelings of revenge, but in my association with Western Indians I think I never heard of anything of this kind. If acts, such as you allude to, ever took place among the Western Indians they were, in my opinion, the result of some special occurrence, and in revenge for some particular injury thought to have been received by the group. There was practically no torture of captives by the Western Indians. I have been told of many cases where captives were kindly treated and even adopted into the tribe.

I have always been somewhat skeptical about many stories of torture reported as practised by the Eastern Indians.

The Western Indians, of course, wished to destroy their enemies, men, women and children, but I think they never practiced torture, except, possibly, in some cases where they were still very angry over some injury they believed they had received.

      Yours very truly,
      (Signed) Geo. Bird Grinnell

No. 7.
WAR STORY: A BRAVE CROW WARRIOR IS KILLED

Sitting Bull early performed a feat which added greatly to his fame among the Northern Sioux. The Sioux and Crows were having a battle on the Yellowstone, not far from the mouth of the Rosebud.

One of the Crow warriors was very brave, and when he found himself surrounded by his enemies, he stood them off on foot with his bow and arrows. He was so brave and such a good shot that none of the Sioux dared go near him. They hung back and shot arrows at him from a distance, and he shot back at them.

But they could not hit him, for he was as active and quick on his feet as a boxer. They kept on shooting, nevertheless, and pretty soon the Crow had used up all his arrows. Then the Sioux thought they had him and tried to charge him. But the Crow snatched up the arrows they had fired at him, shot them back and hit some of the Sioux. They began to think they could never get at him.

Just then Sitting Bull rode up.

"Haven't you killed that one yet?"

"No," they said, "he uses our own arrows against us. We shoot them over, and he shoots them back and is killing us that way."

"Well," said Sitting Bull, "I have some good arrows he might like to use. You boys stand back. I'll show you how to fight."

Sitting Bull took three arrows from his quiver and dismounted. Running forward, he shot one arrow at the Crow, but the Crow dodged and, running to where the arrow had stuck in the ground, snatched it up and placed it on his bowstring. Sitting Bull followed and, drawing his second arrow back to its head, let fly again.

But once more he missed. The Crow was too quick for him, a good fighter and hard to kill. And now he had Sitting Bull's two arrows, and Sitting Bull had but one.

Sitting Bull dared not risk another miss. He ran forward. The Crow loosed one of his arrows at his enemy, but dodging is a game that two can play. Sitting Bull was not hit, and still rushed forward. When he was close enough to be quite sure, he drew back his arrow and took good aim. *Twang* went the bowstring. The arrow sped on its way, hitting the Crow in the throat. Sitting Bull snatched up his two arrows. Two more shots—one in the shoulder, one in the crotch, finished the Crow.

Sitting Bull was victor.

After that, whenever there was a battle and some reckless young man expressed a wish to go in alone and strike the enemy, some other fellow would nudge him in the ribs and answer:

"Hold on there! You're not Sitting Bull."

No. 8.
MOVEMENTS OF THE HUNKPAPA SIOUX CAMP FROM THE SPRING OF 1870 UNTIL THE CUSTER FIGHT 1876

So much discrepancy exists in the published accounts as regards the location of the camp of the Indians under Sitting Bull that I thought it worthwhile to check the movements of this camp during the five years preceding the Custer Fight, June 25, 1876. Here follows Chief Joseph White Bull's statement of these movements as known to him, supplemented by some information from other old men of the Sioux Nation for periods during

during which Chief White Bull was absent from Sitting Bull's camp.

After the thirty Crows were killed on the Big Dry River in the winter of 1869-70, the Sioux moved north almost up to the Missouri River. Spring found them not far above the mouth of the Yellowstone River.

Spring of 1870

The camp moved south to the Yellowstone, passing the spot where the thirty Crows were killed on the Big Dry, until they crossed the Yellowstone. Crossing the stream some distance above Powder River, they returned within a few days to the north bank of the Yellowstone and moved down to the mouth of the Powder River. After camping here some time they followed buffalo up the Yellowstone for a considerable distance, remaining on the north bank. Then they turned back down the Yellowstone and made camp at the Shallow Crossing, which is perhaps seventy-five miles below the mouth of Powder River. They remained in camp there until the rosebuds were in bloom.

Summer of 1870

White Bull cannot say how long Sitting Bull's camp remained at the Shallow Crossing of the Yellowstone, for White Bull was away with a war party during the early summer. When he returned he found the camp had crossed the river to the south bank and was heading toward the mouth of Tongue River. The camp crossed the Yellowstone to the north bank and followed the Yellowstone down to a point well below the Shallow Crossing. During the summer the Indians remained on each camp-site two or three nights. During all this time the people were busy hunting and stopped only long enough to jerk the meat they killed. Having sufficient meat for the winter the Sioux moved back to the Shallow Crossing of the Yellowstone, and there turned to the north and made their winter camp, south and east of the Horn Buttes.

Winter of 1870

The Sioux remained in their camp southeast of the Horn Buttes during most of the winter. But before the snow was gone they moved southwest to the mouth of Tongue River. Following up the Yellowstone, they passed the mouth of the Rosebud River to the Big Bottom, somewhat above, where they found a large camp of Sioux (Oglala, Minniconjou, Sans Arc) on the south bank. The combined camps set out to the west.

Spring of 1871

This large camp continued toward the west until they reached the foot of the White (Big Horn) Mountains. After a time they turned back and camped on what was later to be the Custer Battlefield.

White Bull here pointed out that all this country had once belonged to the Crow Indians (See treaty made at Fort Laramie, 1851), but that the Crows had been forced farther west by this time. White Bull says that the camp remained at the White Mountains only three or four days. After passing the Custer Battlefield the Indians went north to the Yellowstone and made camp once more in the Big Bottom.

Summer of 1871

The camp remained at Big Bottom about a week. From Big Bottom it moved down the Yellowstone and crossed to the north bank below the mouth of the Rosebud River. From the crossing the camp moved to Horn Buttes, there turning back south to the Yellowstone. By this time it was the end of June. At that time White Bull left Sitting Bull's camp and went to live with the tribe of his father Makes Room—the Minniconjou—and did not return until the summer of 1874.

Summer of 1874

On his return he found the camp moving north from the forks of Powder River. It proceeded to the southeast to the Big Bottom and remained there four days. Four tribes of Sioux were camped together; the Hunkpapa, Oglala, Minniconjou, and Sans Arc. The camp remained there until the Yellowstone was in flood and the roses in bloom. White Bull then left Sitting Bull's camp and was gone all winter.

Summer of 1875

On White Bull's return he found Sitting Bull's camp at the Big Bottom on the Yellowstone. Soon after, it moved northwest to the White Mountains, then, following the game, turned eastward down the Yellowstone to the Shallow Crossing. By that time it was autumn and White Bull went away.

Winter of 1875

On his return White Bull found his uncle's camp at the mouth of Powder River. It was then mid-winter. Four other bands of Sioux were camped far up the Powder (Little Powder) almost due east of the site of the village destroyed by Colonel J. J. Reynolds (March 17, 1876). Sitting Bull's band moved down to join the four bands on the Little Powder, but remained there only two sleeps.

Spring of 1876

At this time there was still some snow. Sitting Bull's camp moved over to Box Elder Creek, (known also as Hangs-Up-Pack-Creek) which flows into Thick Timber River (the Little Missouri). From the Box Elder the camp moved to Beaver Creek in the Blue Mountains on Powder River. Here Sitting Bull's camp received the refugees from the village burned by Colonel Reynolds on March 17. Afterward the camp moved to Tongue River and held councils with the other Sioux and Cheyenne bands. From the camp on the Tongue River Sitting Bull sent his summons to the Agencies calling for volunteers to fight the white troops. He mentioned the Rosebud River as the point of assembly and the hostile camp formed there sometime in May. Early in June the combined camps moved from the Rosebud to the Greasy Grass (Little Big Horn) River. They remained three nights on the Little Big Horn, moving to the north, but camping on the stream every night. Finding little game, they returned to the Rosebud and remained there until the game and the grazing for their horses were used up.

The chiefs then decided to return to the Greasy Grass in the hope of finding buffalo. The distance to be covered by the Indian trail from the Rosebud to Greasy Grass was approximately twenty miles. Large camps necessarily traveled slowly. That night the Indians made their camp on the elevated divide between the streams, on Ash (Reno) Creek, at a point six or seven miles from the Greasy Grass. While at this camp that night news was brought that soldiers were on the Rosebud River. Next morning Sitting Bull engaged General George Crook in the Battle of the Rosebud, June 17, 1876. Following the Battle of the Rosebud the Indians moved over to the Greasy Grass or Little Big Horn River where they remained on the same spot until Reno and Custer attacked them, on June 25. Then Sitting

Bull led them to the White (Big Horn) Mountains, where they arrived four days later and held their first Victory Dance. The movements of Sitting Bull and Crazy Horse after that dance have been set forth in my biography of Sitting Bull.

The movements of a camp of buffalo hunters sometimes seem erratic and purposeless to one who does not understand their methods of hunting. A single camp of Indians must follow the buffalo and at the same time search for suitable camping places, where wood, water and grass can be found. To one who knows the country as it was in those days, it is apparent that the Indians followed a fairly definite routine in their hunting. Scouts such as Frank Grouard, who had lived with the Sioux for some years, could readily tell at any given season where their camps could be found.

One of the most absurd notions held by the white men was that the Plains Indians were nomads. The Indian, as a matter of fact, was no more a nomad than a New Yorker who spends the summer in the Adirondacks and the winter in Florida, or than a traveling man who makes certain cities in the course of conducting his business. For the Indian made his camp regularly upon the same streams — very often on the same spots, and unless conditions forced him to vary his routine, generally hunted in the same regions at the same seasons. History is full of incidents showing the Indian's love for his home country, proving the great sacrifices he was ready to make rather than leave his fatherland and the graves of his ancestors. War to the death was usually his answer to any attempt to move him.

Young Indians sent away to school frequently died of homesickness. Today educated Indians find life on the reservations very hard and unfavorable, yet nearly all prefer to live there, rather than leave their own people and find an easier livelihood. You will nowadays find plenty of white farm boys in our cities, but you will find very few Indians there. Indeed the Indians form perhaps the only group in the United States which may be said to *love* their native soil as—for example— an Englishman loves it. How many, even of our rural people, care anything about the flora and fauna of their county? How many can name or tell the characteristics of the plants and animals? But if you pluck a flower and show it to a Sioux, his face will light up, he will smile, and tell you its name, its use, and—very probably —a legend concerning it. And he takes the same lively interest in the native animals. The deep resentment which all real Indians feel for the white men is due, not so much to the fact of conquest or disinheritance, as to the wanton waste of the country's natural resources, and the callous indifference towards the land shown by most white settlers. As Sitting Bull said, "*I want you to take good care of my country and respect it.*"

The white man's inability to understand that sentiment is manifest on every hand. He has cut or burned the timber, gutted the hills, fouled the streams, massacred the animals, ploughed the grass under, turned whole valleys into deserts of sand and gravel, whole ranges into badlands—and wasted half, at least, of the products for which he has made this frightful devastation. No wonder the Indian hated him. It was only too obvious that the white man did not love his country as the Indian understood it. Yet the white man called the Indian a nomad!

As a matter of fact, it was the white pioneer who was the nomad, who was willing and eager to shift his base once in a generation from East to West, ready and willing to jump a whole continent on the chance of finding a nugget, or a free farm, or for the mere love of wandering and adventure. For such men to call the Indians nomads is one of the absurdities of history.

The hunting of the Plains or Teton Sioux differed in one respect from that practiced by other, smaller Indian nations in the buffalo country. This was doubtless due to the fact that the Sioux were so numerous, and that their great confederation comprised so many bands and tribes that co-operation became desirable. But whatever the cause, it is certain that, during the last century, when buffalo became more and more difficult to find, there grew up the beginnings of an organized system of inter-tribal hunting. The bands or tribes would camp along the same stream—usually the Yellowstone—each camp about a day's ride from the next in the series. The band at the end of the line would then make a buffalo hunt. In planning their surround, they would try to rush the herd in the direction of the band down the river. The frightened buffalo would often keep going in the direction away from the hunters, and would in due time arrive at a point near the next camp, where the game scouts would see them coming. It was then the turn of the second camp to make a hunt, and the hunters, in their turn, would try to pass the herd on to their brothers below. In this way a large herd of buffalo was sometimes passed down a line of camps, providing good living for each in turn, and even—on occasion—was turned back again by the last camp of the series. Such systematic hunting was probably accidental at first, but would undoubtedly have hardened into a regular custom had the Indians remained masters of the game country for another half century.

No. 9.

OLD BULL'S BATTLES

Old Bull has one of the best memories among the living Hunkpapa warriors and is generally known as "the Hunkpapa historian." Here follow some brief notes—stories of fights he engaged in.

(a) *South of Arrow Creek; Fight with the Crow.*

There were six tribes of Indians camping together at the time when this battle south of Arrow creek took place. These tribes were Cheyennes, Oglala Sioux, Brulé Sioux, Hunkpapa Sioux, Minniconjou Sioux, Sans Arc Sioux. Old Bull and his brother-in-law, Sitting Crow, were chosen as scouts. They found the enemy (Crow) camp and reported it to the chiefs. The warriors then set out, each tribe under its own leader. Sitting Bull led the Hunkpapa, Chief Circling Bear the Sans Arcs, Chief Steamboat (Fire Boat) led the Minniconjou, Chief Crazy Horse led the Oglala, Chief Tiramnamna led the Brulé Sioux. The Cheyennes had a chief of their own.

When they reached the Yellowstone river they swam it and camped overnight pretty close to the enemy's camp. The Sioux attacked before sunrise, but did not fight long. Two Crow Indians were killed and several Sioux were hit: Swift Bird was shot through the leg and wounded otherwise; Sitting White Bull was shot through the hip; Good Crow was shot through the leg; Brave Crow was shot through the chest. Some of the Sioux warriors were daring. One of them counted a first *coup* on a Crow under fire. Iron Bull followed him and counted the second *coup*. Fool Heart struck third. The fight did not last long. The Sioux had had no breakfast and were hungry; besides it was a very hot day, and their horses soon played out.

(b) *On the east side of the Rosebud, 1873.*

Another fight took place on the east side of the Rosebud River in the year 1873. Sitting Bull and Fool Bull led the warriors. These two and Red Crow sang as they rode into the fight:

> We are looking for His Big Shield,
> That is why we are advancing.

On the way into this fight Sitting Bull honored certain men by calling out their names and telling them to be brave and fight hard. This was a way of calling attention to warriors of distinction before a fight. It centered people's attention upon them and stimulated them to valor. On this occasion Sitting Bull named Bear's Horn, Old Bull and Bears-Charge-at-Him. After these men had been named all the warriors sang together.

There were about four hundred enemies, half of them horseback, the others on foot. Good Bear, Old Bull, and Bird Bear were among the bravest of the Sioux in this affair. Black Crow was killed, but nobody was injured.

(c) *Baker's Fight, August 14, 1872, Mouth of Arrow Creek.*

This is Old Bull's account of the celebrated Baker Fight, August 14, 1872, near the mouth of Pryor creek on Yellowstone river. The story of this battle will be found in my biography of Sitting Bull, Chapter XVIII. White Bull's account appears in my *Warpath* in the

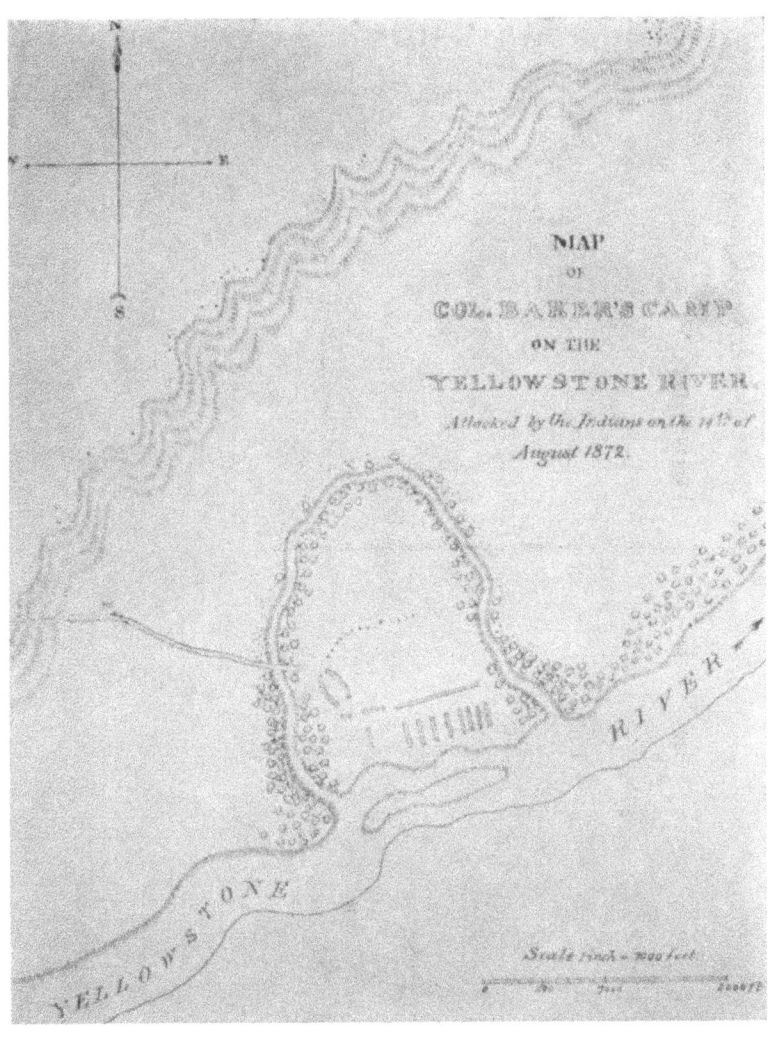

COURTESY, CHIEF OF ENGINEERS, U. S. ARMY

Map of Colonel Baker's Camp on the Yellowstone River, August 14, 1872

chapter entitled "Bullet Proof." Old Bull, however, adds several items of interest here:

"There were four different bands of Sioux in this fight. Sitting Bull led the Hunkpapa; Steam Boat led the Minniconjou; Crazy Horse led the Oglala. The leader of the Sans Arc was Circling Bear. Less than a thousand warriors rode with these chiefs to defend that country and protect their wild game from the soldiers. Six days before this battle (August 8) these tribes were encamped on the Yellowstone river at Big Bend, holding a Sun dance.

Fire White Man was the leader of the dancers. Little Bird and Bull-on-the-Ground, who had been sent out as scouts, returned during the dance and reported that soldiers were coming. Immediately Chiefs Steamboat and Sitting Bull, after counciling with other head men, ordered the Indians to break camp and move about sixteen miles to the southeast, to the mouth of Fat Horse creek. At the same time the fighting men prepared to ride out and meet the soldiers near the mouth of Arrow (Pryor) creek.

Next day the camp moved east along the Yellowstone to Fat Horse creek, the day following to Rosebud river, and after that to the mouth of Tongue river, there to await the return of the warriors.

The war party found the soldiers at dawn on the north bank of the Yellowstone west of the mouth of Arrow creek. Before the Indians could attack, Crawler, Running Enemy, and In-the-Front came in with two horses and three mules captured from the military camp during the night. When the warriors appeared, the soldiers fired at them; they fired the first shot. Plenty Lice was killed outright and Good Weasel wounded. Good Weasel recovered and lived to be an old man.

Two Crows' horse was shot dead under him and the fight became general. Both sides fired heavily, the Indians maintaining the ridge and the soldiers defending the flat below. The Indians were facing south. At last the Indians moved back perhaps half a mile to the north on the high ground. From that point they watched the soldiers.

Old Bull says, "We could see the soldiers building a fire close to where Plenty Lice had fallen. They built a fire and then four of them took his body and threw it into the fire. Sitting Bull, Running Bear, Charging Hawk, Two Spears, Horned Thunder and I all witnessed the burning of his body. Later the relatives of Plenty Lice went to that place after the soldiers were gone. They found only scorched bones left of that burning.

The Sioux counted no *coups* that day. The fight lasted only a short time."

(d) *On Scarf Creek.*

There was a fight at Scarf creek or War Bonnet creek. It flows into the Yellowstone north, below the mouth of Powder river, at the place where you can walk across. Sitting Bull was in this fight and other great leaders like Fool Bull, Long Dog, and Swift Dog. This was in the summer of 1870. They fought the soldiers on foot. They fought from dawn until noon. Thunder Hawk and Old Bull were among the bravest in this fight. Nobody was wounded, but Tawahancakawanyankapi (Appearing-Shield) was killed. Sitting Bull gave good advice to his warriors that day. He rode a black horse and carried his rifle. As he rode into the fight he sang a song:

This is my land;
I will not give it up.

There were over one hundred Sioux in this fight. Old Bull was only a youngster and could not fight like more seasoned warriors.

No. 10.
CHASING HORSES IN CAMP
1871

The Hunkpapa Sioux were encamped between the Rosebud River and Fat Horse Creek, near a butte which is known to the Indians by an unprintable name—being a reference to a dog. The men had been out hunting all day, and when they returned at night-fall, Kills-Enemy reported that he had had a narrow escape, had been almost surrounded by his enemies, the Crows. Old Bull immediately prepared to round up his ponies for safety, other hunters hastened to consult their shaman or medicine-man, Wants-To-Die-Quick. They asked him to divine what would happen. He agreed.

Soon after, one of these hunters came from the door of the shaman's tipi, and seeing Old Bull starting after his ponies, said, "What are you up to? The shaman says the Crows are already within our camp. Get ready!"

Old Bull put an arrow on his bowstring, and lay low behind a stump. He saw a Crow coming, driving away a bunch of Sioux ponies. As they came towards him, he crouched behind the stump, trying to get a fair shot. But the Crow saw Old Bull, let out a yell, and threw the herd another way. Old Bull loosed his arrow, but missed his enemy.

Then Old Bull, who is lame, ran after the Crow, but could not overtake the horses. The Crows were soon lost to sight in the darkness, and the Sioux could not be sure which way they had gone. They soon lost the trail. The Crows got away with nearly all the Sioux ponies that night. Next morning, even by daylight the Sioux could not pursue, for nearly every man was left afoot.

It was so unusual for the Crows to raid the Sioux camp and steal so many horses that the year 1871 is remembered in the Hunkpapa Calendar or Winter Count as Chasing-Horses-in-Camp.

No. 11.
SITTING CROW IS KILLED
1873

After the big fight with the Slota or Red River Half-Breeds from Canada in 1873, the Hunkpapa had an all-day battle with the Crows. These Crows, having despaired of aid from their supposed allies, the white troops, appealed to the Nez Percé Indians beyond the mountains to the west. Soon after, the Sioux found the two tribes encamped in Sioux country, killing Sioux meat. Their tipis formed a big circle near the mouth of the Rosebud River.

The Hunkpapa and Cheyennes attacked these intruders, rode right into their camp—right in among the tipis. Sitting Bull led the charge on his black horse with white stockings—one of the two black horses presented him by Makes-Room. He carried his shield on his back, riding back and forth through his lines, encouraging his men. Old Bull, now living, was close beside him all the time; he was a sort of aide to the chief. Sitting Bull's voice, his advice and commands, could be heard above all the noise, "high up in the air."

With the chief rode ten picked men, the leaders

in this fight: Old Bull, Sitting Crow, Middle Bull, Iron Thunder, Fish-in-the-Kettle, Little Horse, Rain-in-the-Face, Scout, Catch-the-Bear, Strikes-Him-as-He-Runs. It was hand-to-hand fighting.

Sitting Bull counted a *coup*. So did Little Bull, Iron Bull, Fool Heart, Holy Eagle. But the Sioux suffered many casualties. They lost Sitting Crow—a very brave, public-spirited man, one of the founders of the Silent Eaters Society. Also Middle Bull, hero of a dozen fights. And Lone Man, Hail Bear, Eagle Bear. For all that they kept right on fighting until Sitting Bull's resonant voice called out, "Stop fighting!" Then they stopped. They obeyed.

Two Crows was killed, and Swift Bird—shot through the breast and shoulder—died later from his wounds. Many Hunkpapa horses were shot down that day. Four Nez Percés and a larger number of Crows were killed.

That night the Crows kept watch. But their vigilance was useless. Little Bull, Crawler, and Middle stole ten head of horses from their camp—and all without being seen or shot at!

The Sioux and the Crows were like two dogs fighting, the old men say; if you pull them apart and then let them go, they will be at each other's throats again. They will fight; they cannot stop. That is why the Crows were always begging for guns and field-glasses—to fight the Sioux. Their chiefs kept saying to the white officers, "You ought to wipe the Sioux out. Kill them all, or throw a bad disease on them."

No. 12.

A FAT ENEMY KILLED
1874

The Hunkpapa Sioux took part in one skirmish with

the Crows in 1874. The Crows came to steal Sioux horses —and did so. The Sioux chased the Crows ten miles, clear into the hills on the north side of Tongue River, near the mouth. One of the Crows was a fat, heavy, huge man. In the Sioux herd he had found a curly horse, and took it. All the nations greatly admired curly horses. Unluckily for the fat man, this curly horse was one of the slowest in the herd, and saddled with that shaking mountain of flesh, it soon played out. The Sioux began to overtake the fat man, although he kept lashing his staggering mount for all he was worth. Before long he saw that it was hopeless; they were right behind him. Jumping off the heaving, lathered animal, he drew his knife and stabbed it to death (whether from anger, revenge, or spite, or wishing to do all the harm he could to his enemy, is unknown). Then he ran off afoot. Within a few seconds the Sioux were on top of him. He was the fattest man they ever killed. For this reason his death was used to mark that winter in the Hunkpapa calendar.

No. 13.

NOTE ON CURLY HORSES

In the old days, when capturing horses was a major industry on the Plains, the Sioux and Crows particularly admired what were known as "curly horses." Young Eagle, a Sioux survivor of Custer's Last Stand, gives the following description of the curly horse. It is printed here through the courtesy of Frank Zahn.

"These horses were raised by the Indians as far back as anyone can remember. Most of them were dark in color, with hair 'singed.' Hence their name, which is *Sung-gu-gu-la,* literally 'horses with burnt hair'."
The Hunkpapa Calendar owned by Old Bull refers to

curly horses, as in the story of how the Fat Enemy was killed.

No. 14.
THE FATE OF THE HORSE-THIEF

It is a curious fact that everywhere on the Western frontier the penalty for stealing a horse was death. Inasmuch as no such penalty was inflicted in Europe, where white men came from, various explanations have been offered. It has been said that, on the Plains, a man afoot was in danger of losing his life—from enemies, buffalo, wild cattle, prairie-fires, or starvation. Undoubtedly this is true. But I think it probable that in this respect, as in many others, the white frontiersman was simply following the custom of the country. It must never be forgotten that white frontiersmen were strangers in an old, established Indian civilization, and, like other immigrants, they borrowed a great many of the customs of the natives among whom they found themselves.

Among the Plains Indians, the horse was not merely the companion and indispensable aid of the wandering warrior and his family, but the only property—strictly speaking—upon which an Indian placed any value. Everything else he owned was home-made. The horse was not merely his safety in flight, and his living in the buffalo hunt; it also ranked him as a warrior, since the men on the fastest horses invariably won the most honors, other things being equal. Therefore, horses were prizes for which men were willing to risk their lives, and naturally the owner of a good horse did what he could to repel and destroy horse-thieves. The horse was prize of war—booty—hence death came into the picture. Horsethieves were killed and cut to pieces when caught.

Of course, the severe penalty did nothing to stop the thieving—for that was held the most honorable way of acquiring horse-flesh. Horses were very temporary possessions in the Old West. White frontiersmen, after some experience of Indian horse-stealing, soon adopted the only measures which would deter the thieves: they shot to kill. Later, when the Indian's day was over, and white horse-thieves had to operate against men of their own race, the good old European punishment of hanging was substituted for shooting and mutilation— as being more humiliating, or more civilized.

Makes-Trouble tells the following story of how the Sioux treated horse-thieves in the old days.

It was winter. The Hunkpapa were in camp on the Yellowstone River. Some Crow Indians came on foot during the night, killed one of the Hunkpapa sleeping, and got away with a herd of Sitting Bull's ponies.

However, he had one good horse left, which had been tied up close by his tipi. Mounting this animal, he set out across the snow after his enemies, all alone. He rode hard, but the Crows had such good horses that he could not catch them. But he did discover, from their trail in the snow, that one of the Crows was afoot, having had no luck. With this good news Sitting Bull turned back to his plodding comrades, who were following him on foot. All the Sioux then pushed hard on the trail of the luckless Crow, following his foot-prints in the snow. The lone Crow saw them coming after him, and took refuge among some loose rocks on the top of a small butte. The Sioux circled round, trying to shoot him.

Afraid-of-His-Track was a crack shot, and had a

good gun. Sitting Bull called to him, "Get that Crow. Don't misplace your shot. Watch your chance, and make a direct hit."

Afraid-of-His-Track nodded. He leveled his gun, took careful aim, and when the Crow showed his head among the rocks, let him have it. That shot killed the Crow. Sitting Bull saw him tumble, and called out to Catch-the-Bear, "The Crow is dead!" At once all the Sioux raced to the top of the butte, to count their *coups*.

When they got there, they found the Crow lying on his side, stone dead, shot through the forehead. Sitting Bull was angry. Said he, "Cut him to pieces. They killed one of us." So they all took their butcher-knives, cut the dead Crow limb from limb, and carried his various members back to camp to show the folks that they had got even with the Crows.

Another time, I have heard, Sitting Bull decapitated a Hohe (Assiniboine) horse-thief. But no eye-witness is known, so the story may be omitted here. Stealing horses was a dangerous game, calling for all the cunning, skill, endurance, and courage a man could show. Many of the Sioux were adept at it. Some men made it a regular business, and never went to war for any other purpose. Among those experts were Dog Eagle, Flying Cloud, and Tree Top.

No. 15.

TAKING ENEMY HORSES
1875

After the Fall hunt, 1875, Sitting Bull proposed a war party against the Crows—to take horses. Now that he was getting on, he preferred raiding for horses to the mere violent exertions and excitements of hand-to-hand conflict. Ten men volunteered to go with him, among them three from his own band—Standing Cloud, One Bull, and Has-Bob-Tail. They set out from the camp on the Powder, and travelled fifteen days to the Crow camp on Musselshell river. Sitting Bull left his shield at home. He wore a gray striped blanket coat with hood attached, and carried his six-shooter. There was as yet no snow. After crossing the Yellowstone, they rode by night and lay hidden during the daytime.

Very early on the morning of the fifteenth night they reached the Musselshell, and found a camp of thirty Crow lodges. The horses were grazing around the camp, within a hundred yards of the tents. It was still dark. Sitting Bull left his party concealed two miles distant, and went into the Crow camp alone. He crept noiselessly in among the tipis, for he knew that the best horses would be picketed close beside the owners' tents. He cut as many lariats as possible, quieting the dogs with meat taken from a drying rack. He started the horses away at a slow walk, without arousing anyone. When he was well away from the camp, he mounted a gentle horse, rounded up the bunch, and drove them quickly off to the place where his young men lay waiting. He brought thirty good horses from the Crow camp, and divided them among his warriors. One Bull received a fine horse from this bunch. Sitting Bull kept nothing for himself. The party reached home after six days of hard riding. The Crows did not pursue.

No. 16.
NOTE ON THE REYNOLDS BATTLE, POWDER RIVER, MARCH 17, 1876

Through the kindness of Senator Frank T. Kelsey, State of Montana, who owns the battlefield where Reynolds attacked the Indians (near Moorehead, Montana)

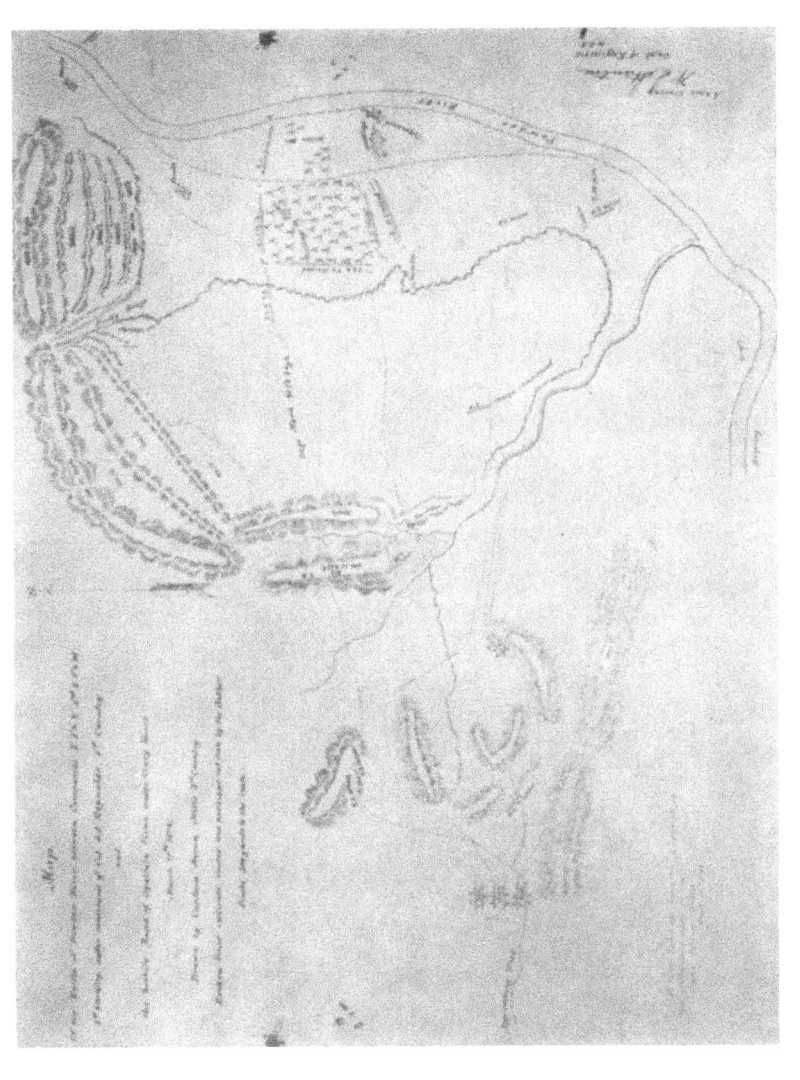

Map of the Reynolds Battle on Powder River, March 17, 1876

on Powder River, I offer the following description of the site.

"The site of the camp is on the west bank of Powder River in a low, flat bottom, quite heavily timbered at that time with cottonwood, willows, buffalo berry and rose brush. It is surrounded on the west by high broken hills rising to perhaps a thousand feet within a half a mile, almost impassable except to a man on foot, and crowned with red scoria. The Indians retreated up these hills when Reynolds surprised them. When we acquired this site thirty years ago, it was covered with Indian sign, partially burned tipi poles, etc.

"Later a former government scout who was with Reynolds in the battle described to me the surprise attack, the fight and the retreat. The scout was a very old man but on the whole he gave a good account of the action. His account in brief was that he and another scout located the Indian camp and reported to General Crook on Otter Creek, twenty miles west. Reynolds made a night march over the divide and down a rough creek bed, arriving at the camp at daybreak. Here Reynolds divided his force, aiming to surround the camp, but one part of the troops encountered deep canyons of which Reynolds probably knew nothing. This part of the troops did not arrive in time. . . . .

"There are tipi poles lying on the high hills west of the battle ground, and undoubtedly here is where the chief left his non-combatants while he drove Reynolds and Crook to Fort McKinney. Mr. T. J. Gatchell of Buffalo, Wyoming went over this site with one of the scouts forty years ago. It was also mapped some years ago by an army officer."

A number of historians appear to be under the impression that the village attacked by Colonel Reynolds was a Sioux village containing a few Cheyenne lodges, and give Crazy Horse credit for leading the Indians in the fight that day. Indians who were present, both Sioux and Cheyennes, state that the village was a Cheyenne village under Chief Two Moon and that only a few Oglala Sioux lodges were in it. Chief Crazy Horse was not present during the fighting on March 17, 1876. Chief Two Moon of the Cheyennes deserves credit for this victory. His nephew, Young Two Moon, now living, was present. An account of this fight, as the Sioux and Cheyennes tell it, will be found in my *Warpath*, Chapter XVIII.

No. 17.
LIST OF INDIAN SURVIVORS OF CUSTER FIGHT. STANDING ROCK AGENCY, 1929

One Bull	Looking Elk
White Bull	Fearless
Circling Hawk	Pretends Eagle
Little Moon	Low Dog
Shoots Walking	Flying By
Little Soldier	Good Dog
Black Bear	No Two Horns
Bear Soldier	Bobtail Bull
Grey Eagle	Elk Nation
Old Bull	Kills Hawk
Hona	Crazy Hawk
Black Prairie Dog	White Face Bear
White Cow Walking	One Elk
Two Bull	Cross Bear
One Hawk or (Young Hawk)	Mary Crawler
	Young Eagle

COURTESY, BUREAU OF AMERICAN ETHNOLOGY

The Cheyenne Chief, Two Moon

No. 18.
NOTE ON THE CUSTER FIGHT
Through the kindness of Mr. Frank Zahn my attention was called to the fact that, following the fight with Major Reno in the bottoms of the Little Big Horn on the morning of June 25, Sitting Bull had an accident. It happened soon after the troops fled to the bluffs. At that time some of the pack-mules were shot, or ran away to be captured by the Indians. Sitting Bull saw a pack-mule on the ground. Supposing the animal was dead he went up to it, whereupon the mule kicked Sitting Bull on the shins. The chief was not seriously injured.

No. 19.
INDIAN CRITICISM OF MAJOR McLAUGHLIN'S BOOK *MY FRIEND THE INDIAN*
The Sioux at Standing Rock respect the memory of Major McLaughlin as that of one of the best agents they ever had. However, old warriors complain that in his book he quotes the story of the Custer Fight from the lips of Mrs. Spotted Horn Bull—a woman. They feel that he should have taken the story of this fight from a warrior who was in the fight rather than publish an account by a *woman*. In their opinion war is the business of a man and not a thing which women should be quoted on.

No. 20.
"YOUNG-SITTING-BULL" IS KILLED DECEMBER 17, 1876
After the Battle of the Little Big Horn, June 25, 1876, rumors of Chief Sitting Bull's death were frequent. A lame Indian was found lying in state in a

burial lodge, and for some time it was supposed that this was the chief. And somewhat later, (winter of 1876-77), a young Oglala named Sitting Bull was actually killed. He was not related to the chief. This is how it happened, White Bull says:

It was the policy of the chiefs of the hunting bands, at that time, to keep away from the soldiers and avoid war. They fought only in self-defense, or to drive away poachers or those who scared off the game. But some of the young men could not resist temptation; one day, some of them ran off horses belonging to the soldiers at the mouth of Tongue River. As soon as the chiefs found this out, they sent the young men to restore the animals. They carried a white flag to Fort Keogh, December 17, 1876.

"Young Sitting Bull," the Oglala (also known as Drumpacker) went with five or six others. It was midwinter, very cold, and the soldiers were not visible as they approached Fort Keogh. However, Hollow Horns (a Sans Arc) saw some of the Crow Indian Government Scouts hanging around; he said, "These Crows are tricky; maybe they will start something."

Just as the Sioux reached the fort, the Crows fired on them. "Young Sitting Bull" fell first, then Fat-on-the-Beef, Lame Red Skirt (both Minniconjou), and two others named (in the books) Tall Bull and Bull Eagle. Hollow Horns had a very fast horse, he was not hit, and away he went. After him came the Crows, on fresh ponies. Hollow Horns went the wrong way, and was held up by the thick brush in the bottoms; the Crows caught up with him and killed him, and his horse too. It was all over before the officers at the fort knew what was up. This unlucky chance made further efforts at peace unpopular in Sitting Bull's camp; for the young men killed had relatives in all the bands.

No. 21.
NOTE ON "SITTING BULL'S BOYS"
by Frank Zahn

Sitting Bull is said to have selected his personal bodyguard from men all of about the same height. Those living are nearly all about five feet six inches in height. Examples are Male Bear, Old Bull, One Bull, White Bull, Elk Nation, Bear-With-White-Paw.

No. 22.
NOTE ON THE WHITE HORSE RIDERS

The White Horse Riders, or White Cavalry, was an order of warriors among the Hunkpapa Sioux. It was organized, or perhaps reorganized, by Sitting Bull shortly before the Custer Fight, 1876, at a camp near the White Buttes on the Little Missouri River. Sitting Bull and Hollow were the chiefs. Among the charter members at that time were Makes-the-Enemy, Feather Mane, Running Hawk, Fool Bull, Running Horse, Brown Eagle, Black Bull, Charging, Thunder Spotted Horn, Red Horn, Brave Thunder, His-Horse-Looking. This society is still flourishing and some years ago contributed funds to purchase a stone and pay for an inscription to the memory of Chief Sitting Bull, their founder. Owing to official interference or, some say, to a mistake in the carving of the inscription, the monument was never erected and the stone still lies in the barnyard of one of the members. The following men now living contributed a horse or money for this monument: One Bull, Old Bull, Little Eagle, Circling Hawk, Bobtail Bull,

White Horse, Did-Not-Butcher, Iron Dog and Male Bear.

No. 23.
NOTE ON THE FOX WARRIOR SOCIETY

The following Sioux warriors are members of this society: One Bull, Eagle Boy, Rosebud, Old Bull, Bobtail Bull, and Red Legs. They say that their society sometimes sings the following song in honor of Sitting Bull, formerly chief of the society:

> "Friends, take fresh courage.
> This, my country, I love."
> Sitting Bull, saying this, has passed away.
>
> "Friends, take fresh courage.
> As for me, I am helpless."
> Sitting Bull, saying this, has passed away.

II. PROBLEMS OF PEACE

No. 24.
THE GREAT TREATY COUNCIL AT FORT LARAMIE
1851

1. The Election of Stirring-Bear.

The Autumn of 1851 the Indian nations assembled at Birch Grove on Horse Creek, for the great treaty of Fort Laramie. Sitting Bull rode down the three hundred miles from Grand River with the other Hunkpapa, who—as they moved south—picked up in turn delegations of each tribe of their Teton relatives: Blackfeet Sioux, Two Kettles, Sans Arc, Minniconjou. The Oglala and Brulé Sioux were already in camp on the Platte. All the Teton tribes would be represented there.

This treaty was a great event in Prairie Sioux history, and had a profound effect upon Sitting Bull's views and later policy. His later speeches show that he had a very good grasp of what it meant to his people. But at the time he was only twenty years old, and certainly was unaware of all the causes which led the white men to make it. Some of these causes went back a long way.

Twenty-odd years before Sitting Bull was born, a hard-up Corsican adventurer sold most of the Sioux country to a Virginian doctrinaire for a substantial sum in cold cash. Neither of these gentlemen had ever laid eyes upon the lands they haggled over, and the Sioux had never even heard of them. Yet, by the convenient fictions of European diplomacy, Sitting Bull's country was thereafter considered to belong to the United States, the remainder being ceded by the British. It was as though the King of Siam should sell Texas to the Grand Lama, merely because certain Siamese gentlemen had visited Texas and thought he might like it. The absurdity of the transaction never seems to have occurred to Thomas Jefferson or Napoleon Bonaparte. Yet if Jefferson had suspected how much it was going to cost to get Sitting Bull to agree to the sale, he would have beat Bonaparte down to a much lower figure! The Sioux campaigns cost far more than the Louisiana Purchase.

Soon after, Jefferson sent Lewis and Clark up the Missouri River to see what he had bought, and from that day the troubles of the Sioux began. For a long time the Sioux had been friends of the Red Coats, but now the Red Coats had pulled out, and so the Hunkpapa signed a treaty of amity with the white Americans in 1825. After that, traders and trappers multiplied like rabbits in their country, and when Sitting Bull was only one year old, in 1832, a steamboat actually navigated the Missouri River all the way up to Fort Union, at the mouth of the Yellowstone. About the same time the United States passed Intercourse Laws, and forbade the introduction of liquor into the Indian country. But this prohibition never came to the notice of the Sioux.

The steamboat brought plenty of trouble up-river. In 1837, it brought smallpox, a plague which carried off some twenty-five thousand red men with frightful speed, leaving lodges standing on every hill, with never a streak of smoke rising from them. The farmer tribes, who lived in palisaded towns of beehive earth-lodges on the bluffs along the river, were almost wiped out. Nine-tenths of the Mandans perished, one-half the Hidatsa, and some three thousand Rees. Before long these three tribes had to combine and fortify themselves in one town, to keep from being carried into slavery by the Sioux. The Blackfoot Nation and the Crees also suffered terribly. But the Sioux all scattered at the first alarm, and so saved themselves. Thereafter they became the scourge of their less fortunate neighbors. Many persons of the Village tribes committed suicide from grief or despair, or in horror at seeing their flesh rot while they were still alive.

On top of that, there was trouble at the Ree village with the trader, F. F. Girard, and the Sioux would have rubbed out the whites to a man, if the Rees had not interfered. In 1840 the Cheyennes and Sioux made peace, which lasted thirty-six years. In 1842 the Sioux went to war against white trappers, rubbed out Frapp's party, and scared Kit Carson into making his will. Two years later the price of buffalo robes went down, and the Indians suspected that the traders were cheating them. This state of affairs was not helped by the cholera epidemic brought up the Oregon Trail by white men in 1845. That same year General Stephen Watts Kearny threatened the hostile Arapaho, but on finding his words were empty wind, they went to war again the next summer. In 1847 the Mormons marched across the Indian country to Utah, and two years later two "soldier houses" were built on the Platte: Fort Kearny and Fort Laramie.

All these things meant trouble for the Plains Indians, but the worst was yet to be. In '49 came the gold rush to California.

The Sioux along the Platte had never seen such

hordes of white men (100,000 or more), and decided that vast hunting grounds must now lie vacant toward the rising sun. But along the Oregon Trail the buffalo promptly disappeared. And soon after, a second scourge of cholera swept away almost half the remaining Indian population of the Plains.

Those footloose farmers who trekked up the Oregon Trail beside the white tilts of their prairie schooners brought with them a ready-made notion of the Indian, a notion gained in the long struggle for the Dark and Bloody Ground east of the Mississippi, a notion that every Indian was a lying, thieving, skulking murderer, who would delight to torture any unfortunate wretch who fell into his clutches. It was a notion which did not fit the Plains Indian at all, but it was a mighty agreeable notion to all those who wanted to dispossess the Indian, and the emigrants passed too quickly through the Plains to discover how false it really was.

As a matter of fact, the Plains tribes were generally men of their word, scrupulously honest, and too courageous to rejoice in wanton cruelty. It hardly becomes white men, who have taken everything the Indian possessed, to call him a thief. Nor, considering the way white men broke the treaties, can the Indian be branded a liar. Time and again I have left all my possessions lying on the prairie in the middle of an Indian camp of three thousand persons for as long as a week, and when I came back found everything just as I had left it. Unless whiskey is flowing, a town of Plains Indians is the most law-abiding community in America. When gangsters have made our cities uninhabitable, there will still be peace and order in Sitting Bull's home town. Moreover, though atrocities did sometimes occur during the Sioux campaigns (as in all wars), the Sioux never reserved prisoners for torture. They either killed them at once, put them to ransom, or adopted them into the tribe.

Another droll idea cherished by these homeless farmers was that the Indian was a "nomad." Now Sitting Bull died within twenty miles of his birth-place, and but for a flood which prevented him crossing Grand River, would have built his house on the very spot where he was born. He loved his home country, and fought for it with a stubborn tenacity which has made him memorable among the patriots of all ages. Yet these wandering farmers, who had changed their base at least once in every generation for a century, and were even then jumping clear across a continent, called Sitting Bull's people "nomads." As a matter of fact, a farmer cannot love the soil as a hunter does, because he is bound to it. The cities are full of farm boys now, but you will find very few Indians there.

The emigrant farmer was, as a rule, a man of small imagination, hard and thrifty, who marched with a rifle in one hand, the Old Testament in the other, and a jug of "likker" in the wagon. He always had a grievance, and knew nothing and cared less about the feelings and customs of the Indians. He was alternately arrogant and panic-stricken, and tried to make up for the boredom of plodding along the endless trail by writing home highly-colored accounts of imaginary Indian raids. Who can blame him? Any officer who censored soldier mail overseas during the World War knows how often bored soldiers behind the lines wrote home glowing accounts of battles they never saw. Evidently, the emigrant did the same thing, and by 1850 the tribes along the Santa Fe and Oregon Trails had received a thoroughly bad name in the East.

The number of white persons killed by Plains Indians before that date was negligible, and the tribute exacted by the tribesmen from emigrants was rather less than the motor tourist pays when passing through the same region today. But the emigrant was tight-fisted. He aroused the nation. Uncle Sam decided that something must be done, and sent the Reverend Father Pierre-Jean De Smet, S.J., to summon his red brothers to the council. And when the Black Robe, as the Indians called the good father, asked them to attend, the Prairie Sioux could not refuse.

Those Indians who lived by the side of the road to Oregon were anxious to attend. They wanted to adjust their growing difficulties. They were surrounded by enemy Indian nations with whom they must fight, if they left their own hunting grounds for game. The buffalo had vanished from the Platte. White men were cutting all their scanty timber, burning off their grass, turning what had lately been a great meat-producing country into a barren desert. Yet when the Sioux hunter, hungry and poor because of these same white men, ventured to approach a wagon train and ask for a little present of food or tobacco, these inhospitable devastators of his country warned him away, or even fired on him.

When white Americans visited Sioux camps, the people always entertained them freely for as long as they chose to remain, with no thought of asking payment: the evidence of the white men themselves, as shown in early Western books, is absolutely clear on that point. And it seemed pretty rotten when the men who were ruining the Sioux country, men rich beyond the dreams of Indian avarice — men with *guns* and *steel knives*;—refused to do the same for them. They could see no reason for that. Among the Sioux any man was welcome to drop in at meal-time and eat his fill, quite without invitation. Stinginess was the lowest, meanest vice they knew. Yankee thrift, Yankee caution, Yankee sharp practices were all alike abhorrent to the Sioux. And seeing how the white man behaved, the Sioux could only decide that this stranger was a mean, stingy, inhospitable rascal. The Sioux did not like the way he treated them, and they began to resent it. If, today, hordes of Chinese millionaires passed through the States, consuming our supplies, wasting our resources, enjoying our hospitality, and then—when an opportunity offered to return our entertainment—treated us as spongers, beggars, and thugs, what should we do? Probably we should be less patient than the Sioux were under like conditions.

The proud Oglala Sioux, the touchy Brulé Sioux, the friendly Cheyennes, the unstable Arapahos—all these were willing and eager to smoke with the chiefs sent out by the Grandfather from Washington.

Sitting Bull's people, however, away north on Grand River, cared little about the treaty. They went down to Laramie because the Black Robe asked it, and to see their relatives. They were always ready for a holiday. As for white men, they saw very few and wished to see none—except traders. "All we want from the white man is his hatchet, his knife, and his gun," they said. "We made one treaty; why make another?" That was what the Hunkpapa said. In fact, the sorriest vagabond in the Hunkpapa camp, with only a gee-string and a piece of old tent-cloth to cover him, thought himself infinitely better than any white man. He despised the traders as a lot of unwarlike, timid weaklings, who brought trade goods produced by more cunning people beyond the big water. Why trouble to go all the way to the Platte to smoke again with them?

Why indeed?

The civilization of the Plains Indians was established long before white men saw their country. It was ancient then. But with the coming of the horse from Europe, every phase of it received, as it were, a shot in the arm. Life became freer, richer, bolder, more picturesque, colorful, prosperous. The change wrought by the introduction of the horse in Indian life can only be compared with that brought about in our own civilisation by the invention of the automobile. A static world became dynamic. Men who had lived laborious lives, plodding after game with heavy packs on their backs, who had slept huddled in wretched, leaky bark lodges or cramped tents barely ten feet across, men who had and hoped to have no property, who never travelled, never traded, never had enough to eat, and to whom war was little more than self-defense, now suddenly found themselves emancipated in a grand and glorious world.

Their range now extended from the Rockies to the Lakes, from Mexico to the Barren Grounds. They packed their burdens on animals, enlarged their dwellings to stately dimensions, got food with ease and in abundance, had something to trade, something to give away, and their warfare developed into a glorious sport. For more than a century they lived like kings.

This rich, colorful, free life of the Plains Indian entranced all men who beheld it. It penetrated the eastern forests: farmer tribes (like the Cheyennes) took to hunting again, and even the most sedentary nations hunted and lived in tents half the year. The horse, the tipi, the camp circle, the *coup*, the Sun Dance—all the typical traits of Plains Indian culture spread like wildfire; into the woods eastward, over the mountains westward; northward almost to the country of the Eskimo; southward into the Spanish settlements, where (early in the eighteenth century) the Spanish governors had to issue edicts to *compel* their subjects to till the soil and to hunt buffalo *only* at stated seasons.

Plains Indian culture bade fair to sweep the continent—until the coming of the English-speaking ploughmen. It had absorbed some of the Spaniards, had swallowed the French Canadians bodily. The Hudson's Bay Company men, and other trappers, were hardly more than Indians in thought and habit. Old Bill Williams is said to have offered his corncob pipe to the sun, like any shaman. Kit Carson lived in a tipi and counted *coups*.

To this very day, when an Indian in New York or California wishes to dress the part, he puts on the scalp-shirt and war-bonnet of a Plains Indian. So great is the prestige of that far-flung civilisation still. Now, the Prairie or Teton Sioux formed the very hub and center of that civilisation, and of the most powerful Indian nation on the continent. Why should they care for the wishes of a far-off white Grandfather? Not all of them could be induced to attend the treaty.

Yet many of the Sioux went. Recently the Crows had been making trouble, having been well supplied with guns by their traders, and the Hunkpapa had had so much to do that the old communal government had nearly broken down. The people were too numerous now to be looked after by a "soldier lodge," Little Bear was too old to direct matters. It was decided to appoint a chief for each band. Accordingly, four chiefs were named to control the four major bands of the tribe.

These chiefs, named that very year, 1851, were Red Horn, Loud-Voiced-Hawk, Running Antelope, and Sitting Bull's uncle, Four Horns. Probably this new honor and responsibility were what led Four Horns to attend the treaty council. He was a man who took his public duties very much to heart.

He and his delegation arrived at the council grounds on Saturday, September 6, 1851.

On the point formed by the junction of Horse Creek with the Platte River, stood the tent of the United States Commissioner, and all about this, up-stream and down, on both banks of the river, were the camps of the assembled nations: Sioux, Cheyennes, Arapahos, Crows, Shoshoni, Mandans, Hidatsa, and Rees. Also the camps of the traders, of the Indian agents, of the Dragoons and Mounted Rifles. It was the largest encampment young Sitting Bull had ever seen. It was estimated that not less than eight thousand Indians were there.

As the Hunkpapa and their companions rolled down the valley from the northwest, the young men—a thousand strong—painted up, donned their finest clothes, uncovered their shields, mounted their best horses, and formed in column of fours. Led by their chief carrying an old American flag, and filled with barbaric pride of arms, they rode tumultuously in careless order, with war-bonnets nodding, lances flashing with steel and lustrous eagle plumes, all singing and shouting in chorus. Sitting Bull, bearing lance and shield, rode on his bay charger among the other young men of his Warrior Order, his deep voice resonant and strong in the chant. The cavalcade made a fine appearance, and struck admiration into the hearts of the white men who saw and recorded it. When they reached the tent of the Commissioner, they halted, dismounted, and received his welcome, his tobacco, his vermilion. He told them that the council would begin at the firing of the cannon, two days later.

While the women were pitching the tipis, the Oglala and Brulé Sioux, already on the ground, entertained their cousins from the north with feasts and dances. The wagons bringing supplies for the council had been delayed, and there was no buffalo meat on the starving Platte. And though the Commissioner drew heavily upon the post sutler's stores at Fort Laramie to fill the bellies of his hungry guests, Indian dogs went into the kettles by the thousand.

The next day was the white man's *wakan*, or holy day—Sunday—and Sitting Bull had ample time to see the sights, while the women were erecting the great shelter for the council. He saw the white men put up a tripod of lodge-poles to support their big flag, and observed that they treated the flag just as he did his own shield, displaying it to the sun in the daytime, and taking it in at night.

That day he first saw a young man by the name of Red Cloud, who was afterward to become the famous war chief of the Oglala Sioux Bad-Face band, but was then better known as a medicine-man, having ended a cholera epidemic at Pine Ridge only three years before, by administering a decoction of cedar leaves to his ailing people. Maybe Sitting Bull saw the lodge of Red Cloud's father there also, a lodge painted with a vision of a buffalo and a red cloud, from which the family took its name.

But to Sitting Bull much the most interesting sight was the white man and his belongings. Long before, his people had bestowed various descriptive epithets upon the white men. In the first place, the name Was-e-chun, or Guardian Spirits, had been given them, because of the wonderful things they had and did. But after familiarity bred contempt, other nicknames were applied.

It was noticeable that one white man smelled like two porcupines, that many of them were apparently in mourning, with hair cut short, and that they had much hair on their faces and bodies. Hair on face or body was offensive to the Sioux, perhaps because he went naked so much. Because of this hirsuteness, the Sioux sometimes called the whites Dog Faces—an uncomplimentary title. Sitting Bull's people also had noticed that the white men turned out their toes in a ludicrous manner, and therefore dubbed them Crooked Feet.

Perhaps it was only their short hair which made the ears of white men seem to stick out so far, but the Sioux thought it must be due to ill-treatment received when children. While visiting caravans along the Oregon Trail, some of the Sioux had seen white parents punish their own children by pulling their ears until they cried, and the terrible cruelty of people who could so abuse their own flesh and blood profoundly shocked the Indians. An Indian who punished his own child would have been considered crazy; such a thing was almost unknown. Therefore, when a Sioux called the white men Flop Ears, it was no mere derisive nickname: it suggested that dark cruelty of which no decent Indian parent was ever guilty.

The Sioux had heard terrible tales of how white men, when starving, would eat each other (as sometimes happened among the trappers, or in the case of that unfortunate Donner party). And so, when pork was offered to the young men, an old chief advised them not to touch it. Sitting Bull wished to sample this new dish; he had a curious mind. But the old chief pointed to the inspector's stamp in indelible blue ink on the meat.

"It is well known that white men eat each other," he said. "This is strange flesh they offer us. I have hunted all my life, but I have never seen an animal with flesh like that. You can see in this camp how many of the white soldiers are tattooed. Well, look at the tattoo marks on that meat! Perhaps this is the flesh of some white man they have given you. Do not touch it."

After that, Sitting Bull and his young friends would not have touched that pork with a ten-foot pole.

The white man's beef seemed very insipid to him, and he found that a few pounds of it made him sick. Even the mere sweetish smell of the cattle made some of the warriors puke. And so Indian dogs continued to go into the kettle by the hundred. All in all, Sitting Bull saw little at Fort Laramie that attracted him to the white men, though he admired their guns, their knives, their big, strong horses. For the sake of trade goods, he was quite ready to be friends; in fact, he considered that his people had always been friends—ever since the treaty of 1825. So far as white men's society went, he could be quite happy without that. His exciting life of hunting and warfare made whiskey quite unnecessary: he was never bored. But one thing he must have: iron, guns, ammunition.

For the Crows who came to that treaty council were all well armed, and now here came Chief Washakie and his Shoshoni, uninvited, stirring up trouble, and demanding back the scalps the Cheyennes had just taken. All the enemies of Sitting Bull's people had guns, but "not one in a hundred of the Sioux had guns" at that treaty, as Lowe has recorded. It was necessary to be friends with the people who could supply such things.

When the cannon roared next morning, the chiefs assembled at the council house, followed by their delegations. There an ominous thing happened.

A prolonged discussion took place as to the precedence and seating of the various nations. The Sioux, being most numerous, insisted upon having the place of honor. The Cheyennes, basing their claim on deeds of valor, would not yield. And the other nations all put in a bid for the chief place. At last, in despair, the Commissioner arbitrarily settled the matter, and indicated the section to be occupied by each nation.

Immediately a new wrangle began, for in each nation were several tribes and bands, all of which had some claim to consideration, and all of which desired the first rank. The Commissioner settled this dispute in the same manner, arbitrarily.

But then began a third palaver as to the relative rank and merits of individual chiefs and braves within the tribe or band. This was a thorny problem, bristling with personalities. Two men might have the same number of *coups*, but were they first *coups*, or seconds, or mere fourths? Was a wound more creditable than a captured weapon, or a rescue better than a stolen horse? It began to look as though the council could never be seated. But at last the Commissioner intervened a third time and seated them all without regard to rank.

That little comedy was portentous. If the Commissioner had been as knowing as he was well-intentioned, he must have realized then that his treaty would prove a failure. But he did not. Briefly he explained the proposition. Then he dismissed the council, giving them one day to think it over.

It was a hard task he had assigned them. Heretofore the Hunkpapa had been ruled by the Strong Hearts, and now—when the feathers were hardly dry upon the new-fledged chiefs—the Commissioner was asking them to assume a power and responsibility such as no Indian chief had ever dreamed of.

The chiefs sincerely wished for peace. How pleasant to sleep sound, never to worry over the safety of women and children, nor to have to watch the horses in the night! They wanted to trade with the whites and with each other. If some way could be found to keep other Indian tribes out of their hunting grounds, they were willing to be friends with them. But, as one chief put it, "War is indispensable. Of course, we lose a few men every year, but so do our enemies. If we smoke with them, they will crowd into our hunting grounds, and we shall starve. Anyhow, I don't believe that our old enemies will keep the peace, if we make it. They cannot be trusted, and then we shall be blamed for fighting."

However, Sitting Bull's people agreed to make the best of that.

The second point—the white men's demand to be allowed to build roads and forts in Sioux country—was a great difficulty. That was hard to grant. Roads meant more trouble, more hunger for the Indian. In fact, it was a road—the Oregon Trail—that had caused all the trouble which made *this* treaty necessary, and now—instead of closing that road—the Grandfather asked them to let him make certain others. That might mean starvation. Yet the Sioux were eager for peace, they had confidence that the Grandfather would not let them down. They conceded the point.

The payment of damages to Indians for white depredations was all very well, but how catch the criminals? And as for turning over Sioux criminals to the white men—that *was* a problem. What chief would dare do it? It was contrary to custom. No chief had ever turned over a Sioux to another nation. If he did, the man's relatives would probably kill the chief. Yet this might never happen; they risked this point, also.

Boundaries of the various nations were readily settled. Their boundaries were clearly marked—by the graves of their young men.

But the great crux came when they considered the demand of the Commissioner that they should elect *one* chief for the whole nation. *That* was staggering! *One* chief who would be responsible to the Grandfather at Washington, *one* chief whom all the Sioux would obey! That was a glittering ambition, indeed, a dream, an impossibility—like the United States of Europe, the League of Nations, the Federation of the World!

The Sioux government really existed only for the duration of some emergency, and as soon as that emergency was ended, it automatically ceased to be. And it was local government, intensely so. What a problem the Commissioner had set those new-fledged chieftains!

If all the Sioux could have agreed upon a chief, he could not have enforced his sway over that great, far-flung people.

The organization of the Sioux nation reminds one irresistibly of the man who was going to St. Ives. Seven (or more—usually many more) family tents made one band; seven bands made one tribe; seven tribes made one grand council fire; seven grand council fires made up the Sioux nation. The area occupied by all these scattered groups, each with its own local and independent government, was about that of the State of Texas, or of the German Empire before the World War, with Austria Hungary thrown in. How could such a population, (each unit entirely self-supporting), speaking three different dialects, part Christian, part pagan, part tame, part wild, agree upon *one* man to lead them? How could such a man, if chosen, manage to enforce the treaty clauses upon bands which had only a distant rumor of his name? There was no machinery for such enforcement, even had the chief been acknowledged.

From the beginning the white men consistently confused the hereditary chieftaincies of the American Indian with the monarchies of Europe. They called chiefs "kings"—King Philip, King Massasoit—and held them responsible for matters over which they had no control whatever. No chief ever held more than a personal authority, a personal prestige, and this was endangered every time he failed in an enterprise, or disregarded the wishes of his people. He could not tax, or imprison, or punish his people. Such discipline as there was lasted only while a ceremony or a hunt, or some other public business, was going on. And the chief's duty was that of a mouthpiece, a spokesman, an arbitrator. He was supposed to keep the peace, adjust disputes, and provide for the common defense. He was supposed to see that the people had enough to eat. He was helpless to cross public opinion. The Indians obeyed literally the scriptural injunction: *If any man be great among you, let him be your servant.*

The real power of the Prairie nations lay in the Warrior Societies, and a chief could do nothing with them when their blood was up. They had magnificent *esprit de corps*, and on occasion they even fell upon their chiefs and flogged them severely, as happened to the Keeper of the Cheyenne Medicine Arrows, in 1838.[1]

The Sioux had been doing as they liked for too many generations to submit readily to dictation. They could never act together in large numbers. They were as touchy as so many Irishmen, and had a perfect genius for disintegration. By 1851, the nation had already sloughed off the Oto, Osage, Ponka, Iowa, Winnebago, Omaha, Quapaw, Crow, Hidatsa, Kaw, and Hohe tribes, not to mention long-lost relatives in North and South Carolina and in Mississippi. Already the Western (Teton) Sioux felt themselves almost a distinct nation, and looked with contempt upon the Santee Sioux and other bands to the east of the Missouri River, who had knuckled under to the white men, and had even adopted some of the customs of their enemies, the Chippewas.

Even one tribe or band of Tetons could seldom pull together very long. Sitting Bull's own band, the Icira (pronounced Itchy-krah) gained its name from this fact. There is no exact English equivalent, but the name may be approximated by Sneerers, or Jeerers. It has been translated "those who laugh at each other," or "those who quarrel and come together again." The central idea seems to be ill humor, or humor of a grim and unpleasant kind. The band so named was supposed to be mean, quarrelsome, dangerous. Its members were so warlike that they even picked fights with each other. A jealous lot.

And it was so with other Hunkpapa bands. Wherever, in old records, you come upon the name Hunkpapa, you will find these people mentioned as making trouble, committing depredations, fighting, or refusing to make peace. And not content with their own natural aptness

---

[1]. Grinnel, *The Fighting Cheyennes*, page 42.

in this way, they had freely intermarried with those terrible scrappers, the Cheyennes. All through Sitting Bull's life, he had to contend with bitter factions in his own camp, and such factions still exist on the Standing Rock Reservation.

Therefore, the Commissioner was asking an impossibility. Chief Red Horn expressed his misgivings in these words: "All our people are not here. Some of them are out west hunting in the mountains. There is no use trying to do anything until they all come back."

What wonder that, when the council met again, the spokesman of the Sioux declared: "We have decided differently from you, Father, about this chief for the nation. We want a chief for each band, and if you will make one or two chiefs for each band, it will be much better for you and the whites. Then we will make soldiers of our young men, and we will make them good to the whites and other Indians. But Father, *we cannot make one chief.*"

That treaty of 1851 was probably the fairest ever made with the Prairie Sioux. Everyone present was full of good-will, and no shady tricks (such as were afterward so common) were used in order to induce the chiefs to sign. But it was doomed to prove a failure. "*Father, we cannot make one chief.*"

There were too many candidates.

But the Commissioner would not be balked. He named a chief himself, Mato-wa-yuhe, Stirring Bear, translated in the newspapers of the time as Frightening Bear.[2] Then he railroaded through a unanimous vote

2. The name Mato-wa-yuhe means, literally Stirring Bear. The name refers to a bear which engages in a rough-and-tumble—the kind of fight which the Sioux call "stirring gravy"—the kind of fight we call a "mix-up." I have heard it translated Bear-that-Digs. Grinnell translates it Bear-that-Scatters (a Cheyenne approximation). The name is spelled "Mah-toe-wha-you-whey" in the official records of the Council.

from a constituent assembly, organized like an American legislature, each member representing a certain number of lodges.

Stirring Bear was overwhelmed. "His nomination was wholly unexpected, and came upon him like a clap of thunder from a clear sky." The new chief declared that he had no wish to be chief of the nation, that he had not been attending councils, that there were older and wiser men than himself, men who knew the whites better. He said he was just a buffalo hunter, and that—if he had known they intended to make *him* chief—he would never have come to the treaty council.

He foresaw what would happen to the man who assumed such sway over his people: "Father, I am not afraid to die, but to be chief of *all* the nation, I must be a *big chief*, or in a few moons I shall be sleeping (dead) on the prairie. I have a wife and children I do not wish to leave. If I am not a *powerful* chief, my enemies will be on my trail all the time."

Then, in a more manly tone, he went on: "I do not fear them. I have to die sometime, and I don't care when. If you and the Grandfather insist that I become chief I will take this office. I will try to do right to the whites, and hope they will do so to my people . . . . I know the Great Spirit will protect me, and give many spirits of my enemies to accompany me, if I have to die for doing what you and the Grandfather ask."

The band to which this chief belonged were the last to vote for him. He himself threw away his ballot-stick, and refused to accept anything from the presents distributed in the assembly, not even allowing his relatives to partake.

The Commissioner was highly pleased with this arbitrary arrangement. But without an army behind him, no man could be arbitrary with the Sioux and get away with it. The Indians knew very well that this paper chief could not stand, and nobody knew it better than the man himself. In a short three-minute speech he refers to his approaching death no less than six times.

Perhaps he thought the unexampled dignity of being named chief of *all* the Sioux was compensation enough for martyrdom. Earthly glory could no further go . . . .

In all this, Sitting Bull saw much that was instructive: the absurd, unreal arrangements of the white man, the jealousy of the chiefs and warriors, the danger of assuming power over such a prestige-mad community, and especially the folly of pretending to be chief without the solid backing of the warrior societies. At that council he saw (though he may not have realized it) the whole glory and failure of his own career, and the cause of his violent death. It was all displayed for his instruction on that little stage under the arbor. He remembered that lesson, referred to it in later speeches. The moral of the speech of Stirring Bear was not lost upon the thoughtful, stocky youth who sat behind his tall uncle, Chief Four Horns.

He had plenty of time to observe and consider these matters. The councils went on for some time.

But at last the treaty was signed, and the long delayed wagons corralled on the dusty, wind-swept plain, while the Indians gathered to receive their presents. Twenty-seven wagons were unloaded, the property stacked in one place. The cannon roared, the stars and stripes waved on high, and everybody turned out dressed in his best, to take his place in the immense circle surrounding the goods, the women leading pack-mules or horses dragging travois.

First of all, uniforms and swords were given to the chiefs, who struggled into pantaloons for the first time in their lives, and strutted around proud as peacocks, with their long hair floating over the high collars of the new uniforms, and the swords banging against their shins. Then the chiefs proceeded to distribute the presents to their people. All went forward without impatience, without apparent jealousy or haste, in decorous silence.

They ate the beef because they were starving. The bacon they burned.[3] The soda and flour they threw away for the sake of the containers. The coffee-beans they could use—some of them—but bed-ticking, thread, and flimsy cotton cloth were of no interest. However, there were plenty of knives, kettles, awls, paints, brass buttons, rings, beads, blankets, and twists of tobacco. The women had so many kettles that nests of them were left behind when the camps pulled out for the forks of the Platte, where fat buffalo were said to be numerous. Packing mules is no pastime, and copper kettles are heavy plunder for a long jaunt. Enough is plenty. And three hundred pounds is about all one travois can carry.

Thus ended the great treaty, which, after all, came to nothing but trouble. For the Senate amended the treaty, cut down the amount of money promised the Indians, and because the Crows would not sign the amendment, it was never fully carried out.

Sitting Bull had an uneasy feeling that universal peace was not quite all that the white men—and the old men—seemed to think. It was not clear just where the Strong Hearts and a rising young warrior would figure, if there were no more big wars to make ambition

---

3. When buffalo were plenty, the Sioux were used to burning tallow with their fire wood.

virtue. Universal peace meant that young men would never have a chance to rival their elders, that the end of promotion and honor had come. Sitting Bull tried to imagine a world in which there was no war, no glory, no captured horses. Tried—but failed.

Four Horns, swanking along in his officer's coat, the gilt sword whacking his pony's ribs at every step, was pleased at his nephew's intelligent interest in the treaty councils. He offered the young man advice.

"Nephew," he admonished, "be a little against fighting. But when anyone shoots, be ready to fight him back. White men will come among your people and try to deceive you and fool you. Don't let them do it. They will bring goods to trade to the people, but some of them will be liars."

II. The Fate of Stirring Bear.

Peace on the Platte did not last long.

One day in 1853 a visiting Minniconjou Sioux fired across the river at a soldier in a boat, near Fort Laramie. The soldier was unhurt, but the commanding officer had issued an order that no one should fire a gun near the post "lest alarm be created among passing emigrants." Accordingly, Lieutenant H. B. Fleming took a detail into the camp of the local Oglala Sioux, and demanded the man who had fired the gun. Of course, he had skipped, and the local Indians could not produce him. Thereupon the Lieutenant, forgetting all about the alarm he might create among passing emigrants, ordered his men to fire into the camp. Most of the Oglala men were away, but the few that were left ran, covering the retreat of their women and children by firing at the troops. Several Indians were killed, but no soldiers. Nevertheless, no immediate hostilities followed. The

Oglala rightly supposed that the young officer was a foolish young man, and that the Grandfather at Washington was not to blame. They were frightened, of course, and complained that the soldiers who had been sent into their country to keep the peace had been the first to make trouble.

The Cheyennes, however, who hated the post trader, made this affair an excuse for running off his horses. And so there was ill-feeling on both sides.

The Sioux chiefs, nevertheless, were anxious to keep the peace. And so, when an Indian shot a worn-out, abandoned cow, to get a piece of rawhide which he needed, the Brulé Sioux chief, Stirring Bear, immediately reported the matter to the post commandant, and asked for soldiers (according to the treaty) to go with him and arrest the guilty man. Hearing of this, the emigrant who had abandoned the cow returned to the post and put in a claim, hoping to get a little cash from the government. As before, the offending Indian was a visiting Minniconjou, not a member of the local camp. But the commandant rightly estimated that the cow was worthless, and paid small attention to the matter.

One of the officers at the post, however, took a different view. He was a young Irishman named Grattan, full of fight, wholly ignorant of Indians and of Indian warfare, but eager to show his mettle. He begged so hard to be allowed to go after the man who had killed the cow, that the commandant reluctantly allowed him to. His orders were strictly limited, but no sooner had he got them than he seemed to lose his head. He called for volunteers "for dangerous service," took ten more men than he was authorized to take, and two howitzers, and went into the Brulé camp. He told the men at the post that he was going "to conquer or die," and marched away, evidently believing a dead cow sufficient excuse for launching an Indian war.

In the camp, he talked for some time with the chiefs, who could not produce the Minniconjou at the moment, and begged him to wait until their agent could come and settle the matter. They offered good horses in payment for the worn-out cow, and promised to make all amends possible. But Lieutenant Grattan would not listen. He went back to his men, who fired into the camp, shooting down Stirring Bear, the very chief who had first reported the killing of the cow.

That was a little more than the Brulés were prepared to stand. They immediately attacked Grattan's force, which retreated and ran into the Oglalas, who were coming to join the fray. In a few minutes, Grattan and his thirty-nine men were all dead. Not a single man escaped the Sioux arrows.

Afterward, the Indians looted the store of the unpopular trader, but made no attack upon the Army post.

The officers of the post later testified that Grattan had exceeded his authority and was responsible for the tragedy. But the newspapers in the East had by that time inflamed public opinion. Misled by the false stories in the newspapers, the public demanded reprisals.

The Indians, of course, had no newspapers. Had they been wiser, they would not have accepted annuities when they sold their lands. A controlling interest in the *New York Herald* would have been far more valuable to them.

Had they had it, they might have published their own story of the "Grattan Massacre," a story which is in substantial agreement with the findings of the War Department—after the mischief was done. George

Bird Grinnell has printed the Cheyenne version in his book *The Fighting Cheyennes*. No Sioux account has appeared heretofore. I offer the Sioux version here: it comes from Chief White Bull of the Minniconjou, who received it from one of the brothers of Chief Stirring Bear.

White Bull says that at Fort Laramie there were two leading candidates for the office of head chief of the Brulé tribe—Stirring Bear and Iron Claw. Apparently the Minniconjou never realized that Stirring Bear was supposed to be chief of *all* the Sioux: the notion was so fantastic that they probably thought it a mistake of the interpreter's, if they heard of it at all. At any rate, when the ballot-sticks were counted, Stirring Bear had the most votes; he was made head chief. Therefore, when the cow was killed, the soldiers put the matter up to him, they say. They sent their Interpreter, a breed, to talk to the Chief. The Interpreter said, "Whoever these men are who killed that cow, they must give it back, or pay for it." The Chief said he had tried hard, but could not find the guilty man.

A second time the Interpreter came to interview the Chief, and again he said that he must produce the guilty man, the man who had killed that worn-out cow, and send him to the Captain at the fort. Once more the Chief told him that he did not know who had done it, could not find him, and so could not produce him. Twice the Interpreter came with such messages. The third time he came, he said to Stirring Bear, "Soldiers are coming. If you do not produce the man who killed that cow, you had better not come out when the soldiers come, for they will surely kill you." Stirring Bear told his friends what the Interpreter had threatened, and they prepared to defend themselves, if necessary. And so, when Grattan brought his troops to the camp, and asked for the chief, they were ready. The chief, just as brave as he had told the Commissioner he would be, came out to talk to Grattan. His warriors were around him, ready to protect him. The officer said he wanted the guilty man. The Chief replied, "I cannot produce him. But I will give you two of my best ponies."

Right after that the soldiers began to shoot. They fired together, and killed Stirring Bear the first thing. Then his friends began to fight. The soldiers found it too hot for them, they tried to run away. But they were all surrounded and killed right there. Not one got away.

The Interpreter jumped on a horse and made a run for his life back toward the fort. But the Indians took after him, they chased him, and caught him. The Interpreter kept saying, "I am part Indian. Don't kill me. Let me live!" But they knew he had come there with the soldiers; he had known all the time that the soldiers were coming to kill the Chief. The Sioux did not take pity on that Interpreter. They killed him at once.

That is the Sioux story, as given by Chief White Bull.

Colonel William S. Harney was sent to "punish" the Sioux. When he arrived on the Platte, he repeated the conduct of Fleming and Grattan, but with better luck. Not being able to find the "murderers" of Grattan, he pitched into the first Sioux he could find (and of course only friendly Indians would ever allow themselves to be found), killed a lot of innocent people, destroyed their camp, and carried off seventy women and children. Harney himself, in his own report, admits that these people were blameless, and says, "if it had been any other band it would have been the same." He was no hair-splitter when it came to killing Indians:

he killed them quite impartially. Ignoring the provisions of the treaty of 1851, which provided for damages for depredations, he declared to the chiefs in council, "We will have blood for blood." Whose blood hardly mattered.

This sort of thing was repeated with tiresome regularity on the Plains. It was nearly always impossible for the troops to find the hostiles, and always easy to reach friendly bands. It happened, as we have seen, twice at Fort Laramie; again when Harney attacked Little Thunder's band at Ash Hollow, 1855; at Sand Creek, 1864; at the Battle of the Washita, 1868; in the Baker fight on the Marias River, 1870; and on Powder River, March 17, 1876. Indians have been much criticized for taking vengeance on innocent parties, but the troops consistently did the same thing.

When Sitting Bull's people, away to the north on Grand (Ree) River, heard what had been happening on the Platte, they made up their minds that the soldiers could not be trusted, and that any Sioux who would voluntarily go and camp in their neighborhood was a fool.

They themselves, now that the white men had broken the treaty, committed a few depredations around Fort Clarke, and finding a trader's wagon with some Rees whom they were after, broke it to pieces. But they were much too busy with their old tribal wars to give more than a passing thought to the Flop Ears at that time.

III. "White Beard's" Council at Fort Pierre.

General Harney's attack on Little Thunder's camp struck terror to the Southern Sioux. Therefore, when "White Beard," as they called him, demanded the "murderers" of Grattan, five young men rode into Fort Laramie, dressed in their war clothes for burial, singing death-songs. Two of them, Red Leaf and Long Chin, were brothers of the dead chief Stirring Bear, whom Grattan's men had killed. Stirring Bear had met the fate he foresaw when appointed head chief of all the Sioux at the treaty council of 1851. Two others of the five young men, Red Plume and Spotted Elk, offered themselves in place of the two who could not come in. The fifth was Spotted Tail, afterward the well known chief and ally of the white men, who, as a friend, was to be murdered in his turn.

But "White Beard" was not content. He sent out runners asking the chiefs of all the Tetons to a council at Fort Pierre, at the mouth of the Bad (Teton) River on the Missouri. Little Thunder was anxious to recover his captured women and children, and urged the chiefs to attend. Accordingly, Four Horns once more rode southward to smoke with the white men. The council was held in March, 1856. In General Harney's verbatim report of the proceedings will be found a complete statement of the views of both parties to the proposed agreement. It gives a very clear picture of conditions at the time.

"White Beard" was a man of impressive bulk, strong character, and intelligence. He held an iron rod over the Sioux, and he knew it very well. They were humble, ready to do what they could to make amends, honestly anxious to keep the peace. "White Beard" began by threatening them with dire penalties. But before he got through he was so impressed by the character and good will of the chiefs that he actually apologized for having attacked Little Thunder's camp!

Yet he began by threatening them. He demanded

"the man who killed the cow," the return of the captured horses. He said there must be no more payments to traders to "cover dead white men," swore he would "have blood for blood," and declared, with terrifying emphasis, "Big Head's band shall not live upon the face of the earth!" Vain threat!

Harney was furious with the traders at Fort Clarke, who had brought ammunition up the river and afterward instigated the Indians to compel their agent to let them buy it, after such trade had been forbidden by the Superintendent of Indian Affairs. He accused Peter Sarpy, a trader, of persuading the Ponkas to go to war. He proposed that thereafter all traders *must* remain near military posts, so that they could no longer act as "fences" for property stolen by the Indians, sell liquor or ammunition, or foment inter-tribal wars. He proposed to settle the Indians on reservations, put them to farming, give them annuities in payment for their lands.

But his first and most original proposition was to appoint *chiefs* for *every band*, who should command organized companies of Indian policemen, with uniforms and arms issued by the United States. These chiefs and these police he proposed to back up with the authority of the Army, which was also to have supervision of the issue of annuities.

A good plan—if it could have been carried out. But the United States government, having been created in fear of tyranny, was too full of checks and balances to permit any one department to manage the Indians. The War Department was balked by the Indian Bureau, which in those days filled its posts with political appointees, who went to the Indian country—as a rule—determined to enrich themselves from the Indians' annuities. For many years it was a tug of war between the Army, with its talk of "Wars of extermination," "nits make lice," "the only good Indian is a dead Indian," and the Indian Bureau, with its humbug of "progress" and "humanity," concealing a long and almost uninterrupted series of frauds. From the point of view of the Indians, it was generally a toss-up as to whether the Army was to kill them, or the Indian Bureau was to rob and starve them. However, an impartial compromise was effected, so that these enterprises were attempted alternately and in rotation. No real attempt was ever made to put General Harney's scheme into operation.

The chiefs also had their grievances, and felt that "White Beard's" demands were too hard. They had tried to keep the peace. The Yankton chief, Struck-by-the-Ree, explained that when one of his young men had killed a white man, he himself killed the offender. Long Mandan had done the same in two instances, in punishing mere insults. And Bear Ribs I, the Hunkpapa chief, who spoke for the delegation, mildly rebuked General Harney for his blood-thirstiness, reminding him that when the whites killed Bear Rib's brother, he had let it pass. That put Harney in a corner: he had to confess that he was not as great a chief as Bear Ribs, for *he* could not forgive wrongs done to the Grandfather at Washington.

The chiefs complained that the white soldiers had not protected the "good" Indians, as promised in 1851; that they were starving; that their agents stole everything, and that their traders had been taken away. To his proposals that they assist him in rounding up the Sioux criminals, they replied, "All of us here don't wish and don't pretend to fight our brothers." It was impossible for Sioux to fight Sioux. But Harney insisted that the chiefs control their young men, and that—if their enemies would not keep the peace—they must fight them. Another war to end war!

The chiefs' cry was "help us to do what you want us to do!" Said one, "I was so hungry that when I saw your cattle I could not help eat them, and that's what kept me alive." Said another, "I am a man, and I am not going to beg for my life." Another—with regard to the Indian agents sent out from Washington: "You pick out the poorest man you have and send him up here to give us our goods. When an agent comes here he is poor, but he gets rich; and after he gets rich he goes away, and another poor one comes." Another: "You came here and whipped me, and after that you starved me." And Smutty Bear had a laugh at the expense of the elaborate pretences of the Indian Bureau. Said he, "The chief on the Platte told me I would be like a white man; but he told me a lie, for I am not like a white man yet."

The General's most startling proposal was that the Sioux aid him by catching deserters from the Army. He offered a reward for each deserter brought in. And when a chief suggested that the deserter might shoot him, if he tried to make the arrest, General Harney replied, "You must shoot him first, and if you kill him, you shall have the reward by telling me where he lies."

General Harney saw clearly that what was needed in the Sioux country was a strong, organized government, with the backing of the United States Army. For a long time the Sioux nation had been falling to pieces of its own weight and size, and this had been hastened by the conflict of authority. Every trader had some reliable warrior in his pay to protect his wares, and this warrior was given a medal and a paper stating that he was a chief. The Indian agents, in order to protect themselves, also gave medals and commissions. The military officers at the various posts were accustomed to do the same thing. And even missionaries played politics sometimes, for reasons best known to themselves. In every tribe there was therefore a considerable number of men who claimed to be chiefs, but were not elected by the nation itself. What wonder that there was confusion?

Harney proposed to remedy this condition by naming *more* chiefs (of his own!) But, like the traders, the agents, and the missionaries, he named as chiefs *not* those who were actually powerful and rightful chiefs, but such as were obedient to his suggestions. And then, to make these paper chiefs weaker than they already were, he demanded that they cast out of their bands all who would not obey them, thus breaking in two the very authority he was trying to create!

In fact, some of the sub-chiefs of each band were really much bigger chiefs than the ones he named as their superiors. Thus, Bear Ribs was made head chief of the Hunkpapa, though Four Horns and three others (not present) were all more important. Fire Heart, named head chief of the Blackfeet Sioux, was certainly less important than Used-as-a-Shield, the father of the celebrated John Grass, or than High Eagle. However, a great number of the most important men of the Teton Sioux were present, they were under "White Beard's" heavy club, and for the time all went smoothly.

However, the Sioux is tough-minded, with an overwhelming sense of reality. Only facts impinge upon his mind. White men might attach great importance to a piece of paper saying that a man was a chief; but unless the Sioux could see that the man *was* a chief, the paper meant nothing.⁴

Probably Sitting Bull found much food for thought in the deliberations of the chiefs at Fort Pierre. Only one remark of his made at that time has come down to us. After hearing of the frauds of the Indian agents, he said, "I would have more confidence in the Grandfather at Washington, if there were not so many bald-headed thieves working for him."

General Harney's council at Fort Pierre in 1856 is well-remembered by the Sioux. They respected his common sense and straight-forward methods, and more than one old man has told me that "White Beard" (as they call Harney) was the only white man they had ever met who could talk sense or tell the truth, with the exception of Father De Smet. The thing which convinced them of his intellectual powers is a remark he made at that council—a remark not found in the official minutes. (Generally speaking, the most important statements made at Indian councils were usually left unrecorded, it appears!) Harney prophesied that, within ten years, the Sioux and the whites would be fighting again. Killdeer Mountain and Red Cloud's War were the fulfillment of this prophecy, and old Indians remember it as a true saying. Therefore, of all the soldiers

---

4. Among the Minniconjou chiefs named by the General at this treaty council was Ki-yu-kan-pi, The-One-That-Makes-Room, usually translated Makes-Room, but better translated as Make-Room-For-Him, or Welcome. This man was the husband of Good Feather, Sitting Bull's sister, and the father of the "famous fighting nephews," White Bull and One Bull. About this time Ki-yu-kan-pi left his wife and moved away to camp with his own tribe, the Minniconjou. Good Feather brought her sons home to live with Sitting Bull.

Soon after, Sitting Bull's first wife, Scarlet Woman, died, and with her their little son, just four years old. Sitting Bull adored his son, as only an Indian father can. He used to spend whole afternoons sitting on a buffalo robe in the shade, playing with the roly-poly warrior, singing and talking to him, teaching him to dance. Now he was hard hit by his loss. Good Feather's younger son, One Bull, was the exact age of the boy who had died, and so Sitting Bull adopted him and reared him as his own. One Bull resembles his uncle, and this may have pleased Sitting Bull. At any rate, they remained together until Sitting Bull was killed.

who fought and talked with the Sioux, General William S. Harney stands pre-eminent in their memories as a wise man and a soldier.

But the only result of all that talk and fighting was a lot of dead men. Of them all, we may perhaps remember Chief Stirring Bear with most respect and admiration, as one who—for the sake of his people and his own honor—went open-eyed to his death in the endeavour to perform an impossible task. Betrayed by the whites who had promised to back him up, he became a warning to the Sioux who might otherwise have followed his peaceful trail.

But that trail led only to the Indian's grave. Stirring Bear, Bear Ribs, Crazy Horse, Spotted Tail, Sitting Bull, Big Foot, Dull Knife, White Antelope, Black Kettle: they all met violent ends as a result of their making peace with the white men. The white man was more deadly to his friends than to his enemies.

No. 25.
THE "TREATY OF LARAMIE" AT FORT RICE
1868

One of the most important treaties ever made with Indians in the territories of the United States was that made in 1868 at the end of the hostilities known to history as Red Cloud's War. This treaty brought to an end a long series of engagements between white men and plains Indians and was the foundation of the treaties which followed. It is not only a famous treaty but is, in fact, unique in the history of the United States. It is the only treaty made by the United States in which nothing but peace was demanded of the other signatory. Moreover, it was remarkable for the courage shown by Father Pierre-Jean De Smet, S. J., who was daring enough to visit the hostile camp of Sitting Bull at the mouth of Powder River and persuade him to send delegates to Fort Rice to meet the commissioners. The story of Father De Smet's unselfish journey has been repeatedly printed. Notwithstanding, the actual minutes of the later council at Fort Rice have never been published, and indeed the proceedings of that council are so little known that in most histories it is referred to as the "Laramie Treaty", though Sitting Bull's delegates signed the treaty at Fort Rice on the Missouri River.

The leader of the delegation sent by Sitting Bull and his fellow chiefs to Fort Rice was Gall, who also bore the names Red-Walker and The-Man-Who-Goes-In-The-Middle. The name Red-Walker had been given Gall in boyhood after a ceremony made by his father in his honor in order to show love for the boy. At such a ceremony the lad honored is dressed entirely in vermilion with long trailing streamers, and parades up and down before the assembled guests, who are afterwards rewarded for their admiration by rich gifts presented by the lad's father. It is not known how Gall earned the name The-Man-Who-Goes-In-The-Middle, but it was evidently won in battle with some enemy tribe. Gall was proud of this name, as is shown by the fact that he used it to sign the treaty at Fort Rice. Historians have been puzzled by the fact that though Gall was known to have headed the delegation from Sitting Bull's camp to this council, the name Gall did not appear among the signatures on the treaty. Mr. Lewis F. Crawford first identified Gall as The-Man-Who-Goes-In-The-Middle. The name Gall (Pizi) was given him McLaughlin says, in boyhood when the lad was discovered eating the gall of a freshly killed buffalo.

Major McLaughlin in *My Friend The Indian* idolized Gall to such an extent that, as Col. Charles Francis Bates has put it, "It is clear that he could see no other Indian on the horizon." Inquiry among the Hunkpapa (Gall was a Hunkpapa) has failed to reveal any very remarkable exploits performed on the warpath by Gall. It is therefore interesting to consider why Gall should have been chosen by Sitting Bull to represent his people on such an important occasion as the treaty council of 1868.

There were a number of reasons. First, Gall was as much an agency Indian as he was hunter and warrior. He was constantly moving back and forth from the buffalo country to the agency according to the dictates of his stomach. When game was plenty he preferred the plains, but in hard times he could generally be found at some agency beef issue. He was, in fact, a mere man of action, incapable of any settled policy or any definite philosophy of life. His whole career, both before surrender and at the agency, abounds in instances displaying his unstable character. Therefore he knew the agency people better than wilder Indians: they thought him better able to deal with the white man.

Besides, he wished to carry the flag which Father De Smet had given the Indians on Power River. At heart he was still Red-Walker.

But there was a better reason why Gall was chosen for this embassy. It happened that a Sioux named Long Mandan went up to the Ree village at Fort Berthold, and took a Ree wife. Gall thought this a disgrace—a kind of treason—for a Sioux and a head man to go and live with the Rees. Gall went up there and ran off some of Long Mandan's horses, in retaliation. Such an affair could not be kept secret—probably Gall boasted of it— and Long Mandan soon found out who had taken his ponies. He bided his time: Gall was in the habit of coming in to trade at Fort Berthold.

Some time after, Gall came with other Sioux, and camped near Fort Berthold to trade, as there were then no soldiers at that fort. Long Mandan hastened to Fort Stevenson, only twenty-seven miles away, and brought a detachment of soldiers to arrest Gall. There was already an order out for his arrest. One hundred soldiers went along, and reached Fort Berthold about 2 A. M. They surrounded the sleeping Sioux camp, and the interpreter called out, "We have you surrounded. Nobody will be hurt. Come out between our lines. We want Gall." Someone pointed out the tipi where Gall was sleeping, and the soldiers surrounded it.

The commotion roused Gall, who stuck his head out of the door of the tent. Immediately, one of soldiers fired at him at close range with a revolver. Gall was not hit. He jumped back into the tipi, drew his knife, slit the back of the tent, and leaped out, hoping to get away. But the soldiers, armed with bayonets, were all around. One of them stabbed him, ran him through. Gall fell to the ground, shamming death, and the soldiers trampled him and kicked him, covering him with bruises. They stabbed him through and through, back, breast, and neck. The soldier had to put his foot on Gall's body in order to withdraw his steel. Everyone supposed he was dead, and after a time the soldiers went off to Fort Berthold to get warm. Gall lay there, unconscious and almost naked on the snow. None of the Sioux cared to touch his body. They struck their tipis and cleared out at once.

When all had gone, Gall came to. It was still dark. Gall was a Hunkpapa of the Hunkpapa, and had all that wonderful indifference to cold, hardship, and ex-

COURTESY, BUREAU OF AMERICAN ETHNOLOGY

Long (Tall) Mandan, Two Kettle Sioux Chief

posure characteristic of the old-time Sioux. He managed to get to his feet and staggered away. Snow was falling, and it grew bitterly cold. His friends had gone, and he dared not remain near the village of his enemies, the Rees, until morning. His nearest friend, Hairy Chin, lived twenty miles away.

When he reached the timber on the Missouri River, he was lucky: he found a fire, left by some herder. He warmed himself, and prayed to Wakan Tanka to take pity on him and save his life. Then he drank water, and felt stronger.

At daybreak, after the soldiers had gone, the Rees came down to scalp Gall's dead body. Finding it gone, they called out the soldiers, and set out on the bloody trail across the snow. But the snowfall covered his trail, and they had to give it up. Gall was not taken. Early next day he reached the lodge of his friend Hairy Chin, the doctor, and staggered in, half-dead, shaking, his scanty clothing thick with clotted, frozen blood. With every breath, bloody froth bubbled from his lips. But Gall's magnificent constitution and Hairy Chin's skilfull treatment saved him. He pulled through. What a man he was!

It was long before those terrible wounds healed. A year later, one of them was still open. They troubled him until the day of his death, which they hastened.

After that, Gall hated the whites. As soon as he was able to go on the warpath, he went, and returned with seven white scalps, which he had taken in retaliation. Even that revenge could not satisfy him. All the flattery lavished upon him in later years failed to remove that deep-seated indignation. Some say he died from taking an overdose of Anti-fat, others because of a fall from a wagon. But the truth is, his wounds destroyed him, and he died regretting his half-hearted friendship for the white men. This incident at Fort Berthold made the Indians think Gall a fit envoy to go to Fort Rice.

When Gall and Bull Owl reached Fort Rice, they found only three of the members of the Peace Commission awaiting them. The Commission had divided its forces, in order to make several treaties at the same time. However, General "White Beard" Harney was there, General Alfred H. "Star" Terry, and General John B. Sanborn. Sanborn was spokesman for the whites. He warned the Sioux that their hunting days were numbered, that the soldiers had never really tried to conquer them (good stuff to feed the troops), and said that steamboats and forts on the Missouri could not be removed, as they were needed to protect the Indians from white invasion. He offered attractive inducements to Indians who would settle down and farm: rations, clothes, cattle, implements, schools, permanent agencies, rewards—and punishments. These benefits, however, were to be available only during the time they were learning to support themselves. The treaty put a premium upon laziness, and it was always the lazy Indian who preferred the agency to the hunting grounds.

Sanborn proposed to create a great Sioux reservation (South Dakota west of the Missouri River) to include the Black Hills. All title to lands outside was to be relinquished. But far more interesting to the Sioux were the provisions of Article 16:

"The United States hereby agrees and stipulates that the country north of the North Platte River and east of the summits of the Big Horn Mountains shall be held and considered to be unceded Indian territory, and also stipulates and agrees that no white person or persons shall be permitted to settle upon or occupy any portion of the same; or without the consent of the Indians first had and obtained, to pass through the same; and it is further agreed by the United States that within ninety days after the conclusion of peace with all the bands of the Sioux nation, the military posts now established in the territory of this article named shall be abandoned, and that the road leading to them and by them to the Territory of Montana shall be closed." Article 11 provided that the Sioux had the right to "hunt on any lands north of the North Platte River . . . .so long as buffalo may range thereon in such numbers as to justify the chase."

The government proposed to pay for all roads built through the Sioux Reservation, if the Indians did not oppose them. And it was provided that in future no treaty would be valid unless it had been signed by three-fourths of the adult males of the tribe.

The Sioux, on their part, were asked to keep the peace, not to oppose railroads then being built or to be built outside their Reservation and unceded hunting grounds; not to raid white men, nor carry off women and children from the settlements, nor kill and scalp white men, nor molest the military posts south of the North Platte River.

When Sanborn had explained all this, he yielded the floor to the Sioux. Gall spoke. His answer to the commissioner was the most ambitious speech by him on record. Most of Gall's recorded speeches are brief and to the point; and their burden is "when do we eat," though sometimes he varied this military formula by threatening to kill anyone who disagreed with him.

The stenographic record of his speech at Fort Rice in '68 has never been published, though Mr. Lewis F. Crawford in his *Rekindling Campfires*, has given a white frontiersman's recollection of an Indian's report of it. Without prejudice to Mr. Crawford's great services to Western history, we may perhaps prefer the official minutes of the council in seeking an accurate version of Gall's speech. It follows:

"God raised me with one thing only, and I keep that yet. There is one thing that I do not like. The whites ruin our country. If we make peace, the military posts on this Missouri River must be removed and the steamboats stopped from coming up here. Below here is the Running Water,[5] which is our country. You fought me and I had to fight back: I am a soldier. The annuities you speak of we don't want. Our intention is to take no present.

"You talk of peace. If we make peace, you will not hold it. We told the good Black Robe (De Smet) who has been to our camp that we did not like these things. I have been sent here by my people to see and hear what *you* have got to say. My people told me to get powder and ball, and I want that.

"Now, many things have happened that are not our fault. We are blamed for many things. *I* have been stabbed. If you want to make peace with me, you must remove this Fort Rice, and stop the steamboats. If you won't, I must get all these friendly (Agency) Indians to move away. I have told all this to them, and now I tell you."

Gall, the majestic, was not conciliating that day. He ended with a demand for twenty kegs of powder.

Bull Owl echoed these remarks, asking that forts and steamboats be taken away, "so that the buffalo will come back."

Running Antelope spoke third: . . . . "I am only a

---

5. Southern Boundary of the proposed Reservation, as explained to the Sioux.

Gall, the Hunkpapa Sioux

small man among my people. White Beard, I saw you when you came to Fort Pierre (in 1856). I keep in my heart the talk we had then—it is thirteen years ago. I have never met a white man with any sense since then, except the Black Robe. . . . . . We want Galpin to stay in this country and be our trader. . . ."

When the three Hunkpapa had finished, men of other Sioux tribes and bands talked: Fool Heart, Black Eye, Chief, Black Catfish, all Upper Yanktonais; Two Bears, Mad Bear, and Lousy, Lower Yanktonais, catering to the whites, eager for peace; Wapasha, the Santee yes-man; Thunder Bull, Wanneton, and All-Over-Black, Cut Heads; Lone Dog, the Two Kettle; Fireheart, a chief of the Blackfeet Sioux; Pretty Lodge, representing the Sisseton; The-Man-Who-Has-No-Horn, a Sans Arc; Magpie, Long Soldier, and Bear Ribs II, of the agency Hunkpapa.

From much repetition, a few statements may be gleaned to show the temper of the Sioux: "Now, if you have power to stop whites from coming into our country, that will put an end to trouble. . . . We have been raised by the traders. . . . . The Blackfeet Sioux are quite satisfied. . . . A great many things that the Commissioners tell us I don't believe. I am much afraid that both sides are going to tell lies again to each other. . . . Ever since the war with the whites began, a great many of our best young men are laid in the ground. . . . . I want peace, but not to sell my land . . . . It is the whites who will break the treaty, not we. . . . It was the fault of the whites ten times where the Indians were to blame once. . . . .

"Tell the interpreters and half-breeds and white men with Indian families not to tell so many lies after this. . . . I have met a great many white men, and never saw one who would not lie except the Black Robe. . . . . Everyone wishes to live; it is so with the Sioux. . . . We have met big chiefs before and after they went away, everything went wrong. . . . Let us choose our own agent. . . . Stop chopping wood and setting beaver traps in our country. . . . Let us buy ammunition. . . . In times past whenever the Indians wished to do anything, they all tried to do it together. Now our nation is divided. What caused this? The whites. . . . Everything that goes wrong is blamed on the Hunkpapa. . . . We have been abused by the traders. . . . I don't like a man who talks with two hearts and two faces. . . . The agents have done bad things. . . . Give us guns. . . . The blood has been washed away. . . . I can only say yes."

Bear Ribs II[6] presented his claims as Pretender to the head chieftaincy of the Hunkpapa, on grounds of primogeniture. But his real power and influence is shown by his place on the program: his was the fourteenth speech. Nevertheless, his arrogance was inclusive: "I want everything the whites have got, and if I cannot get it, I will not stay here." The bray from beneath the lion's skin.

At last the delegates talked themselves out, signed the treaty, took the presents, and went away. The Hunkpapa signers of this treaty were not men of much importance, with a few honorable exceptions: Gall, Bear Ribs II, Running Antelope, Looking Crow, Long Soldier, Shoots-Walking, Magpie, Plenty Crow, Iron Horn, Wolf Necklace, The-Man-Who-Bleeds-from-the-

---

6. Bear Ribs I was killed at Fort Pierre in 1862 by jealous Indians who found that Bear Ribs was after all not to be protected by the white men to whom he had catered. The name Bear Ribs, sometimes translated Side-of-Bear, should be translated Front-Part-of-Bear.

Mouth, Elk Head, Grindstone, Fool Dog, Blue Cloud, Red Eagle, Bear's Heart, Chief Soldier.

So ended the "Laramie Treaty" council held at Fort Rice, July 2, 1868. Other members of the Commission met the Comanches, Apaches, Kiowas, Cheyennes, Arapahos, and the other Sioux bands elsewhere; all accepted the terms offered. No wonder. For this was the only treaty ever negotiated by the United States after a disastrous war begun by the government, which granted everything to the hostile power and gained nothing in return. The hunting bands of Sioux had triumphed: Red Cloud's War ended in complete success. Red Cloud rather rubbed it in, too. He refused to sign the treaty until the forts had actually been abandoned.

True, the steamboats still ploughed their lone way up the turbid Missouri, and the forts on that River remained to guard their endless course. True, the Yanktonais ceded their lands east of that river, and moved across into the hunting grounds of the Tetons. Yet, in the main, Sioux demands had been met: the old status had been restored. And Sitting Bull probably dared not hope that the white men would keep the terms of the treaty long, in any case. From his point of view, the "Laramie Treaty" was simply and solely a treaty of peace.

But when Gall, "loaded with presents" came back to the camp on Powder River, some of the head men were jealous of him, and complained that he had talked big about forts and steamboats to the Commissioners, and then, when they offered him bribes, had signed on the dotted line just the same. There are still old men among the Hunkpapa who hold that Gall gave in too easily, that he was hood-winked, or sold out. Others, say that Gall's arrogant oration was simply intended to remind the white men of his injuries at their hands, and to show what a *great thing* he was doing in overlooking these injuries and making peace with them. Gall seems to have rated himself very high. Considering that he had already taken seven white scalps in retaliation for his bayonet wounds, one might suppose that he was satisfied. Certain it is that he did not insist on the demands, did not carry out the instructions of his chiefs. He signed and took the presents.

Sitting Bull, however, had pledged himself to accept the terms made by his representatives at the council. He had no intention of breaking faith with the Black Robe. When the other chiefs complained of Gall's weakness, he laughed at their fears. In his joking way, he chaffed them, saying, "You must not blame Gall. Everyone knows that he will do anything for a square meal."

In some books, one finds the statement that Sitting Bull signed this treaty in person. That is an error. The Sitting Bull who signed was an Oglala, and his name will be found among the Oglala signatures on that document. This Oglala Sitting Bull is the man who somewhat later accompanied Red Cloud to Washington, and was supposed by many people (and some historians) to be the famous Hunkpapa. But the Hunkpapa Sitting Bull's first visit to the east was in 1884.

The "Laramie Treaty" was ratified by the Senate February 16, 1869, and proclaimed by President Andrew Johnson eight days later.

Bull Owl accompanied Gall to the council at Fort Rice in 1868 where the "Treaty of Laramie" was signed. Bull Owl was an old warrior, part Cheyenne, part Hunkpapa Sioux.

No. 26.
THE SILENT EATERS
1869

No one can go far into Sioux Indian history during the last century without encountering some mention of a society known as the Silent Eaters. It was founded among the Hunkpapa Sioux soon after Sitting Bull was made a chief (1867) by a few of the leading members of the Strong Heart Warrior Society, who wished to meet together and discuss how they could best help and advise their people. Many problems had arisen in those difficult times, when the Sioux nation was falling to pieces, and often the people went hungry, or got into trouble. Accordingly Iron Bull, Sitting Crow and a few others organized a men's dinner club with a membership limited to twenty.

Because of the serious purposes of the club, it held no dances, and seldom sang songs. Joking and storytelling were barred. The members generally met at night, in any lodge where it was convenient, and without any public announcement. Nobody could buy his way into that club, and a single "black-ball" was enough to exclude a candidate for membership. Because of the peculiar customs of this society, and the fact that its members merely dined and never danced or sang, it became known to the tribe as the Silent Eaters.

Crawler was their herald, and when he circled the camp, bringing news of a meeting, the members would gather quietly at their rendezvous, each man bringing his own dish. There was an usher and a servant appointed to serve the feast—these offices were held by the members in rotation. Leading men from every band were members, and four of these acted as chairmen, whose duty it was to declare what the concensus of opinion was before the meeting broke up. Persons not members, women, children, and dogs were not admitted to the lodge during the meetings, which took place at irregular intervals—whenever something came up which had to be settled.

Such was the repute of the club that the chiefs very often called upon the Silent Eaters to decide what should be done in an emergency, what treaties should be made, what movements of the camp should be undertaken, what hunts organized, what war parties launched.

Private individuals also relied upon the Society for advice. For example, if a man wished to give away a horse to benefit the people, and was in doubt how best to bestow his benefaction, he would lead the animal out before the crowd and say, "I give this horse to the Silent Eaters. They will know how to use it to the best advantage of the tribe."

Other societies among the Sioux worked for their own members, but the Silent Eaters worked for the good of the nation, without pay and without much public honor. Only men known to be very brave and very generous could become members. Experience and intelligence were of the first importance, for the club had thoughtful aims. It was not a part of the tribal government, it had no means of enforcing its wishes upon the people; influence was its only means of control. Sitting Bull was elected a member some two years after the club was founded, and the fact that he was made a member is one of the finest tributes to his character as a man and a warrior. Thereafter he and the Silent Eaters acted as one man. They backed him until the day he died. Some of them died with him.

Because of the high character of this club, and the

great influence it exercised upon the destiny of the Sioux for a generation and more, it is no more than just to record here some of the names of distinguished old-time members. Among these were Crow King, Crawler, Lone Man (Gall's brother), Grabbing Bear, Red Thunder, Strikes-Him-as-he-Runs, Eagle Bear, Shooting Eagle, Little Bear, Rock, Shell King, Jumping Bull or Little Assiniboine, Strikes-the-Kettle, Circling (Turning) Hawk, White Bull, Black Bird, Enemies.

All of these men were known for being in the thick of things in a fight, all of them brought home enemy horses, all were generous, and many had been wounded or had had horses shot under them.

This club had a large blank book (obtained from some white man) in which members were permitted to draw pictures of their exploits, their *coups*, if they expressed a wish to make a permanent record. That book, if it could be found and properly annotated, would make a thrilling history. Perhaps it was lost when the cabins of Sitting Bull's camp were looted after his death. Perhaps it was buried with some old man who had cared for it. Perhaps it still is cherished, packed away with medicine-bundles and old weapons, at the bottom of a trunk in some Indian cabin.

The Silent Eaters club was imitated in some of the other Sioux tribes, it is claimed, but the Hunkpapa had it first. When Sitting Bull fell, the Silent Eaters became a memory.

No. 27.
TRADE WITH THE SLOTA
1873

During the campaigns against the Indians just following the Minnesota Massacre (1862), the American officers in the field complained repeatedly that the Red River Half Breeds from Canada, who crossed the line to hunt buffalo, were supplying the Sioux with arms and ammunition. The controversy as to how well the Indians were armed in their battles with the troops has been discussed at some length in *The Fighting Cheyennes* by George Bird Grinnell, and in my *Sitting Bull*. But as nothing has been published from the Sioux point of view on this matter of trade with the Red River Breeds, the following note may be of interest.

The Sioux knew these Canadian Breeds as the Slota, or Grease People, and often had fights with them, as with the Canadian tribes generally. One famous scrap took place on the Rosebud in 1873 (described in *Warpath*), when the Sioux got much the worst of it. Occasionally, Sitting Bull traded with the Canadians. But this was only during the rare truces, as when he bought a fine horse just before the Battle of Killdeer Mountain from them—the horse he rode in the fight. For two years Sitting Bull had been in the employ of Pierre Garreau, trader at Fort Berthold, and therefore had no occasion —and perhaps no liberty—to trade with any other importers. But finding that Garreau wished him to connive at the cheating of his people, Sitting Bull threw up the job. After that he would not come in to Fort Berthold to trade. When he did come to trade, he camped far off on the prairie, and made the traders come to him. The Sioux would have nothing to do with a trader who had once cheated them. They preferred such men as Galpin and Tom Campbell, who could be trusted, and would trust them. I have asked in vain for recollections of regular trade with the Breeds from Canada. The Hunkpapa (who lived farthest north, and were nearest them in those days) have very few memories of friendly contact with the Slota.

However, Chief White Bull recalls one occasion, which he has described to me. It was cold. The snow was two feet deep that winter of 1870. But a train of laden one-horse sleds came through the snow from the north, their lashed cargoes covered with hoar-frost, their swarthy drivers puffing great clouds of frozen breath. On they came, right into the circle of smoke-browned tipis, where the Sioux, huddled in their woolly buffalo robes, stood waiting, looking on.

Sitting Bull entertained the traders in his camp, taking three of them into his own snug lodge, where they could thaw their fingers at the brisk little blaze. For some days the Sioux traded with these men, traded for tobacco, knives, files, guns, powder and ball, and —more rarely—for red and blue blankets and woolen cloth. A good gun cost from two to five dressed buffalo robes, and a single robe brought only two pounds of gunpowder. It was at this time, when the camp was near Spoonhorn Butte, on a creek that flows towards Powder River, that Sitting Bull bought a gun.

White Bull, the chief's nephew, traded for two guns. These were single-shot breech-loaders, using percussion caps. He wanted them for stalking deer and antelope. For running meat horseback at short range, he thought a bow quite good enough. The Sioux were good shots from the saddle. They had steady hands, were always riding bareback, and habitually shot so. Once White Bull killed an aged toothless wolf with a knife, leaning from his saddle and stabbing the running wolf.

The trouble with guns was that the Indians had few tools for making repairs and no gun-oil. They had to use oils made from the marrow of a deer's foreleg.

That is the only time White Bull ever knew of the Sioux trading with the Red River Breeds from Canada. He was born in 1849.

No. 28.

HOW THE SIOUX MADE FRIENDS IN CANADA
1877

No sooner had the refugee Sioux entered Canada in 1877 than Sitting Bull began to take measures to protect himself. He feared that Bear Coat's soldiers might rush across the line and attack him. Moreover, he was surrounded by the ancient enemies of his people: Red River Mixed-Bloods, Plains Cree, Blackfoot, Bloods, Piegans, Saulteaux, and Canadian Hohe (Assiniboines). He at once set about forming a defensive alliance with these peoples.

There were several villages of Red River Mixed-Bloods near Wood Mountain; they had often made truce with the Sioux, that was quickly arranged. The Canadian Hohe also made no difficulty. Sitting Bull's Hohe "brother" Jumping Bull led him to their camp, introduced him to his cousin Big Darkness and other relatives, and all went smoothly. Sitting Bull was astonished and delighted with what he heard of the Red Coats. The Indians told him that when a white man shot an Indian, the Red Coats would *hang* him; that their *own chiefs* were accustomed to hand over Indian criminals to the Red Coats for trial, and that *none* of the Indian tribes in Canada would be a party to any war with the Grandmother's soldiers! Sitting Bull told the Hohe chiefs, "I came to this country to make peace; I am not going to make any trouble." That was the first tribe he talked to after he reached Canada; that was even before the Red Coats saw him. Big Darkness says Sitting Bull had lots of horses then: he gave many to the Hohe. The two tribes camped in one circle. Jumping Bull told his cousin that Sitting Bull had been good to him, didn't like to let him go, and that was why he stayed with the Sioux. They camped together for almost a moon. The Hohe knew Sitting Bull for a mean warrior, but very kind to his own people and their allies. He loved Jumping Bull very much, they say.

The most powerful tribe in that country was the Blackfoot. Sitting Bull took a party of Sioux to visit them; One Bull, Long Bull, Many Sacks, Loves-War, and White-Crow-Blanket were among the Sioux who sat in council. The Blackfoot were in camp near the Cypress Hills, or 'Big Desert,' east of Medicine Hat. Chief Crowfoot, the cool-headed, tactful, wise ruler of that unruly people, made Sitting Bull welcome. They merely smoked and made peace. Both of them were glad to be friendly, for neither wanted a fight. The Blackfoot, High Eagle, remembers this council: he was in the tent. Sitting Bull told Crowfoot, "We will be friends to the end of our lives—my children shall be your children, and yours mine. From now on we shall be friends forever, and never fight again." Crowfoot said, "Yes." Afterward, there were dances and feasts. Sitting Bull then named his young son Crowfoot after the Blackfoot chief, whom he admired and liked. Only recently the name (*Kangi-Siha* in Sioux) was again conferred by One Bull upon a grandchild in the family.

The Blackfoot High Eagle says that, somewhat later, Crowfoot's people visited the Sioux near Fort Walsh, and that some of the Blackfoot horses disappeared. Thereupon Crowfoot walked around his camp, yelling aloud that Sitting Bull was a liar and an enemy. But the living Sioux seem never to have heard of this, and certainly Sitting Bull always regarded Crowfoot as a firm friend, as is well shown by the interview he gave to the *Toronto Globe*, August 24, 1885, when with Buffalo Bill's Wild West Show in Canada. The peace with the Blackfoot was never broken, though there may have been difficulties between individual Sioux and Blackfoot.

The Crees, however, presented a more difficult problem. They were ancient enemies. Sitting Bull first ran on to them in Canada in the sand hills, just after he crossed the line. He was riding hard; as Chief Feather says, "His stirrups were hot!" One of Sitting Bull's men gave horses to an old Cree woman, and others followed his example, until they had donated twelve head to the Crees to create good will. Sitting Bull said, "I want to be friends. But I am going to move my camp away from you. Some of my boys might make trouble." The next time the Crees saw Sitting Bull was in the Little Rockies, but they ran away, for they were wearing necklaces of another tribe, and they feared that Sitting Bull would mistake them for enemies. Some of the Cree were killed by the Sioux, after Sitting Bull had returned to the States (1881). They could not keep from strife.

In '77, some of the Sioux were still hostile to the Crees. One day Chief Feather, then a young man, heard that the Sioux had killed a Saulteaux Indian near the Cypress Hills, and with thirteen companions rode over to White Cap's Sioux camp to talk it over. White Cap was friendly, and gave them four horses. Hoping for more gifts, the Crees started for Sitting Bull's camp, which was on the headwaters of Poplar River, north of the boundary. White Cap had warned them that Sitting Bull was "a bad man." But they carried a peace pipe. They went ahead.

When Feather reached the camp of the Sitting Bull Sioux, the first person he met was an old woman. She said, "The men are all away hunting. Only one chief is here." They rode into camp.

But the chief would not smoke their pipe. He talked with his own people, but said "These Crees ought to be killed." He would not look at them. He had a hooked nose, he was tall.[7] He called another Sioux into the tipi, and soon after two more came in; both were painted black about the eyes and mouth. The Sioux took the weapons and clothing of the Crees, and kept them sitting there in the tent all day, without food or water, waiting until the hunters should return. Feather was nervous; the Sioux who sat beside him had a big, keen butcherknife in his hands, ready to stick it into Feather's naked ribs.

"One of us is out hunting. As soon as he returns, we shall kill these Crees." That was what the chief said. At sundown Feather and his companions heard the hunters riding in. They thought their time had come. The hunters crowded all around and filled the tent.

Presently the hunter they had been waiting for came into the tent. He was short and broad in the shoulders, and limped a little. He took hold of the chief and said, "Here, feed these people; we must have no fighting in the Grandmother's country." The chief said nothing. But the Crees did. They said, "That's right. Leave us alone." The stocky man gave them back their guns, and that night they held a dance. Feather forgot all about his anxiety that night; he had a good time with the Sioux girls.

Feather is under the impression that it was Sitting Bull who wished to kill him. But from his description

---

7. This chief may have been Four Horns.

of the two men, it is clear that he is mistaken; it was Sitting Bull whom they waited for, and who saved him from death. Sitting Bull had no trouble with the Crees, and wanted none. There are stories in print telling how Sitting Bull had trouble with various tribes in Canada, and with the Red Coats also. But none of the Indians—Sioux, Blackfoot, Cree, Saulteaux, Hohe, or Red River Mixed Bloods can recall any such incidents, nor do they figure in the official records of the Mounted Police. They are sheer romance; the last thing Sitting Bull wanted was strife and trouble. His whole mind was set on making allies and friends to defend him against attack by soldiers from the States. It is too bad that these yarns cannot be substantiated, as some of them are very dramatic and admirably told.

No. 29.
CHIEF JOSEPH'S PEOPLE JOIN SITTING BULL
September, 1878

General Nelson A. Miles received the surrender of Chief Joseph, of the Nez Percé tribe, September 30, 1878. However, not all the Nez Percés with Joseph surrendered at this time; some escaped into Canada and joined Sitting Bull's camp there. Nothing has been published about how this union of former Indian enemies was effected. Here follows the account of Sioux and Nez Percé survivors who were witnesses of the treaty. The arrival of the Nez Percés had a very decided effect in determining the attitude of the Sioux chief towards the United States Commissioners, who came to Fort Walsh a few days later to induce him to return to the States. His indignation and distrust of the Americans were there expressed in no uncertain terms. Therefore this treaty and union with the refugee Nez Percés

COURTESY, BUREAU OF AMERICAN ETHNOLOGY

Chief Joseph, of the Nez Percés

has an historical significance, as well as the interest to be found in any account of old Indian customs.

One day, about September 28, 1878, Sitting Bull saw mirror signals sent by his scouts from a hill to the south of his camp, and he knew that someone was coming. Soon after, a crowd of people horseback and afoot came pouring over the hill and down into the narrow valley where the Sioux were camped. To his surprise, he saw that they were his old enemies, Nez Percés, hurrying along, and with them rode some Sioux hunters who were bringing them in. As they swarmed down the slope, he saw that many of them were wounded and bloody, some in travois, some tied in their saddles; the tired, haggard women were crying, the men looked grim, and babies whined from their cradles slung from saddlehorns. They did not stop, but rode right into the middle of his camp, looking for protection. Then they halted.

Robert Moses, a Nez Percé who spoke English, said, "There are more of us coming. Bear Coat's soldiers have cornered our chief, Joseph, at the Bear Paw Mountains. We want to be friends with the Sioux."

Sitting Bull's heart was touched. He took pity on the refugees. He knew just how they felt. In Canada there could be no war, the Red Coats had warned him. "You are welcome," he said, and everybody shook hands. The strangers gave Sitting Bull eight head of horses. They had a lot of horses, but nothing else, except some meat tied on their saddles, and the clothes they wore.

All the Sioux were angry and pitiful to think how these poor people had been treated; the soldiers had chased them since midsummer, all the way from their old home beyond the mountains, had fought with them in five battles and several skirmishes. Many of their women and children had been killed, and most of the warriors were wounded. They had been trying to get to Sitting Bull's camp in Canada, they said. But so many of their people were wounded that Chief Joseph would not leave them behind; he said he had never heard of a wounded Indian who got well in the care of the soldiers. But White Bird had brought away his wounded, he would soon be here. "Here he comes now."

A second crowd of Nez Percés came pouring down the hillside, and their chief White Bird was with them. Sitting Bull said, "Before Long Hair (Custer) died, we killed four Nez Percés, but now I want to be friends with you. You can stay with us here as long as you please. The Red Coats say that as long as we obey their law, we can stay. If the soldiers want me, they will have to start the war. All I want is to be at peace."

Sitting Bull's camp looked like home to those war-weary Nez Percés, who had fought harder and marched farther than any Indian nation known to history; whipped the troops almost every time, marched more than fifteen hundred miles through strange mountainous country. The Sioux made them welcome. Big Mane, and others, made feasts for them. One of the Nez Percés had his broken arm in a sling; another, a big warrior, naked to the waist, was bleeding from a bullet wound just over the right nipple. Sitting Bull did what he could to make them comfortable. He said, "I wanted my women and children to sleep sound of nights, so I came to this peaceful country. There is plenty of meat here, and traders."

George Peo-peo-tal-likt, one of the Nez Percé survivors, says, "Sitting Bull was a fine man. He was very kind to us and to his own people. He was a good hunter, and lived mostly on deer. The Sioux served dog at their ceremonial dances and feeds; only noted warriors were allowed to partake. Sitting Bull always thought things over before giving an answer."

The hundred refugee families were happy with the Sioux; they say, "The Sioux were having a good time, and we joined in." They stayed with them two years and more; one of the Nez Percés married a Sioux woman.

When the Red Coats arrived (called by the Nez Percés Captain Scobey and Captain Morton), they had with them a breed named Bullhead. Bullhead asked the newcomers if they were Nez Percé Indians. They said they were, that they had just arrived in Canada. The Red Coats said they were astonished at the way the Americans kept chasing their Indians into Canada, driving them out of the country, and told the Nez Percés it would be all right for them to remain north of the line. "You may select some land and live on it." Accordingly some eighty Nez Percés chose parcels of land. But they left them when they returned to the States after a year or so.

After the people had rested a few days, Sitting Bull led a scouting party of ten Sioux, nine Nez Percé men, and three Nez Percé women back to the Bear Paw Mountains to see if the soldiers were still there. They were out four days, but found no soldiers. Sitting Bull was anxious, for he could not understand what it was kept the soldiers from coming into Canada, "the Grandmother's country." It was certainly not the two dozen Red Coats at Fort Walsh, or the tiny detail at Wood Mountain. Knowing how tricky "Bear Coat" Miles was, Sitting Bull probably expected him to rush over the line and attack the Sioux, now that the Nez Percés had joined them. He was taking no chances.

He visited the battle-ground, and carried away some ammunition which the Nez Percés had buried before they fled to the north. At Chinook, on Milk River, where the French Chippewas lived in log houses, he was told that the soldiers had said the war was over, and had gone away the day before. Chief Joseph had held out four days in his trap, hoping that White Bird would bring aid from Sitting Bull's camp. But Sitting Bull dared not risk the displeasure of the Red Coats; he had to look out for his own people first. And so at last Joseph had surrendered to Bear Coat Miles under a promise that he would be sent back to his own country—a promise which was not fulfilled, as the captives were sent to Kansas and afterward to Indian Territory, where many died of malaria. Bear Coat, however, did not resign his commission, excusing himself to Joseph by saying, "If I resigned, it would do you no good. Some other officer would carry out this order." Bear Coat knew that even the resignation of a general could not shame the United States into keeping faith with an Indian in those days. Yet Joseph was no savage. He and all his people were Christians, and they waged war in a civilized manner.

The chief had led his three hundred warriors and their families through nearly two thousand miles of wild mountains, living off the country, fighting eleven engagements with the troops, five of them pitched battles, in which the soldiers' casualties sometimes ran as high as thirty-five percent. The total number of troops sent against him was nearly two thousand men, but he whipped them or evaded them every time, and only surrendered out of pity for his wounded and freezing women and children. It would be hard to match the march of the Nez Percés for courage, resource, or speed. Even with the telegraph and railroad available, the troops could hardly ever catch up with him, once he had passed them. Chief Joseph was one of the greatest of American generals.

After visiting the battle-field where Joseph surrendered, Sitting Bull led his scouting party back to Canada, to his camp on Witsa River, as the Sioux called it. The Nez Percés were much impressed with his knowledge of the country and his influence with the French Chippewas. "He seemed to be almost their leader, too," they say. The refugees were well content to camp with such a man.

No. 30.
THE SIOUX ACCOUNT OF HOW SITTING BULL'S SURRENDER CAME TO BE MADE
1881

Much has been printed by officers and officials of the U. S. Government, by The Royal Northwest Mounted Police of Canada, and by various other white men about the negotiations leading up to Sitting Bull's surrender. Here follows the Sioux account of some phases of this business heretofore neglected or misrepresented in our histories.

About the first of November, 1880, Scout E. H. Allison came from Fort Buford to Sitting Bull's camp at the mouth of Frenchman's Creek, on Milk River. He had conceived the idea of reaping the glory of getting Sitting Bull to surrender, and had succeeded in getting the U. S. military authorities to back his venture. With him went a private soldier, dressed in citizen's clothes, to drive the wagon loaded with hard bread, sugar, bacon, coffee, and tobacco. He has left an interesting account of his attempt to bring the chief in.[8]

The Hunkpapa, however, are unwilling to accept

---

8. See E. H. Allison, *The Surrender of Sitting Bull*, Dayton, Ohio, 1891.

Allison's book as entirely authentic. He had been among them for a long time, spoke Sioux fluently, and was known to them as "Fish," because he was such a slippery customer, or—as they put it—"such a liar." On one occasion, they say, the Hunkpapa backed him against a squawman at Standing Rock in a contest to see which could tell the biggest lie. The Yanktonais backed the squawman, who was married to one of their women. But though both did wonders, the match was declared a draw!

Inasmuch as the Indian agent in 1875 reported that "Fish" had been thrown into jail for theft, and appealed for authority to throw him off the Reservation for "carrying on an unwarranted and prejudicial intercourse with the Indians," there seems to be some reason to accept the Hunkpapa opinion of his character. One thing is certain, he begins his book by telling how he deliberately lied to Gall, and how Gall did not believe him. If Gall, who knew him well, would not believe him, I cannot see why we should. There is a framework of truth behind his story, but he was more dramatic than the facts warranted, made himself out a bold, heroic figure, and gave no credit to the U.S. soldiers, the trader LeGare, or the Red Coats, all of whom also claim to have brought about Sitting Bull's surrender.[9]

9. ALLISON THE SCOUT.—"A Wail from the West."—The following letter from "Little Muddy," west Missouri Slope, is interesting to say the least: Editor, Tribune:—I have the *pleasure* of writing to you to give a statement of the condition of the crops. There has not been any rain here since the first of June and the crops will be a complete failure. The grasshoppers did considerable damage in the early part of the season, and the drought and hot weather destroyed the balance. Prairie fires are raging in all sections and there are no signs of rain. Cattle men are coming in with herds and are looking almost in vain for small patches of grass to cut for the winter, and farmers will cut some of their grain for hay, leaving the remainder on the field.

There was a shooting affray here on the 13th; a half-breed named "Parky" Ward being shot in the mouth with a 38-calibre revolver, the ball lodging in his neck. The shooting was done by ALLISON, the Scout and interpreter, who brought in Sitting Bull.

G. S. Bartlett, Little Muddy, Dakota

(Comment of the Tribune: "If there is any affliction or crime, scourge or contagion which Mr. Bartlett has failed to enumerate, it is hoped he will make the correction at once.")

(From *Bismarck Daily Tribune*, Saturday, July 24, 1886, page 3, column 1).

These claims present a jungle which at first appears impenetrable. But the Hunkpapa old men know the paths through it, and in their story each man's part becomes clear. And—as might have been expected—it also becomes clear that it was Sitting Bull himself who determined upon leaving Canada, and no one else.

Allison had promised Gall that, if he would help bring Sitting Bull in, the Grandfather would make him head chief of the Sioux, and says that Gall, plain, blunt man of action, had swallowed the bait whole. It was the same bait used to win over Spotted Tail, and then offered to lure Crazy Horse to the agency. Allison is also responsible for the story that Sitting Bull and Gall quarrelled in Canada, and were never friends afterward. None of the Hunkpapa know anything of this alleged quarrel. Gall and Sitting Bull "got along fine up there," and when Sitting Bull came to Fort Yates a prisoner, Gall was the first man to meet and embrace him. All the chiefs were jealous of Sitting Bull at times, of course, but Gall was not the man to betray his leader. He was straight as a string. He was passionate and outspoken, no doubt, and anyone unfamiliar with the constant carping and back-biting which goes on in an Indian camp might have supposed at times that he was a mortal enemy of his chief; but it was not so. "Fish" naturally wished to reap whatever glory there might be in bringing Sitting Bull in, and made a good story of it. Bob-Tail-Bull, now living, was Allison's guide.

Sitting Bull, who was perfectly aware of Allison's identity and knew what he had come for, entertained him in his own hungry, crowded lodge. "Fish" and the disguised soldier ducked through the door-slit, and found themselves facing a nest of pots and pans, with the fire beyond. On the left of the door was the firewood, then the bed of the chief's younger wife and the twins, now four years old. Crowfoot, just seven, gave up his bed and was wedged endways into a narrow gap in the duffle on that side. Beyond Crowfoot, Sitting Bull's two daughters, seventeen and fourteen, slept at the back of the lodge to the left, and after another partition of household goods, came the bed of "Fish" and the soldier. Nearer the door on the right side Sitting Bull slept with his elder woman. The ten of them rather filled the big tent.

"Fish" makes no mention of the councils held to consider his proposal to surrender. Perhaps he was not told of them, for he seems to think that Gall engineered the whole thing in an underhand way, quite out of keeping with the known character of that forthright warrior.

However, Old Bull, One Bull, and others who attended these councils tell a different story. At these councils Crow King, Fool Heart, He Dog, Big Road, No Neck, Running Horse, Fool Bull, Turning Bear, and Gall were present and discussed the matter with Sitting Bull. It was agreed that all would go in and surrender.

Sitting Bull said, "Go, if you wish; I am coming too." But (as Allison also admits) a summons had come from Major Walsh, who was back from Fort Qu'Appelle with an answer to Sitting Bull's plea for a Reserve in Canada. Sitting Bull told the council of this summons, and said, "Just now I am called to visit the Red Coat garrison. I want to go there first. I will come where you are soon." Gall, loyal to Sitting Bull, and perhaps hopeful of remaining in Canada after all, returned with his chief to interview the Red Coats. "Fish" Allison was allowed to carry 20 lodges back to Buford with him;

he would have us believe that he slipped them away without Sitting Bull's knowledge or consent!

Incidentally, it is interesting to observe that "Fish" is also the author of the yarn about Sitting Bull's son's name The-One-Who-Was-Left, given him because he was said to have been left behind in the tipi when Major Reno struck the camp on the Little Big Horn in '76. Only this time it is the child's *mother* who abandoned him. Sitting Bull's defamers had not yet thought of saying that the chief himself had run away.

The Red Coats interviewed Sitting Bull and other chiefs on November 18 and 23. They were delighted to learn that he intended to surrender, and reported that he would soon do so. Learning that there could be no Reserve for the Sioux in Canada, Gall led about four hundred people down to Camp Poplar, and went into camp in the timber, within two miles of the post. Gall then found that his people would not go farther, and proposed to postpone their surrender until Spring. It was then (according to the military thermometer) every day from 10 to 30 degrees below zero, and too cold to travel. Gall's people wished to await the return of Crow King, whom Sitting Bull had sent with "Fish" to Buford to see how the Sioux who had surrendered were being treated. Moreover, the chiefs of the Poplar River Sioux wished to merge Gall's camp in their own, with a view to increasing their own importance, and therefore talked against going to Buford.

Meanwhile, Allison was back at Wood Mountain, trying to get Sitting Bull started south. Low Dog had already pulled out, December 11, '80, and Sitting Bull started soon after. Allison gives a most picturesque account of this march over the snowy plains, and the Indians say he told the truth about that. Sitting Bull's people had barely enough horses to pack their camp, even colts had burdens, and most of the grown folks walked. Most of the mounted men were in the rear, and at intervals sent out half a dozen men to ride on the flanks a mile or two. These flankers would then halt, sit down, and smoke until the column came up with them, when a new detail would start forward. There was no game, the supplies were exhausted, and the cold became intense. Allison was called aside by a young warrior, who beckoned to him. Sitting Bull rode over with "Fish," who asked the young man what he wanted. "He seemed embarassed, and stood for nearly a minute, silent, holding the muzzle of his rifle in his hands, while the butt rested on the ground. At last he said, looking at me, while his lips quivered and his voice trembled with savage emotion, 'Where are you taking these people?'

" 'To Fort Buford.'

" 'Then why don't you feed them, don't you know that they are hungry?' "

Says Allison, "I was about to reply, but Sitting Bull, realizing the situation, adroitly placed himself between me and the speaker, and while indicating by signs that I should move on, he engaged the young man in conversation. And when, a little later, he overtook me, he simply said, 'The young man's heart is bad; his little sister is crying for food.' Only for the intervention of Sitting Bull, I have no doubt that the young man would have attempted my life."

Once more Sitting Bull had saved a white man, who promptly went home and called him "coward." "Fish" was employed by the soldiers; he knew which side his bread was buttered on. He went on with his plans for the chief's surrender.

But the time for that surrender was not yet. On Milk River the Sioux found buffalo, and camped there to feed their starving people. Meanwhile Sitting Bull sent Crow King to Fort Buford with "Fish" Allison, to see how the surrendered Indians there were getting on. It was the last week of December, 1880.

While he hunted on Milk River, things happened at Camp Poplar in the States which had a great effect upon Sitting Bull's future actions. Camp Poplar was on his road to Buford.

Major Guido Ilges had just brought in his frostbitten troopers to Camp Poplar from Fort Keogh, and Gall went to see him, and said he would like to go on alone to Fort Buford. His object was to gain information which would reassure his people, some of whom preferred to go to Fort Keogh. Gall was ready to surrender, and asked for an escort to Buford. The Major, knowing nothing about Indians, thought this a time to be firm, refused Gall's request, and thereby destroyed the little authority he had left in the disintegrating camp. It is so much easier to be firm than to understand. Ilges gave the Sioux three days to think it over. At the end of that time, they must surrender and go to Buford.

As Gall had failed, all the headmen waited on Ilges, saying that they wished to await the action of Sitting Bull, "who was their only chief." But just then dispatches arrived from headquarters forbidding Ilges to have any intercourse with the "hostiles," and the interview was ended. Just why Ilges thought these people "hostiles" is puzzling: how any man in his senses could believe that "hostiles" would bring their women and children and camp within two miles of an Army post where there were cannon and cavalry, is past finding out. But Ilges was not a man "to reason why."

Crow King, just back from Buford with Allison, reported favorably on that post, and told the Indians that they ought to go there at once, that this was the wish of Sitting Bull, for whom he was acting and speaking. But the people said it was too cold to drag their families (half-clad and hungry, as Ilges reports) through the snow. They were not in awe of the soldiers, and resented the Major's peremptory tone. Gall was so exasperated that he vented his feelings to the post trader in an empty boast, saying that he would wipe out everybody in the soldier camp. This was reported to Ilges, who immediately had another spasm of firmness. On January 2 he turned out with 12 commissioned officers, 272 enlisted men, 19 Indian scouts, 2 citizen volunteers, all mounted, and two pieces of artillery. About noon Guido began his "march" on the village—two miles away!

Meanwhile, Crow King, Gall, and Allison, who were conversing peaceably at the trader's store, saw the troops moving out. They realized with amazement and horror that Major Ilges was about to attack the camp. If he did, of course, there would be no more Sioux surrenders for many a moon to come. That was certain. Allison sent Gall galloping across the frozen river to his camp to call off his warriors and run up a white flag. Gall "threw himself upon the back of his beautiful black pony and was away with the swiftness of a deer." Allison and Crow King clambered up to the roof of the trader's store and watched developments. They saw the Major place his artillery, and without any attempt at a parley, fire into the tipis. But Gall had arrived in time, and when the troops reached his camp it was empty, and Gall was waving the white flag in the face of the soldiers. An old woman was wounded, and one man killed. By Major Ilges' own report only one shot was fired by the Indians. There were "no casualties" among the whites. Having captured the camp in this valiant manner, the Major ordered the tipis of his captives burned. These poor wretches numbered three hundred, and had only 31 lodges saved from the flames!

If the Indians had attempted to defend their camp, which was admirably located in the timber and surrounded by brush, a good many soldiers might never have answered roll call that evening, though eighty fighting men could not have destroyed the command, more especially as many of them had no arms. Only a few guns were captured, described by the Major as "a few worthless muskets," and "16 rifles and guns of different patterns, and two pistols." These Indians had come in to surrender; many of them had never had guns, and of the rest not a few had swapped them for food in Canada.

But the Secretary of War declared in his Report for the year, "Major Ilges' conduct deserves especial commendation," comments upon his "intelligent obedience" and says he "shares with Major Brotherton the honor of having brought the war to a conclusion." Undoubtedly, the "*war*" was over.

Having conquered Gall, the Major now moved against the Yanktonais camp on Red Water. But the Yanktonais, who had been peacefully camped there under the protection of the troops all winter, hastened to meet him. He demanded the "hostiles" who had fled to them from the burned camp, and they turned over to him eighteen persons, "among them 4 bucks, nearly all of them badly frozen and frost-bitten, and all of them in the most destitute condition." No guns are mentioned.

Meanwhile, Allison sent Crow King posthaste to

reassure the Indians with Sitting Bull, who were certain to hear of this affair and turn back to Canada. Crow King rode hard, and was successful in bringing back 51 lodges to Wolf Point, from which place they were transported to Buford by the soldiers. Crow King brought in "300 people, among them 70 or 80 full-grown warriors, 5 guns, and 13 ponies."

No sooner had Sitting Bull learned of the attack on Gall's camp at Poplar, than he turned back and crossed the line. Crow King might risk surrender, but Sitting Bull would not. He sent Four Horns, his uncle, One Bull, his nephew, and Bone Club to Fort Buford to learn the truth of the matter and see how these surrendered Sioux were getting on. He had meat now, and had no intention of walking into a trap. With these three emissaries went a Red Coat, and at the boundary line they were joined by a United States soldier. The two white men had a jug of whiskey between them, and after they crossed the line the pair of them got quite merry together. One Bull, brought up in Sitting Bull's dry camp, had never seen men drunk before. His curiosity was aroused. He said, "Friends, we're out on a trip together. I want to see how it tastes, and how it feels to be drunk like you."

But the white men would not share. They knew that a warrior generally became homicidal when intoxicated. They kept the jug from him. He asked them why. They replied, "No. We're afraid you'll kill us, if you get drunk!" Bone Club and Four Horns laughed at that, they kept joking One Bull about how scared the white men were of him. He never heard the last of that. This happened northwest of Camp Poplar.

Four Horns and One Bull found that the Indians who had surrendered at Camp Poplar had had to give up their arms and horses, but were given rations and beads. They got all the details of the fight begun by Major Ilges. Then they went back to report, and told how the mounted soldiers had fired guns and cannon over the heads of the Sioux. Because of this, the year 1881 is known in the Hunkpapa Calendar as the Winter-when-the-Sioux-were-fired-over.

On February 7, Major Guido Ilges, still going strong, learned that Jumping Bull, was "casually sojourning at Wolf Point" and asked the Indian agent to arrest him. "The arrest was quietly effected on the following day, and this noted warrior and murderer" (sic) was thrown into the guard-house, "secured by shackles." The Major also seized "his three horses, his gun, and his family"..... The Major goes on to say that Jumping Bull (whom he calls Little Assiniboin) was "a fit subject for Leavenworth prison".... apparently because he was Sitting Bull's adopted brother. Jumping Bull was kept in solitary confinement and in irons during that bitter weather without a fire, until Bull Ghost, then a scout, took pity on him and persuaded the soldiers that there was no harm in the man. But that was some time later.

When Sitting Bull turned up at Wood Mountain again, Superintendent Crozier held another council, and after some talk, Sitting Bull (remembering what Guido had done on January 2) declared, "If I could get a good letter from the soldier-chief at Fort Buford that he will treat us well, I might go. I will see about it." Crozier immediately sent couriers to Major Brotherton, and reassuring letters were promptly forwarded to Sitting Bull through the hands of the Red Coats.

Meantime, Sitting Bull heard what they had done to his brother, Jumping Bull. If they treated him so, for no reason at all, what would they do to Sitting Bull himself? Accordingly when Crozier read the letters he had got from Buford, Sitting Bull jumped up and cried out, "I do not believe a word that is said." He turned and left the room. Crozier was so disgruntled that he called after the chief, "I don't want to see you again; you've made me so much trouble."

Then Sitting Bull said to his aide Old Bull, "I want you to go and find out how the Hunkpapa are getting along down at Fort Buford. Bring me a report about this." Old Bull agreed. He asked Catch-the-Bear to go with him. A white man, a trader (Le Gare?) went along, leaving Sitting Bull camped on Mud Creek at the south end of Wood Mountain near the trading house. This trading house was run by a man who also owned a Roman Catholic Church, and Catch-the-Bear and Old Bull worshipped in this church before starting south into the country of the Christians. They went to the mouth of Yellowstone, and found the Hunkpapa in camp near Fort Buford.

It was spring.

Old Bull and Catch-the-Bear were two days on the trip from Camp Poplar to Fort Buford. All the way in they were followed by Black Pheasant and Swift Bird, who caught up with them just as they reached the Indian camp at the post. There Old Bull met Running Hawk, one of Gall's warriors, and Strikes-the-Kettle, who belonged to Crow King's band. Both invited him to dinner. Old Bull went with Strikes-the-Kettle and sent the other men to Gall's camp. The Hunkpapa at the post welcomed him and Catch-the-Bear. While they were eating a man came from the post on horseback and said he was the interpreter and that his name was George. Just then Old Bull noticed that the bugles were sounding.

The interpreter said, "The guards at the fort have seen three men coming into the post and I have been sent to find out who they are. Old Bull immediately told what he had come for and said that Black Pheasant and Swift Bird were in Gall's camp.

The interpreter immediately replied that the commanding officer at the fort wished to see all of them at once. The Indians prepared to go with him to see the officer. The chiefs of the different bands encamped there were King, Crow King, Gall, Loud Dog, Fool Heart, and Turning Bear. They all accompanied Old Bull, Black Pheasant, and Swift Bird to see the commanding officer. The interpreter led the way. The soldiers were drilling on the parade ground and lined the road leading to the soldier house. The nine Indians and the interpreter passed between their ranks and went on into the office of the commanding officer. There Old Bull saw a middle aged man with hair turning gray in uniform. This man said "How." The Indians said the same, shook hands with the officer and sat down.

Scout E. H. "Fish" Allison was there. He spoke Sioux and asked the Indians to take their arms and give them to the officer. Old Bull got up, took off his cartridge belt, and laid it, with his rifle, upon the officer's desk.

The officer said to Old Bull, "Why are you traveling? These are my orders, to round up all the Indians. Why did you come here?"

Old Bull: "Sitting Bull told us to find out how our people are treated at this camp. These people here are our relatives and we want to see how they are getting along."

Major: After you see with your own eyes how your

people are treated, I suppose you are going back to report?"

Old Bull: "Yes."

Major: "Tell Sitting Bull that his reservation will be from here one half the length of the Missouri River. The north line will be the Little Missouri, as far as it goes, taking in all the little hills and badlands. That will be Sitting Bull's hunting grounds. Also the Grandfather is going to give the Sioux teams of oxen, teams of horses, mares and colts. There must be no more roaming, everybody must settle down. This land is reserved for the Sioux nation. These chiefs with you have already heard all about this. Tell Sitting Bull he will be treated like them. Rations will be issued to all and nobody will go hungry."

The Major then returned the gun and cartridge belt to Old Bull, and added, "Before you go, I want you to see with your own eyes what rations your people are getting today. Also, I want you to come to the mess-hall and eat before you start."

Though Old Bull had just eaten dinner, he was a thorough Sioux. He went into the mess-hall and got round another square meal right away. Afterward, he went outside and saw a steamboat coming up the river, with the stars and stripes at the mast-head. He heard an Indian singing on board, and when the boat came near, he saw it was Chief Running Antelope, of the Hunkpapa. He has been sent from Standing Rock to get the Indians to come down there. A council was called to discuss this. But before the talk, Old Bull went to see the issue. A big wagon came up, with a four-mule team, and it was loaded with meat and other goods. Every family received all the food it could eat, a tent, and other things, even beads. When the issue was over, the interpreter asked, "Well, how do you like it?"

Old Bull replied, "I cannot help but like it, if they are going to treat us this way."

Old Bull went back to the camp of his host, and met Running Antelope. Running Antelope said: "You are one of the men I want to see. Your father wants you to come back."

Next day they held a council to discuss Running Antelope's invitation. They all assumed, apparently, that Sitting Bull would be unable to hold out longer, that he would come down to Buford before long. That was not very welcome news to some of the jealous little chiefs who, having now left his camp, wished to remain outside the shadow of his greatness. They did not want him to return. And if he was to stay at Buford, they wished to go elsewhere.

Fool Heart: I agree with Running Antelope. We should move over there to Standing Rock.

Low Dog: (Oglala) I object. This is a much better location. If you are jealous of Sitting Bull, you can go. I am going to stick with Sitting Bull; if this is to be his country around here, here I stay.

Turning Bear (avoiding the challenge): Lots of my kin are down on that Standing Rock Reservation now. I would like to move down and live with them.

King: I do not think it right to move down there. This is a good place, and there is plenty of game hereabouts. I'm with Low Dog on this question.

Speaking of this council, Moses Old Bull says, "My brother Red Crow always advised me never to tell a lie. Therefore I have not, I have told the truth. This was the worst (this jealousy) that I heard that day. Next day we started back to tell Sitting Bull. The Canadian trader went along. We were two days on the road, but found his camp moved. Long Horns was still there; he said, 'Sitting Bull has gone towards the north, towards the lakes. One Bull and others went along. He'll be back before long.'"

Old Bull left his report with Long Horns. He and his wife and her family went south with the trader in wagons. He fed them well. They reached the steamboat just before it started south. The soldiers were kind to them at Buford, helped them get aboard. Old Bull remembers one man especially—he had a scar on his cheek.

Before they went on board, the soldier-chief gave Old Bull some paper money—one bill. It was the first money Old Bull ever handled. He did not know its value. He took the bill over to the traders, laid it down, and pointed out a bolt of cloth. He wanted to get a piece of that. But the trader gave him enough to clothe a dozen families!

The soldier-chief also gave Old Bull a paper. Old Bull was told that this appointed him chief of this band. But once, when there was a dispute over an issue of shoes, he became angry and tore it up. And so he never learned what the paper said, exactly. Old Bull was given blankets, beads, and other presents, also.

Two years later Old Bull saw Sitting Bull again, and learned that Long Horns had faithfully delivered the message left with him.

No. 31.

NOTE ON LOUIS LE GARE

My old friend, Louis Le Gare, was one of the most picturesque and remarkable men I have ever met. He told me that he was born in France but he must have come to the Prairies at a very early age. As a trader in

Buffalo pelts he made his headquarters at Willow Bunch which became a French-Halfbreed settlement of considerable importance in later years. Le Gare told me his creaking caravans took three months on their way to market, Fort Garry (Winnipeg). He also ran a general store and conducted a rather extensive ranching business when I knew him.

Le Gare was almost if not entirely illiterate; otherwise I think he could have risen to remarkable heights. He was a man of great physical vigor. He combined with characteristically French qualities of character an inflexible imperturbability and a comprehension of and sympathy with Indian and Halfbreed traits that gave him a very commanding influence over an immense if sparsely inhabited territory. I never saw such eyes in anyone else. He gave you the impression that he could count your vertebrae from the front. Usually incommunicative, for a Frenchman, he would occasionally open up and I was fortunate enough to get him into a delightfully reminiscent mood once when I called on him in 1906 or 1907. I already knew from the oldtimers the essential parts of his narrative but took care not to reveal the fact. Everything he told me fitted into the facts otherwise known to me and I have no reason to question the reliability of his statements, so far as they went.

You do not need to be told, however, that even honest men rarely tell the truth. In connection with the Sitting Bull episode the American officials, the Mounted Police and probably Mr. Le Gare, all had an eye to acquiring whatever glory their part in the transactions might entitle them to, so they showed no undue tendency to blow each other's horns. Le Gare himself was hampered by his inability to write for himself and we have to rely almost wholly on the Police records. That these did not wholly ignore Le Gare is indicated by my quotation from Commissioner Irvine's report of February 1882, but Le Gare quite plainly thought that very cold justice had been done him, and in this view he was supported by other old settlers with whom I have talked the matter over.

At the time of the Sitting Bull affair the Northwest Indians and Halfbreeds were in great distress owing to the sudden and catastrophic disappearance of the buffalo herds. By the way, Le Gare himself believed that the migratory herds had been systematically and deliberately annihilated as an incident to the American effort to compel Indians to submit to concentration on reservations. At all events the elusive Sioux when they came to Canada helped to complete the destruction of the chief source of livelihood of the Indian and Halfbreed population and there was much hunger and misery. On the whole the Sioux were remarkably well treated but the local authorities were pretty well at their wit's end to know what to do with the hungry foreigners. Le Gare said that he could not sit back and watch them starve and that for three months or so he maintained about four hundred of them at his own charges. Reckoning these meagre rations at ten cents per diem the trader told me it cost him about forty dollars a day. Le Gare said he lost thousands of dollars in cold cash over this affair. No doubt he expected to be generously reimbursed by Uncle Sam. Of course his liberality gave him great influence with Sitting Bull, who often came to his store to talk his troubles over with the sympathetic Frenchman. Le Gare took advantage of these conferences repeatedly to urge upon Sitting Bull the wisdom and indeed the necessity of surrender. At last Sitting

Bull one day yielded the point and told Le Gare that he was ready to give up. Le Gare immediately notified the authorities and officialdom promptly corralled all the credit.

(Signed) Norman Fergus Black

No. 32.
SITTING BULL AS PRISONER OF WAR
(1881-1883)

Sitting Bull surrendered to the United States troops at Fort Buford, July 19, 1881. On July 29, his band of one hundred and eighty-seven souls boarded the steamboat *General Sherman* to go down river to Standing Rock Agency.

On August 1, '81, the steamboat made landing at Mandan, and Sitting Bull's party were taken ashore for an issue of rations. The chief and his people were held in a hollow square of soldiers. Sitting Bull and some other head men were invited to enter a carriage, to be taken into the town for dinner and a photograph. As the carriage moved away, the women and children huddled on the bank began to wail and cry; they thought they had seen the last of their beloved leader, that he would never be able to help them again. When this pathetic scene began, the soldiers brought their rifles to bear on these defenceless people. But Sitting Bull stood up in the carriage, gesturing and talking, and soon had the Indians quiet again. Then he was driven away.[10]

In the hotel he and his friends had a good dinner, and were paid for having their photographs made.

10. For this story, I am indebted to Mr. J. D. Allen, of Mandan, N. D., who witnessed it.—S.V.

Sitting Bull was suspicious; he kept his back to the wall. Meanwhile, two days' rations had been issued to the Indians at the steamboat landing; they remained there less than three hours, but at the end of that time all the food was gone. They had been hungry so long, they could not be filled up. Many were so destitute they had only a blanket to cover them.

At Bismarck quite a party of white people boarded the boat; H. F. Douglas, then post-trader at Standing Rock, the editor of the *Bismarck Tribune*, Colonel C. A. Launsberry, a number of officers from Fort Abraham Lincoln, and several ladies. The officer in command of the escort introduced the ladies to Sitting Bull. Scout E. H. "Fish" Allison acted as interpreter.

Sitting Bull was in shabby Indian clothing, hatless, and without paint or feathers. But he was cheerful, "and at first disposed to talk freely"—until Allison intervened. "He chatted freely of his family, and seemed very proud of his children. He showed great regard for the ladies," and asked one of the officers how the white men managed to keep their women so good-looking. He was told that the white men did not work their women hard. One of the ladies was a young girl, Miss Emma Bentley. She gave him a fine California pear. Sitting Bull cut out a morsel, tasted it, and liked it. Poor as he was, he could not give up his old habit of being benefactor. He never received a gift without making some return. Taking a brass ring from his finger, he placed it upon one of her own "with as much care as the most devoted lover," and then folded her hand so as to hold the gift firmly.[11]

Meanwhile Professor Haupt had been making a pencil sketch of the chief. Sitting Bull took it and tore

---

11. Mrs. W. A. Falconer (née Miss Emma Bentley) still has the ring. The story was published in the *Detroit Free Press*, August 1, 1881.

Section of Sitting Bull's Camp at Fort Randall, 1882

it up, throwing the pieces on the deck. However, these were afterward recovered and put together. Attempts were made to get him to talk of the Custer fight, but without result. Many "interviews" were later published in the newspapers in which Sitting Bull was made to tell the story of that battle; few, if any, of them have even a shred of truth. Sitting Bull was cautious, and until he went with Buffalo Bill, in 1885, was unwilling to say one word on that subject. While he was running wild on the plains, reporters had to be careful what yarns they published, for everyone knew that the chief was inaccessible. But after he surrendered, the temptation to print stories was very strong, and few writers who went west of the Missouri could resist it. They could "get away with murder" then, for none of Sitting Bull's people could read English. Good interpreters were very rare. And not infrequently, one surmises, the half-breed interpreter, rather than lose his pay, would converse with the chief about the weather, and then tell the eager white man a yarn made of whole cloth. Unless one knows enough Sioux to follow the talk, even good interpreters sometimes make errors and omissions which are never detected. Due allowance also must be made for the extreme courtesy of the old-time Sioux, who will sometimes say what they think the stranger wishes to hear, rather than the truth. It is essential for getting at the truth to avoid all leading questions, unless the ground has been prepared beforehand and the old-timer understands the importance of making a truthful record. Such difficulties made it almost impossible for a brisk reporter, generally without any knowledge of the Sioux or their language, to get the truth. And so the newspaper men did a nobler thing than record history—they created it. The public could not check those outrageous lies, and generally swallowed them whole. But one may say without a second's hesitation that ninety-nine per cent of the "interviews" with Sitting Bull, and the great majority of the magazine stories about him, are without a shred of truth. The only virtue in these yarns is that they contradict one another.

Miss Bentley and her friends found Sitting Bull courteous and anxious to make friends, but "evidently a better fighter than talker." Yet he was "thoroughly subsided," and "likely to be one of the most docile of his band" at the agency.

As the boat approached Standing Rock, the Sioux lined the rail, and many of them began to sing, overcome with emotion at the sight of their old friends and relatives swarming down the bank to meet them. Sitting Bull stood silent among the others. On the bank Gall was standing, with folded arms, and Sitting Bull could hardly wait for the landing-stage to be lowered so that he could embrace his old friend. But Running Antelope jumped on board and hugged Sitting Bull hard, cheeked him on both sides. They gripped hands, *"Hau! Hau!"* and tears streamed down Sitting Bull's face. Fully one thousand Sioux had come to greet their famous leader, and these visitors were eating the Standing Rock Indians out of house and home. Major James McLaughlin, the new agent, cannot have approved this; from his reports it is clear that he was dead against this endless visiting back and forth between the agencies. Standing Rock was filling up with the "late hostiles," and the Major would have his hands full without the added burden of hundreds of Sitting Bull's admirers coming in.

Soon an order arrived from the General of the Army. Sitting Bull and his immediate following were to be taken down-river to Fort Randall, and held as prisoners of war!

Over and over Sitting Bull had been promised that he should share the general amnesty, be treated like other surrendered Sioux, and sent to live on the Reservation. If his life were spared, Sitting Bull was certainly justified in supposing that this would be his lot. General Terry, Bishop Marty, the Red Coats, Major Brotherton, "Fish" Allison, all had told him the same story. Sitting Bull, however, had not trusted the Americans, and he was right. They deceived him, just as they did Chief Joseph.

This order making him prisoner of war was only the first of that interminable series of slights, humiliations, and insults with which the later years of Sitting Bull were rendered miserable. From that day on, certain officials of the United States behaved like spiteful women towards the captive Sioux, and—as Sitting Bull was their undaunted leader—he bore the brunt. Again and again he had spared white men, even honored them, when they fell into his hands. But when he became a captive, few treated him with any respect. He might have been a wild beast instead of a man.

Who initiated this order remains to be discovered. It was certainly not expected by the people—both Indians and whites—who came down on the steamboat with Sitting Bull. It is possible that Major McLaughlin asked to have Sitting Bull sent elsewhere, and—if so—he may have done it without any knowledge of the pledges made to the chief by the military. However that may be, the order was issued, and Sitting Bull always held McLaughlin responsible, and said so on a number of occasions. That was the first rift in their relations—

a rift which was to widen with the years until it engulfed the chief.[12]

A story is told that, when ordered aboard the steamboat again, Sitting Bull protested, and a soldier knocked him out with the barrel of his rifle. If this be legend, it at least dramatizes the existing situation most effectively.

And so Sitting Bull marched aboard with his family, and after him came forty-odd men with their own: Four Horns and One Bull, Kills Charging, the son of Four Horns, Bear-Looking-Back, White Dog, Gray(Roan)-Faced-Bear, Standing Cloud, Bear's Boudin, Black-Prairie Chicken, Red Thunder, Red Thunder No. 2, High Bull, Leaf, Muddy Breast, Charging-Thunder, Bone Club, Mad Dog, Fire Cloud, One Hand, Standing Kill, Yellow Dog, His-Holy-Pipe, Iron Heart, Big Legs, and all the rest. A few days later their thirty lodges were pitched beside Fort Randall.

Sitting Bull was agreeably surprised by his treatment as prisoner of war. Though many of the soldiers and officers there must have regarded him as the man who killed Custer, they showed the old warrior no discourtesy. Though monotonous, the life at Fort Randall was by no means disagreeable. The commanding officer and his subordinates exhibited the qualities and character traditional among officers of the best outfits of the Regular Army of the United States: Sitting Bull and his little band had nothing to complain of on that score. Well-fed on Army rations, and well treated, they had time at last to rest and grow fat.

Every morning about nine o'clock, the Officer of the Day came to count the one hundred and fifty-four souls who made up the camp. This daily check became quite

---

12. See *Saginaw Evening News*, September 8, 1885.

a function, quite as formal as the Guard Mount which preceded it. The women and young warriors and children turned out painted and dressed in their best, and seated themselves before their lodges, waiting the coming of the soldier-chief. Being treated with kindness and respect, they showed respect in turn.

For the rest of the day they were free. The camp was on the open prairie in summer, and in the timber nearby in winter. A sentry paced around, but there was no enclosure.

Occasionally something happened to break the monotony of a prisoner's life. On December 12, '81, Sitting Bull faced an interview which placed him in a rather delicate position. Captain A. Lawson and the missionary Rev. John P. Williamson came to his tipi, bringing with them an old Roster Book of the Thirty-First Infantry containing sketches of Sitting Bull's exploits at war. The drawings, done in color, were copies made by Four Horns from a set by Sitting Bull's own hand, had been sold to James C. Kimball, Assistant Surgeon, U.S.A. in 1870 by a Yanktonais Sioux, who also supplied a key or index (highly inaccurate and incomplete) explaining the pictures. The book was later placed in the Army Medical Museum, and is now in the archives of the Bureau of American Ethnology, in Washington. It had been sent to Fort Randall through official channels, in the hope that Sitting Bull would give a more complete and accurate interpretation of the drawings, in case they were authentic. The two visitors showed him the book.

"Sitting Bull immediately recognized the 55 pictures as scenes from his early life, with the exception of Nos. 39 to 51, and 53 and 54, which he said were adventures of his brother Jumping Bull. As to the scenes from his own life, he says these are all true scenes, and he drew a similar set many years ago and gave them to his brother Jumping Bull. He saw his brother last summer and understood from him that he still had them." Who had made the copies he could not say certainly, but told the visitors, somewhat pathetically, that "he could tell perhaps by seeing his brother, who was at Standing Rock. . . . .

"Sitting Bull verified in the main the index accompanying the pictures," and gave an account of his first exploit with some detail and much gusto. He made a number of corrections as regards the Indian battles, but "as to the particular history of each event recorded we found Sitting Bull rather reserved, especially in regard to scenes 11 to 26 (the *coups* counted upon white men and U.S. soldiers). The interviewers reported to the Commanding Officer that 'if a more full account of his deeds is desired, a better time to secure it would be. . . when his status is definitely determined'." Sitting Bull was cautious; he was a prisoner in the hands of his enemies. He could hardly be expected to say anything which might be used against him. The true interpretation of these pictures was not obtained from him until 1885, when Seth C. Jones, armed with copies, found the old warrior in a reminiscent mood. Unhappily, even Jones failed to get the full story of his deeds, as the series was incomplete. No. 55 was not finished, not having the pictograph of a sitting buffalo attached to the hero's mouth by a line, which identified him in each of the other pictures.

The foreign artist Cronau, who visited the captive chief, reports his anxiety to see the President and present his case in person. Cronau (called Iron Eyes because of the spectacles he wore) quotes the chief as follows: "I never was afraid of my enemies and did my best. My successes I owe the Great Spirit. Iron Eyes, when you go to the Great Father (President of the Union), I beg you speak in my interest, for I am of the opinion, that up to now no one has brought my wishes before the Great Father. Tell him, that he may allow me to visit to speak with him personally, tell him that I should like to live like a white man and own a farm that could feed me (Would make a living), for I do not want to live on the rations given to us daily. I like to help myself. I should like to live on the Cannon Ball or Grand River. There is good land, water and wood. There also is the place where I was born. I wished that teachers might live there who would teach my children and those of my warriors; further I should like that blacksmiths and traders would settle there with whom I could establish connections. Tell the Great Father that I do not speak, only to speak; my heart is just and wants what I say."

So day followed day at Fort Randall, until in September of '82, Lieutenant Colonel George P. Ahern, then a young lieutenant fresh from West Point, came to join his regiment, the Twenty-Fifth Infantry. Colonel George Andrews, commanding, found that Ahern was something of a linguist, and asked him to take charge of Sitting Bull's fan mail, which was becoming abundant. Letters addressed to Sitting Bull were being received not only from people in the United States, b utfrom many foreign lands. They were, for the most part, requests for his pipe, knife, tomahawk, and especially for his autograph! By that time someone had taught him to write his name in English, with a large dot over the "i" and the "t" crossed at the very top of the vertical line. But Sitting Bull would not answer a letter or send an autograph unless a dollar was sent in advance. The money he received from this source he spent on tobacco, paint, and other little luxuries at the post trader's.

With this information, Lieutenant Ahern sought the tent of Sitting Bull. He found him "a very remarkable man—such a vivid personality. He stood before me square-shouldered, deep-chested, fine head, and the manner of a man who knew his ground. He looked squarely into your eyes, and spoke deliberately and forcefully; with me he never raised his voice or spoke fast, but occasionally in conferences with visiting chiefs I would lose the trend of conversation, as they used idiomatic expressions and spoke rapidly. For several months I was in daily contact with Sitting Bull, and learned to admire him for his many fine qualities."

At first Sitting Bull was rather reserved with the young officer, "but after we two became friends it was gratifying to see the really friendly attitude on his part in all our dealings together. He would visit me in my quarters when I failed to show up in camp. He would enjoy leaving his card; in fact, it was my card I had left purposely in his tipi, and he would return it with his own name written on the reverse side. The nearest he came to being jovial was when he dropped the card on my table with a smile and a twinkle in his eye. Even then I had become acquainted through older officers with some of the great wrongs done the Indian, and I marvelled at the Indian's patience and forbearance." Sitting Bull called Lieutenant Ahern "Two Crows," after an Indian whom he resembled.

At that time, Sitting Bull's lodge contained his two wives, the twins, and his ten-year-old daughter, Standing Holy. This little girl was a favorite with the officers at Fort Randall. Miss Sallie Battles, niece of

Colonel Andrews, visited the post, and made such friends of the Sitting Bull family that the chief named one of his children for her. Standing Holy was great pals with Lieutenant Ahern. She grew into a fine woman, and died only a short time ago.

At Fort Randall, as elsewhere, Sitting Bull dressed simply, in Indian garb, used little paint, and seldom wore a feather in his hair. He carried a plain, undecorated pipe. But "the camp was well administered by the Chief. Never was there any disturbance. The children were well-behaved and apparently never needed disciplinary measures. This was due largely to the love of the children for their parents, and to the profound respect paid the older members and leaders of the tribe."

This love of children for parents was thoroughly reciprocated in Sitting Bull's home. When Captain R. H. Pratt of the Carlisle Indian School came to ask the chief to let him take some of the young folks away to be educated, Sitting Bull—after thinking it over—made answer, "I have seen the results of school. The children who return are neither white nor Indian. Nothing is done for them. I love my children too much to let anything like that happen to them. I will not approve this request."

And again, when Lieutenant Ahern suggested that Standing Holy ought to be sent to a convent at St. Louis, and the little girl came to his side and took his hand, trusting to his judgment, her father said, "No, I love you too much. Nothing but sorrow would come of it." "And," says Colonel Ahern, "he was right."

The story goes that Sitting Bull opposed civilization in all its forms. This is not true. Sitting Bull merely wished to use it for the benefit of his people. Said he, "If you see anything good in the white man's road, pick it up and keep it. But if you find something that is not good, or that turns out bad, leave it alone." If one believes that the world has made no mistake in scrapping most of what passed for civilization in the '80's, then one cannot deny that Sitting Bull was wise. But the old Indian Bureau wished him to take it over, as it was, lock, stock and barrel. No man of intelligence could, or would, do that.

Sitting Bull said, "We must teach the children to read and write, so that the white men cannot cheat us, and we must hang on to our land until the young folks can speak English and look out for our own interests." Nobody with any knowledge of the Sioux can doubt that, if Sitting Bull had been able to carry through this program, the tribe would be far better off today.

One day, when Chief Bear Ribs was entertaining Sitting Bull at his home, the Rev. Father Jerome Hunt invited him to visit the new Catholic school for Indian children nearby. Sitting Bull gladly accepted the invitation, and next day two Indian school-boys drove over after him. After dinner, the chief was shown over the school plant, and was much impressed by all he saw. When he found the pupils in the class-room, he asked if he might address them. The father gave permission. Sitting Bull spoke:

"My dear grandchildren. All of your folks are my relatives, because I am a Sioux, and so are they. I was glad to hear that the Black Robe had given you this school where you can learn to read, write, and count the way white people do. You are also being taught a new religion. You are shown how the white men work and make things. You are living in a new path.

"When I was your age, things were entirely different. I had no teachers but my parents and relatives. They

COURTESY, DEPARTMENT OF HISTORY, STATE OF SOUTH DAKOTA

Sitting Bull, his two Wives (Seen-by-Her-Nation and Four Times) with three of his children, at Fort Randall, 1882

are dead and gone now, and I am left alone.[13] It will be the same with you. Your parents are aging and will die some day, leaving you alone. So it is for you to make something of yourselves, and this can only be done while you are young.

"In my early days I was eager to learn and to do things, and therefore I learned quickly, and that made it easier for my teachers. Now I often pick up papers and books which have all kinds of pictures and marks on them, but I cannot understand them as a white person does. They have a way of communicating by the use of written symbols and figures; but before they could do that, they had to have an understanding among themselves. You are learning that, and I was very much pleased to hear you reading.

"In future your business dealings with the whites are going to be very hard, and it behooves you to learn well what you are taught here. But that is not all. *We older people need you.* In our dealings with the white men, we are just the same as blind men, because we do not understand them. We need you to help us understand what the white men are up to. My Grandchildren, be good. Try and make a mark for yourselves. Learn all you can.

"With all my heart I thank my Black Robe friends for their goodness and kindness towards me."

Those were Sitting Bull's views on the education of Sioux youth. But he was not content with talk. He took an active part in encouraging intelligent boys to push ahead with their education. When young Antoine De-Rockbrain (flushed with the pride of having just completed the available schooling at Standing Rock) was urged by McLaughlin to go to Hampton Institute, Virginia, to complete his education, he boyishly refused.

---

13. Sitting Bull's mother died in 1884.

But Sitting Bull persuaded him to go, and on his return three years later, gave the young man a good saddle horse, inasmuch as he had listened to and followed the advice the chief had given. So long as there was yet a chance to educate the young before the white men had stripped the Indian bare, Sitting Bull was keen on education.

Perhaps because he favored keeping Indian families together, the chief's real attitude towards civilization and education for his people has generally been misrepresented. Later, when at Standing Rock Agency, he showed his hand unmistakably.

To begin with, he obtained permission for his band to settle on the fertile lands along Grand River, forty miles south of the Agency, near the present towns of Bullhead and Little Eagle, South Dakota. His little band, which had followed him through thick and thin, hung upon his words as upon those of an oracle. Though they could not always follow his thought, they trusted to the man's heart, and the fact that he had never let them down. McLaughlin issued a cow, a yoke of oxen, and a wagon to the Chief, and in April '87, he started off to begin his life as a farmer. He was happy to drive down the breaks into the deep, broad valley of that pleasant stream, with its gravel bed and fringe of stately, rustling cottonwoods. It was Spring, and he was home again. As they approached the river, he said to his nephew, One Bull, "I was born at Many-Caches, so we shall settle there."

But Grand River was in flood, they could not cross their wagons. The time for planting was already past, they had to plow at once, and so Sitting Bull settled on the north bank, and his nephew built a cabin some distance below.

Sitting Bull had brought along the gray circus horse given him by Buffalo Bill in 1885, and had bought a bay with the money earned in the Wild West Show. He put in a garden, and within three years accumulated forty-five head of cattle, ten head of horses, and kept eighty chickens in his chicken-coop. He raised oats, corn, and potatoes, had a long double log house, a separate kitchen, and a log barn "fifteen steps long." He learned to make hay, and put up as many as five wagon-loads in a season. He built a big feeding-corral for his stock, and sheds for the farm-machinery and wagons which he gradually got together. William "White Clay" Pomplin, now living, taught Sitting Bull to farm. Sitting Bull encouraged One Bull to follow his example, and One Bull soon had cattle and horses and a fine flock of Barred Plymouth Rocks. So much for his efforts towards self-support—at fifty-six years of age.

Sitting Bull was really keen on education for young Indians.

The chief asked McLaughlin to establish a day school near his home. It was done. And all his children—Standing Holy, Crowfoot, Captures-Horses, William, Potala—attended it. So did the children of Jumping Bull and One Bull. Sitting Bull encouraged Mary Collins, the missionary, to teach young Indians to read and write. And when Andrew Fox came back from school in his uniform and paid court to Sitting Bull's daughter, the fact that he was educated was a strong point in winning the father's consent to the match. Sitting Bull was keen on education; he wished to turn the white man's learning to the benefit of his people.

He also asked to have a sub-agency issue station built on Grand River, so that his people would not have to spend all their time going and coming with slow ox-teams week in week out for rations. "All these things were done at my Uncle's request," says One Bull, "and we were happy."

His efforts to reunite the nation are well-remembered. One day he stood on the bank of Grand River and said, "I was born near where I stand. I want you to hold these lands. I want you to follow me. I want you to pledge yourselves to do as I ask you." And he added, "Keep your land. It will be worth far more. Keep it. Value it at twenty dollars a foot." And all the time he did what he could to maintain old customs and dances—those old familiar folk-ways which reminded the Sioux far better than any words of their past glory and their common blood.

Sitting Bull's program looked to the betterment of the Sioux *as a nation*—and the Indian Bureau looked another way. Farming and schooling were all very well. But McLaughlin was unrelenting in his opposition to Sioux unity, to the old-time religion, to the dances and ceremonies, to chiefs and Strong Hearts and Silent Eaters. He had to divide the Sioux to boss them, and he used every weapon within his reach.

Sitting Bull, though (from his own view-point) constructive and progressive, found that the Indian Bureau lay like a mountain in his path. For that old Indian Bureau was the most un-American institution ever known on the continent. Under its rule liberty was not—neither liberty of person, liberty of property, nor liberty of conscience. Church and State were not separate: the missionaries (who had formerly acted as agents) considered the Red Man their property. Nothing that we call American existed at Standing Rock. No law—only the orders of the agent. No appeal—for the Bureau's acts were not subject to court review. No freedom of speech—for all news, even personal letters, could be censored by the agent. Self-determination for small peoples had not been heard of, the Civil Service was only beginning to extend to Indian Reservations, and the Rights of Man had been lost somewhere between Thomas Jefferson's study and the cabin of Sitting Bull. How any person could expect an Indian to understand, admire, or adopt American institutions on a Reservation where none of them existed is a puzzle.

Therefore, though Sitting Bull's program was really more constructive than the Bureau's, he had no chance of carrying it through. McLaughlin and the missionaries were solidly against him, and as time passed more and more of the Indians fell into line behind the agent. Sitting Bull's following was more and more composed of those who cared nothing for the white man's civilization, who were idle, indifferent, and disposed to depend upon him for protection. He found his old power waning, and the only party which would back him up consisted of wild, untamed men—a reckless set who kept the tame Indians in terror and plagued the agency staff with endless annoyance. Sitting Bull could not drive them from his door, they were relatives, Sioux; they were his backers. And so, willy-nilly, he found himself leader of the non-progressives.

Had the government fulfilled its pledges to the Sioux, there could have been no quarrel, no division as between Sitting Bull and the agent. But, as it was, the chief had to choose between loyalty to the Bureau and loyalty to his own race. To a man like him, there was only one choice.

One day he was sitting with a circle of Silent Eaters, and had a joke at the expense of those whom he had to oppose. His old cronies, Strikes-the-Kettle, Catch-the-Bear, Blackbird, and Pass-Beyond were listening. Said he, "You all remember how when we were boys, we played the game called Whipping Tops? In winter we used to clear a space four or five feet wide in the snow, and make a little corral around this space with willow twigs. On one side a gate was left, about a foot wide. Every boy would try to whip his top through this gate, and the first one who succeeded in making his top spin inside was winner. And so we all tried every way to knock the other boys' tops away with our own, and keep them from getting in. We whipped our tops to knock them away from the gate or out of the circle. You recall that?"

"*Ho*," came the word of assent. Sitting Bull puffed at his pipe a moment, then went on.

"*He-han!* Well, it seems that all the Indians are playing that game now. The corral is the agent's office. Everybody wants to get inside and become a favorite. But no sooner does he do this than all the rest combine against him, and knock him, and try to drive him out. So a good many have failed in their attempt, though a few have managed to get ahead and are now spinning happily inside.

"I stand no show whatever of getting into that corral. But so long as I know I am not betraying my people, I shall be content to remain outside."

So much for Sitting Bull's later views on Indian education and progress. Even as a prisoner at Fort Randall he had plenty of opportunity to speak his mind. . . Says Colonel Ahern, "Indian chiefs from all over the Sioux territory came to seek his advice" and the Lieutenant was always asked by Sitting Bull to attend these conferences. Says he, "I found them most interesting, as they showed the deep respect in which

Sitting Bull was held by his people. From this close contact I came to admire him for his wisdom, his unswerving loyalty to his people, and his frank critical attitude towards the whites in authority over his people. I am afraid my Irish ancestors would not have exercised the patience, and would not have suffered so many wrongs without constant hostility."

That Sitting Bull was patient under his people's wrongs was not due to any lack of heart. Colonel Ahern writes, "One night as I sat in Sitting Bull's tipi, a squaw sat between us holding a one-year-old baby girl. The baby was very ill and had several convulsions while I was present. After one severe convulsion, when it looked as if the end was near, Sitting Bull took hold of its little wrist to feel the pulse, and imagine my amazement to see the tears rolling down his cheeks, and he actually sobbing like a woman. The baby died the following morning at daybreak."

Sitting Bull did not "practice medicine" at Fort Randall. When one of his people was sick, he called in the Army Surgeon. One day there was wailing and lamentation in the camp, and the officers found one of the warriors laid out for burial. But when the Surgeon was called for, it appeared that the man had only fainted, and he was soon restored to life! If Sitting Bull had been the medicine-man some people claim he was, he would not have called in the Army Surgeon as he repeatedly did.

Sitting Bull never drank whiskey there. His diversions consisted in talk with visitors (of whom there were many), talk mostly of hunting buffalo and deer, of his travels, and of the speed and endurance of his horses, which he greatly missed. He also took a keen interest in the problems of his people at the agencies, and urged that stock-raising was the best profession for them. It was not a policy which appealed to the cattlemen, who wanted to run their own steers on Sioux grass. But Sitting Bull was right. Plowing Dakota west of the Missouri has simply ruined a good cow-country and produced more farms in a semi-arid region at a time when the world is swamped in cheap wheat. However, the cattle-industry would not have supplied the numerous agency jobs that a farming program did: Sitting Bull's advice went unheeded. Besides, the Army preferred to keep the Sioux afoot.

As time passed and Sitting Bull regained his normal weight, he became more cheerful. His wounded foot was healing better now, and his limp was hardly perceptible. Moreover, at Fort Randall he held the center of the stage; there were no rival chiefs to compete with him for the precedence which was allowed him by the white men. A soldier himself, he liked to associate with soldiers. His surrender rankled less now; his self-respect was strong and lively. And he had found that, after all, many of the Americans were honest and good-hearted. Likewise, he heard from Lieutenant Ahern how the Red Coats in Ireland had tyrannized over that officer's father's people, and the knowledge of this bit of history made him more tolerant of the Americans.

But Sitting Bull did not pass all his time in the camp, or with the military. He paid visits to neighboring half-breeds, and many amusing stories are told of how he mistook the use of napkins, spreading them on the floor to sit upon, and of wash-basins, from which he drank as soon as they were filled for him. He had always been a "wild" Indian, and the devices and appliances of the white men were strange to him.

Missionaries also visited him, and read from the

Bible in Sioux, explaining how men must love their neighbors as themselves, must give all they have to the poor, take no thought for the morrow, and sacrifice themselves for others. Sitting Bull listened patiently: the stories were interesting, the ideas familiar. When all was over his comment was, "The Sioux were better Christians before they ever heard of Christ than the white men are now."

How long Sitting Bull might have remained at Fort Randall is past finding out, since there was no reason for sending him there in the first place, and all his appeals for release to McLaughlin and others merely resulted in the receipt of "good advice." Popular feeling throughout the country was against him, as it was generally believed that he was the "murderer" of General Custer, and it is seldom that an official will brave popular disfavor for the benefit of such a captive. However, there was at Fort Randall a Civil War veteran, Andrew DeRockbrain, who had mixed with the Sioux, and knew that Sitting Bull was not the man who killed Custer. He brought the facts to the attention of the commanding officer of the post, who straightway took the necessary steps to have the chief sent back to Standing Rock. Popular accounts of this matter say that Sitting Bull "promised to be good." But as a matter of fact there was no agreement. The War Department had ordered him to Fort Randall, and it ordered him away again. McLaughlin claims that Sitting Bull was released as a result of following his "good advice," but in the face of his own statements, it is impossible to believe that he took any active steps to have the chief released, or wished to have him back. Early in May, '83, Sitting Bull and his band boarded the steamboat bound for Standing Rock.

Sitting Bull was eager and anxious to rejoin his people. He was tired of sitting still in one place, he missed the active part in affairs which he had always enjoyed among the Hunkpapa. While at Fort Randall, he had been visited by many white men—soldiers, writers, travellers, artists, missionaries—and all of them had treated him as a great chief. He was daily in receipt of letters from the four corners of the earth saluting him as "Great Chief Sitting Bull," "Big Chief Sitting Bull," "Monsieur Sitting Bull, Grand Chef des Indiens Sioux," and the like. People were paying a dollar or more for his mere autograph, and offering any price for his pipe and tomahawk. From all over the Sioux country other chiefs came to salute him and get his advice upon the problems of the nation. He was, in fact, still chief of the men who had followed him, and it is not surprising that he knew it. For it is not written constitutions or scraps of paper which give a man authority. So long as the Sioux regarded Sitting Bull as their chief, he remained so.

Moreover, he considered that he was "god-chosen," divinely ordained to lead his nation. Sitting Bull's conviction on this point did not rest upon any theory of divine right, nor did he base his claim upon miraculous voices or visions, or any such primitive clap-trap: he was no medicine-man. He based his claim to lead, quite frankly, upon his proven ability, his wisdom, his skill, and his superior intelligence. He had led and maintained his people for thirteen years after Red Cloud gave in, he had never truckled to the white men, as Spotted Tail did. He had not trusted to the whites, only to be destroyed before his time, as Crazy Horse had foolishly done. He had not signed treaties swindling his people of their lands and treaty rights, as most other chiefs had been doing. He had never swallowed the bait held out by those who wished to lure him to surrender—the bait about being head chief of all the Sioux. Why should he? He was already head chief.

There are those, McLaughlin among them, who profess to rate Sitting Bull low in the scale of intelligence. It he was low, the rest of his nation was lower. Read all the verbatim reports of the councils, and try to find one speech—by any Sioux chief—which will compare for logic, force, and oratorical skill with the speeches of Sitting Bull. It does not exist. Check his record by that of any other Sioux chief, and try to find an instance in which he betrayed his people, or was fooled by white officials. All the other chiefs (including Red Cloud) were deceived, and not a few of them sold out for the petty honors of an agency job. If Sitting Bull was not a man of brains, he was at least keen enough to get the best of every white official sent to bully, or cajole, or swindle him. No wonder they say the hard things they do of him: he was too smart for them.

It must not be forgotten that the tenure of chieftaincy among the Sioux was life-long. White men might say this, or sign that, but Sitting Bull *knew* that so long as he drew breath, and a single Hunkpapa remained alive, he was the chief of that Hunkpapa. And of the other Northern Sioux bands as well. That was an unchangeable *fact*. The only way to destroy his chieftaincy was to destroy *him*; that was his view, a view to which he held with the unrelenting tenacity characteristic of a tough-minded Sioux. For seven years the white officials fought that view; eventually they had to accept it. Sitting Bull remained chief *de facto*, if not *de jure*, until the day he died.

When he set out on the steamboat from Randall, he

was full of plans for his people: stock-raising, and all the good things promised him by the treaties of '68 and '76, and reiterated time after time by the men who had urged him to surrender. His mind was filled with a vision of herds of cattle, cared for by Indian horsemen following the herds about their reservation and living in tipis, feasting and dancing and visiting in the intervals of their business, as they had done in the good old days. He was unfamiliar with agency routine and organization, and apparently imagined that he would be allowed to administer his camp at Standing Rock, as he had done at Fort Randall. Naturally, in the face of all the lavish promises that had been made him, in the face of the specific promises made in the treaties, he expected cattle, oxen, houses, clothing, wagons and tools, and all the other items listed in those documents. And he supposed that Major James McLaughlin would be glad to coöperate with the acknowledged chief of the people whom he was sent to help along the road to self-support. But he was to find that an official of the Indian Bureau in those days was a very different creature from the colonel of an infantry regiment.

When the steamboat reached Standing Rock, the boys swimming in the river saw the people swarming down the slope to meet it, and hurried out of the water to watch Sitting Bull walk up the slope between two long lines of hand-shaking Indians, *"Hau, Hau, Hau!"* As soon as an interview could be arranged, he presented himself, with a party of his warriors, at the office of Major James McLaughlin, U.S. Indian Agent at Standing Rock, a stone's throw from the fort named Yates, after one of the officers who fell with Custer.

James McLaughlin was born in Ontario, Canada, of Scotch-Irish parents, in 1842, and had come to Minnesota at the age of twenty-one. He was a blacksmith by trade in those days, and lived at St. Paul, Mendota, Wabasha, and Faribault. In '71 he entered the Indian service at Devil's Lake, where he became Agent in '76. Devil's Lake was a Santee agency, and McLaughlin married a young lady (afterward known as Marie Louise McLaughlin) of that tribe. She, like her husband, was a person of ambition, intelligence, and force, and was afterward the author of an interesting volume of Sioux legends.

James McLaughlin was quite superior to the run of Indian agents of his day, and he lost no time in strengthening his position at Standing Rock. In those days Indian agents were, as a rule, at outs with everybody. The military could not endure them, the missionaries disliked them, the traders objected to their meddlesome ways, the Indians commonly distrusted them, and the public regarded them as thieves and grafters. Many of them came to their posts with a single carpet bag, were paid an annual pittance of $1500.00, and left after a few years with a steamboat full of property. They filled the agency posts with their friends and relatives, and received a percentage on the salaries of their subordinates. As a result, nobody loved them. Though they held the rank of Major, the title did not imply any military experience.

Major McLaughlin, however, could not rest satisfied with such a state of affairs. He was keen to get on in the world, and he made friends on all sides. When the military wished some small concession, he gladly acquiesced; when the traders needed his help, he was obliging. When the missionaries of his Catholic Faith required encouragement or contributions, he extended a ready hand. And the Standing Rock Indians say he was one of the best and ablest agents they ever had. Though charges were once brought against him, they were not sustained, and there is no reason to suppose that he was not as superior in honesty, as in other qualities, to the run of Indian agents in his day. It is true that he filled the Standing Rock Agency jobs with Santee Indians and mixed-blood relatives of his wife. But this was the universal custom of the time, and the Major appears to have exacted full value in services from them for the salaries paid. In short, Major James McLaughlin was an able, efficient, and intelligent man, dealing with new and difficult problems, and as honest as a bureaucrat can be. In spite of the odium which fell upon him after the scandal of Sitting Bull's death, he rose to become U.S. Inspector in the Indian Bureau, a post only a little below that of the Commissioner of Indian Affairs.

He represented fully the Indian Bureau of his day at its best. And being so closely identified with that Bureau he necessarily shared the defects of its qualities.

The old Indian Bureau was, in fact, the boot with which the American nation kicked the Indian into the scrap heap. No attempt was made to help him capitalize his Indian qualities—the only qualities he had. Instead, he was told to become a white man overnight. The only way to cure a fish of swimming, is to take him out of the water. Under the old Indian Bureau, the Indian was so handled.

Major James McLaughlin was sent to Standing Rock to destroy Sioux civilization, and in the brief time he had been there, had already accomplished much. He had put an end to the Sun Dance in '82, and the same year had stood by and watched some of his Indians sign an agreement ceding a large part of their reservation for a song. Fortunately, the way in which the Commissioners obtained those few signatures, the indecently low price they offered, and the bare-faced manner in which they ignored the provision requiring three-fourths of the adult males to sign, caused such a scandal that the agreement could not be ratified.

Having suppressed the great Sioux religious ceremony (in defiance of that clause in the Constitution of the United States providing for freedom of conscience); having offered no serious objection to the taking of the Sioux lands; it only remained for McLaughlin to demolish the Sioux political organization. The moment Sitting Bull came to see him, he struck, and struck hard.

This was not their first meeting. The same boat which carried Sitting Bull to Fort Randall in '81, had brought McLaughlin to Standing Rock. The chief went aboard as the new agent landed. Sitting Bull wished to talk with McLaughlin, to plead with him to let him stay at the Agency, but he was held on board by the guards, and before he knew who McLaughlin was, the white man had gone ashore.

Nevertheless, there was an interview. Years after, in 1910, McLaughlin published his interesting book, *My Friend the Indian*, and gave a brief account of this meeting, describing Sitting Bull as "a stocky man, with an evil face and shifty eyes." If this description is not the revised impression of later years, when Sitting Bull's alleged "assassination" caused such trouble to rise against the Major, it is clear that he disliked Sitting Bull from the start. He himself inadvertently tells us why. The chief "sent" for him. McLaughlin was not a man who liked to take orders from an Indian.

He adds that Sitting Bull spoke "without his usual arrogance" (the chief had had no dealings with McLaughlin as yet), and "was then desirous of making friends."

But it is abundantly clear that on this occasion his desire was not gratified.

Thus matters stood when the military brought Sitting Bull to Standing Rock, May 10, '83. Next day he led his little band up to confront their new agent, who was to become known to them as The-White-Haired-Father.

Sitting Bull saw a man about ten years his junior, a man with searching eyes and a handsome pair of mustaches, a man with ambition written plain to see in his Scotch-Irish eyes. The Indians say that when McLaughlin "had it in for you, you sure knew it." The unfailing indication of his wrath was this: he pushed his hat to the back of his head. After Sitting Bull came to Standing Rock, McLaughlin's hat was on the back of his head rather often, it appears. And judging from his report of this first official meeting, one may surmise that he pushed it back rather early in the interview.

Sitting Bull, "with the greatest *sang froid*," proceeded to explain to the Major the code of regulations by which he and his people desired to be governed, as they had been governed at Fort Randall. Sitting Bull knew all about the abuses at the agencies, wished to correct them, and had heard good things of McLaughlin; he expected his proposals to meet with immediate approval. But in this he was to be disappointed.

He went on to say that he did not wish to plant anything that season, not knowing how (it was already the middle of May), but that he would look around and see how it was done and get ready to farm the next year. McLaughlin represents this as an arrogant stand on Sitting Bull's part, as though all Indians at his agency had been passionately devoted to agriculture (which—on the face of his own reports—is absurd; only "about fifty families"—one in twenty—of a population of 3,755 Indians on the Standing Rock Agency had put in wheat that Spring, and of these nearly half were mixed-bloods. The largest farm was five acres.) The fact is, Sitting Bull should have been commended for his interest; not many of the old-coffee-coolers around Standing Rock ever came in to *offer* to plant. Under the treaties it was provided that Indians who labored, should feed themselves; those who did not, were to be rationed. Taking Sitting Bull's statements at their face value, he was among the most progressive Indians at Standing Rock that day. Moreover, McLaughlin's own report for '82 lauds the "late hostiles" as infinitely superior to the old agency Indians in industry, truth, honor, uprightness. He gives a whole paragraph to this praise of the "late followers of Sitting Bull."[14]

14. Excerpt from Annual Report, Commissioner of Indian Affairs, 1882, pp. 43-44:
Standing Rock Indian Agency, Dakota, September 5, 1882.
James McLaughlin.
Tribes, Population, and Disposition.

The Indians of this agency are composed of the Upper and Lower Yanktonnais, Uncapapas, and Blackfeet bands of the Great Sioux or Dakota nation, classed respectively as follows:

Tribes	Men	Women	Boys	Girls	Total
Upper Yanktonnais	157	213	131	92	593
Lower Yanktonnais	236	311	196	161	904
Uncapapas	387	512	283	281	1,463
Blackfeet	192	227	136	134	689
Mixed blood	27	26	22	31	106
Totals	999	1,289	768	699	3,755

About 1,000 of the above-enumerated Indians are of the late hostile bands who surrendered to the United States authorities during the early part of 1881, among whom are Crow King, Gall, Black Moon, Crawler, Rain-in-the-Face, and Circle Bear, six of Sitting Bull's trusted lieutenants, who have all settled down to peaceful avocations, and are engaged in cultivating fields. They are anxious to possess stock and work-cattle, and with a few ox teams to aid them in farm work next spring, I am confident they would augment very materially the area of land cultivated at this agency.

These late hostiles possess the elements of a progressive people, and have many commendable qualities. They are truthful, upright, and honorable; appreciate kindness; are amenable to firm and just treatment, and susceptible to civilizing influences to a very marked degree. In my whole intercourse with this race, I have never met with any Indians who possessed superior qualities to the late followers of "Sitting Bull." Having become weary of strife with the United States Government, and recognizing their inability to cope with the dominant white race, they surrendered in good faith, and now express them-

It seems odd that he should have known, the very first day he saw the chief's immediate band, that they would be so utterly different from their fellows. How strange that these "honorable, upright, truthful" people who "appreciate kindness, are amenable to firm and just treatment and susceptible to civilizing influences to a marked degree" should have followed Sitting Bull all those years, if he was such a fellow as McLaughlin says! That they were like that we know also from the report of Dr. V. T. McGillycuddy, Agent at Pine Ridge, who praises the Oglala band which had followed Sitting Bull as "progressing in a remarkable manner as compared with the regular agency Sioux. House-building and other labor is carried on by them to a greater extent, comparatively; and I will venture to state that in a few years they will be far in advance of the Indians who have lived for years on the reservation. . . I would at any time prefer to deal with wild Indians just in from the warpath than with the majority of pampered and demoralized agency Indians."

Yet McLaughlin, after twenty minutes talk, knew right away that Sitting Bull's little band was totally different from other "late hostiles." He was a man of singular perspicacity.

Sitting Bull went on to say that he wished to have

---

selves as highly pleased with the change from their past nomadic life to that of their present peace and happiness, and in order to foster this feeling and inspire confidence I endeavor to treat them as men, so that each individual may learn to act for himself independent of chief or band affiliations. Being now in my twelfth year of continuous service in the Indian Department, I have had an opportunity of seeing considerable of Indian life, and observing the peculiarities of Indian character. They are the ideal "untutored children of nature," honest in their convictions, sincere in their expressions, anxious to learn and do what is expected of them, and afraid lest they might do what would be displeasing; and whilst the old agency Indians as a rule, are well disposed, yet they are more derelict, in many respects, than these "late hostiles," whose good intentions I have the utmost confidence in, and who are now so anxious to improve their condition and desirous of taking a firm hold of the white man's civilization, through the present means afforded them, that unless some unforseen calamity befalls them, permanent peace with them is assured and their steady advancement undoubted.

the supplies for his people delivered to him for distribution, instead of having ration tickets issued to individuals. He also asked to have his name put first on the agency rolls, and presented a sheet of ruled paper. This paper, prepared in duplicate by Colonel P. T. Swain at Fort Randall, "at the urgent request of Sitting Bull," contained a list of twenty-four chiefs and head men chosen by the chief from among his tried and true followers, "so that same can be presented to and their respective status confirmed by their Agent." The paper was dated April 13, '83:—

Here follows a true copy of this document:

(*Long ruled notebook paper*)

Notes on back: Sitting Bull's papers May 10/83 From Col. Swain.

Copy for U.S. Ind. Agent.

List of Chiefs, Headmen etc. of "Sitting Bull's" tribe, en route from Fort Randall to Standing Rock Agency, D.T.

"Sitting Bull"	Chief
"Red Thunder"	Old chief, (1st)
"Tall as the Cloud"	Headman
"The man that takes the gun away"	Headman
"Looking back Bear" (*in pencil*) See Crow King	Chief (2nd)
"Young Red Thunder"	Chief (2nd)
"Mad Dog"	Chief (2nd)
"Bone Club" (*marked out in pencil &* Tomahawk *written*)	Chief Head soldier No. 1
"White slow Buffalo"	Chief Head soldier No. 1
"Brave Thunder"	Whom S.B. wants as chief

"Four Horns"	Chief
"Fire Cloud"	Chief (oldest chief)
"One Hand"	Chief Head soldier
"One Bull" (nephew)	Head of police
"Black Prairie Chicken	Head soldier. Policeman
"Standing Kill"	Head soldier. Policeman
"Yellow Dog"	Soldier
"Standing Cloud"	Head soldier (chief)
"Roan faced Bear"	Chief soldier
"Big Legs"	Headman
"His Holy Pipe"	Soldier
"Iron Heart"	Soldier
"Four Horns Jr."	Soldier

Fur Coat (*written on bottom of page in pencil*).

 The above list is made by the Post Commander at the urgent request of Sitting Bull so that same can be presented to and their respective status be confirmed by their Agent.

   (Signed) P. T. Swain
    Lieut. Colonel 15 Infantry
     Commanding

Fort Randall, D.T.)
 April 13, 1883)

 McLaughlin reports, rather stupidly, that Sitting Bull intended these twenty-four subordinates to govern only his little band of thirty-five men. But this is manifestly absurd. Sitting Bull expected to be head chief of *all* the Sioux at Standing Rock, as his request to be placed first on the agency rolls clearly shows. Like any other leader, he naturally chose for his staff those who had stuck to him through thick and thin: his uncle Four Horns, his nephew One Bull, Red Thunder, Iron Heart, and all the rest. He defended his choice by saying that they were all "good and true men—true to him and superior to any of the old chiefs of the agency;" and said that the Grandfather (the President) "had written to him before he left Fort Randall that he, Sitting Bull, was now to return to his own country and to live among his people; that he would be the head man, the big chief, of his agency; that a good house would be built for him to live in; that he might gather his own people from all the other agencies and have everything he desired."

McLaughlin "heard his inflated nonsense through" and gave him "sound advice" saying that to be honest he must be frank, and that the Grandfather had never written any such letter to him, or authorized any such promises to be made; that the Grandfather recognized the most industrious Indian who was endeavoring to benefit his condition and set a good example to his people as the greatest chief, and that Sitting Bull would be treated in all respects in the same manner as other Indians of the agency.

Sitting Bull was "considerably crestfallen," said he "was greatly surprised," and departed to recover from this dashing of his hopes.

McLaughlin did not see him for several days, and meanwhile plowed twelve acres for his band, and told them to begin planting next day. Sitting Bull obediently reported for work with the others, expecting—McLaughlin reports—to boss the job. But McLaughlin divided the acreage, staking off a separate plot for each family. "Sitting Bull worked with the others, using a hoe, but rather awkwardly, and in two days they had their field nicely planted." When McLaughlin went out to inspect their work, he found Sitting Bull "pleased that I found him laboring, and in reply to the question if he found planting so very difficult, he answered, 'No,' that he was now determined to become a farmer in earnest."

The balance of this part of the report (dated August 15, '83,) is devoted to a list of Sitting Bull's shortcomings, with which McLaughlin seems to have become perfectly cognizant within three months, though others, who knew the chief for years, never discovered such qualities.

He states that Sitting Bull "is an Indian of very mediocre ability, rather dull, and much inferior to Gall and others of his lieutenants in intelligence. I cannot understand how he held such sway over or controlled men so eminently his superiors in every respect, unless it was by his sheer obstinacy and stubborn tenacity. He is pompous, vain, and boastful, and considers himself a very important personage, but as he has been lionized and pampered by the whites since the battle of the Little Big Horn, I do not wonder at his inflated opinion of himself. I however, firmly believe that Sitting Bull will never cause any trouble, he having been thoroughly subdued; moreover, his influence is very limited now, and I hope to be able to turn what little he has towards the advancement of his people."

From this opinion McLaughlin never publicly wavered: he professed to despise Sitting Bull until the end, and pursued his memory with opprobrious epithets long after the chief was dead. But it is noticeable that all his adjectives are general. Search McLaughlin's book from end to end, you will not find one specific charge against the chief. And after conversing with many employees—both Indian and white—who were with McLaughlin and Sitting Bull at Standing Rock, I have yet to find one who could cite a single instance in which Sitting Bull lied, or stole, or committed any crime whatever, other than self-defense when attacked. His one difficulty arose from his unwillingness to give up his people's religion in his last days, and if the Constitution of the United States is more than a scrap of paper, he was perfectly within his rights in that affair. As to his ability, his career sufficiently answers that depreciation. And if intelligence is to be weighed and measured, I submit that any competent literary critic would place Sitting Bull's poems and speeches (even in translation) higher than McLaughlin's book. However, the relative merits of the two men is of little importance: their relation is the thing. And no one can fail to see that the two were antipathetic from the start. Sitting Bull was chief; McLaughlin was determined to destroy his influence, to "break" him, as McGillycuddy "broke" Red Cloud at Pine Ridge. There could be no chiefs at an agency in those days—no real chiefs. Only figure-heads who would do what they were told.

Sitting Bull went to work with his hoe, and worked well. McLaughlin's lecture was a cruel disappointment. But Sitting Bull, like the other "late hostiles," had surrendered in good faith; he intended to become self-supporting, if possible. He accepted the terms: he would set the best example, and be chief still. He offered no opposition as yet to the authority of Major McLaughlin.

But if McLaughlin imagined that Sitting Bull had abdicated his chieftaincy, he was soon undeceived.

No. 32.
NOTE ON FORT RANDALL
A. G. 314.71
Fort Randall, S. Dak.
(8-15-27) ORD

FORT RANDALL, SOUTH DAKOTA
Information found in the War Department relating to that post.

Location and name.

Situated on the right bank of the Missouri River in Dakota Territory (now State of South Dakota) about 75 miles by land and 100 miles by water above Yankton. Named in honor of Lieutenant Colonel Daniel Randall, deputy paymaster general, who served in the Army from June 8, 1814 to the time of his death December 17, 1851.

Chronology of principal events.

May 9, 1856 the War Department authorized the establishment of a fort in that region, doubtless in connection with the Sioux Expedition of 1855-1856 into western Nebraska territory.

June 26, 1856 Fort Randall was established.

June 14, 1860, an extensive military reservation surrounding Fort Randall and including land on both sides of the Missouri River was established by an executive order; area about 150 square miles, or about 96,000 acres.

September 9, 1867, the area of the reservation was reduced in size.

October 25, 1870, the area was restored to its original limits.

May 18, 1874, by an act of Congress, portions of land within the reservation occupied by settlers prior to June 14, 1860, were authorized and directed to be confirmed to such settlers by the Secretary of the Interior, with certain provisos.

July 5, 1884, by a general act of Congress (23 Stat., 103) providing for the disposal by the War Department of military reservations no longer needed for military purposes, a portion of the Fort Randall Reservation north of the Missouri River, about 24,503 acres, not already confirmed to settlers under the act of May 18, 1874, the Secretary of War was directed to turn over to the Secretary of the Interior for disposition.

July 22, 1884, that portion of the reservation north of the Missouri River, about 24,503 acres, was relinquished by the War Department to the Interior Department.

October 1, 1890, by an act of Congress (26 Stat., 646) the balance of the reservation lying east and north of the Missouri was directed to be opened to settlers.

October 31, 1892, the post of Fort Randall was turned over to the Quartermaster's Department.

November 9, 1892, Fort Randall was discontinued as a military post,—Special Order No. 102, Department of Dakota.

December 7, 1892, troops were withdrawn from Fort Randall,—a detachment of the 21st Infantry consisting of officers and 43 enlisted men.

October 20, 1893, in pursuance of the act of July 5, 1884 (23 Stat., 103) the remainder of the reservation was relinquished by the War Department to the Interior Department.

Fort Randall was the station proper of troops that served in connection with several Indian campaigns, notably the campaigns of 1855-1856, 1862-1863, 1865-1866 and 1876-1877.

War Department,
The Adjutant General's Office,
August 26, 1927.

No. 34.
THE MYSTERIOUS RED COAT
1884(?)

After the Hunkpapa settled at Standing Rock Agency there was continual pressure put upon them to part with their lands, and it required great efforts on the part of Sitting Bull and his faction to hold the people together and prevent the sale. One trump card in the hand of the chief was the story of a mysterious Red Coat who visited the Sioux and promised them that the Canadians would come to their relief and reconquer the Black Hills for them.

This stranger was a white man in civilian clothes. He visited the agency, inspected the rations and clothing of the Sioux, and declared that the government of the United States was cheating its wards. This was no news to the Sioux, but the stranger had more to offer. He told the chiefs that they, the Red Coats, were coming and would appear in the Black Hills in great force. The Sioux and their country had formerly been subject to the Hudson's Bay Company and many of the chiefs had George III silver medals given to their ancestors by His Majesty's representatives. "Be ready," said this stranger, "expect us in the Black Hills. We will restore your country to you."

This promise, vaguely referred to in the report of the Commission of 1888,[15] had a great effect upon the harried Indians. The Commission failed to buy their lands that year.

Indians who talked with this mysterious stranger cannot tell his name or where he came from and deny that he asked for any presents or took advantage of

---

15. See Senate Executive Document No. 17, 50th Congress, 2nd Session, pp. 1-293 in Vol. I, Nos. 1 to 59.

them in any way. He must have been a very convincing liar and there are old Indians living who still cherish a faint hope that the Red Coats are coming.

No. 35.
NOTE ON THE DELEGATION TO WASHINGTON FROM STANDING ROCK, 1888

The Commission sent to Standing Rock in the summer of 1888 were wholly unable to persuade the Sioux there to sign any agreement or cede any lands. For a month they harangued and argued to no avail. After leaving Standing Rock the Commission visited several other Sioux agencies, but in vain.

The Sioux stood solidly behind Sitting Bull, who had shown them the way. And the morale of the Commission was so broken against the polite stone wall of his opposition that their later dealings read rather pathetically. Even Judge Wright, who was the least sentimental of the three, and certainly bore no love to Indians, became so maudlin that on parting, he quoted *Hiawatha* in the council!!

> We are going, oh! my people
> On a long and distant journey. . . .

Soon after, Sitting Bull also recited a poem—but one of his own composition. It was in a day-coach on the train which carried a delegation of chiefs ordered to Washington, in the hopes that a better understanding might be arrived at. The friends of the Indians in the East were alarmed: a baffled Congress was talking of seizing the Sioux lands without compensation, the papers were full of false stories of an impending Indian war. All this was known to the Sioux chiefs, who kept well informed on Indian affairs through the papers.

As the train sped eastward, some of them became discouraged; they knew that the white men were three thousand to one of the Sioux. But Sitting Bull, heartened by his victory over the Commission, remained undaunted. The fighting spirit of the Sioux was in him, and the dingy day-coach echoed to his impromptu music:

> Friends, what are you saying?
> The Black Hills belong to me.
> Saying this, I take fresh courage.

By such means he prevented the Standing Rock delegation from splitting under the fire of the Secretary of the Interior. To a man they signed the Majority Report, while delegations of some other agencies weakly divided and yielded to the Secretary's abrupt demands. Sitting Bull was very cheery at this meeting, and addressed the white men as "My kinsmen" for, said he, "I am now one of your people. . . . I have plenty that I could say myself, but I wish the other men here to speak for me." John Grass was spokesman for the group, and some of his statements are taken bodily out of Sitting Bull's former speeches: "Look at our people; we are poor and we ought not to be poor. We ought to be rich. You are the cause of our being poor.". . . .

Mad Bear, Gall, Big Head, Two Bears, High Bear, Thunder Hawk, Bear Ribs II, Fire Heart, Crow Eagle, Grey Eagle, High Eagle, Hairy Chin, and Walking Eagle were also in the Standing Rock delegation. The essence of their demand was $1.25 an acre, if the land must be sold.

Sitting Bull shook hands with the President, and came home in high good humor. But the days of his triumph were numbered.

No. 36.
NOTE ON THE SIGNING OF TREATIES

The Indians did not always understand what they were doing when they signed a treaty. "The commissioners bring a paper containing what they wish already written out. It is not what the Indians want, but what the commissioners want. All they have to do is to get the signatures of the Indians. Sometimes the commissioners *say* they compromise, but they never change the document." Sitting Bull said this to the Silent Eaters, in 1888.

At the council of Silent Eaters, in 1889, upon the request of the members, Sitting Bull delivered the following speech.

"Friends and Relatives: Our minds are again disturbed by the Great Father's representatives, the Indian Agent, the squaw-men, the mixed-bloods, the interpreters and the favorite ration-chiefs. What is it they want of us at this time? They want us to give up another chunk of our tribal land. This is not the first time nor the last time. They will try to gain possession of the last piece of ground we possess. They are again telling us what they intend to do if we agree to their wishes. Have we ever set a price on our land and received such a value? No, we never did. What we got under the former treaties were promises of all sorts. They promised how we are going to live peaceably on the land we still own and how they are going to show us the new ways of living—even told us how we can go to heaven when we die, but all that we realized out of the agreements with the Great Father was, we are dying off in expectation of getting things promised us.

"One thing I wish to state at this time is, something

tells me that the Great Father's representatives have again brought with them a well-worded paper, containing just what they want but ignoring our wishes in the matter. It is this that they are attempting to drive us to. Our people are blindly deceived. Some are in favor of the proposition, but we who realize that our children and grandchildren may live a little longer, must necessarily look ahead and flatly reject the proposition. I, for one, am bitterly opposed to it. The Great Father has proven himself an *unktomi* (trickster) in our past dealings.

"When the White People invaded our Black Hills country our treaty agreements were still in force but the Great Father has ignored it—pretending to keep out the intruders through military force, and at last failing to keep them out they had to let them come in and take possession of our best part of our tribal possession. Yet the Great Father maintains a very large standing army that can stop anything.

"Therefore, I do not wish to consider any proposition to cede any portion of our tribal holdings to the Great Father. If I agree to dispose of any part of our land to the white people I would feel guilty of taking food away from our children's mouths, and I do not wish to be that mean. There are things they tell us sound good to hear, but when they have accomplished their purpose they will go home and will not try to fulfill our agreements with them.

"My friends and relatives, let us stand as one family, as we did before the white people led us astray."

No. 37.
SITTING BULL AND AN INDIAN BOY
By
Robert P. Higheagle

I have been into Sitting Bull's lodge several times. Of course he is very agreeable to anyone who goes there. It happened one time while I was camping south of the Standing Rock Agency on the Four Mile Flat; in company with my father we visited him. It was soon after he came back from Ft. Randall. It was winter and I had a home-made sled tied behind my father's sled and came in for issuing of annuity goods. I was with my own father. We went there and Sitting Bull came out and saw my toy sled tied behind the big sled. He said, "If you made that sled yourself you have a good sled, but you must remember that to make it as good as this sled of your father's you will have to spend more time on it." The big sled was one for which my father had paid about $40.00 or $50.00. That was one remark I always remembered.

I went to the chief's place another time when he was living on Grand River. We went there after a stray steer, Lone Man and I. We had the hardest time trying to get the steer out of Sitting Bull's herd. It was during July when the weather was hot and the cattle didn't care to leave the river bottom and the shade. After we got the steer out and away from the rest of the herd Sitting Bull came over on horseback and jokingly said, "I was going to come out and show you how to cut out a steer from the herd, but since you have already done it, why I can't do it." Rather made fun of how long it had taken us to get the one steer out. He always joked any boy who came to his place. I wasn't afraid of him.

When I was going east to school was the last time I saw him. It was during the time when the Indians were camping around the agency. When they were having this treaty proposition coming up, (1889). I was then a boy of about 15. I had been to school and could speak English and could read and write and Sitting Bull knew of it and he didn't like to see other men of Santee Sioux or Yankton Sioux blood come and interpret for the Commission and the agent. He came to Lone Man and told him he was trying to get all his Hunkpapa school boys who could read and write to get up there before the Commission and write down all they said, and listen. "I would like to have your boy go over there and listen and perhaps do some interpreting."

I got scared and told him I couldn't speak enough English and there were too many over there. He wasn't satisfied and went to see my father. They both came to me and Sitting Bull brought me some pencils and paper and said, "Here, take this and go join the other Indian boys and take down what they are saying." But I didn't go in. I stayed out, but I could hear what was being said. It was about the cession of lands and the agreements. That they were to pay so much for land and also an amount of money that would suffice them and also what they were going to do with the money. Going to use it for educating the young people and how long they were going to give annuities to the Indians for cessions of lands. Every now and then there was excitement over it. Of course, before this time I saw Sitting Bull many times. This time he didn't scold me. In fact, I never heard him speak loud to anybody. A chief would send soldiers to make people do things if necessary.

No. 38.
INDIAN TALES OF STANDING ROCK AGENCY

Sitting Bull, if not "progressive," was certainly independent, and did not hesitate to harangue McLaughlin when things went wrong, not infrequently in the presence of a crowd.

One day two boys, Standing Cloud and Knocks-Him-Down turned up. They had been sent to school at Hampton, Virginia. There, they said, they had been sent to work on the farm of a white man, to learn how it was done. The farmer fed them on the leavings of his table, and while milking, one of the hungry boys had been caught drinking from the milk-pail. The farmer was angry, emptied the pail on the ground, and whipped the lad with a black-snake. The little fellow was too small to resist, but the other boy was bigger. He interfered, and when the farmer tried to whip him, took the black-snake and gave him a lashing. Then the two of them fled. They had walked all the way across the continent, following the railroad west, until they reached the Hohe reservation. The Hohe had brought them home to Sitting Bull's camp.

As soon as McLaughlin heard that two runaways were home, he sent the Indian police—twenty of them—after these boys. Then the people were excited, hitched up their teams and followed the Police and their captives back to the Agency. When they arrived, Sitting Bull demanded loudly that McLaughlin come outside and see these ragged boys, who had been so abused while under the charge of government officials. "Tell him to come out and see these boys. We all want to see what he will say."

McLaughlin came out, said he had merely wished to see the boys, and was sorry they had had such an experience. He ordered new clothing and rations issued to them. But Sitting Bull was indignant, and thought words a poor return for blows. He made a speech, dilated upon Indian wrongs, and told McLaughlin, "You are not the only man. You are just a hireling. You can be replaced any time. . . . ."

On another occasion, when White-Faced-Bull was brought from Poplar, Montana, and held prisoner and made to dig ditches, Sitting Bull offered unsolicited advice to McLaughlin. The chief was sitting smoking, watching his friend dig, when the agent came along. "Look here," said Sitting Bull, "the government promised to take care of the Sioux. This man has done no wrong. Let him go. I want you to turn him loose."

These little incidents encouraged members of both factions to carry tales to the agent and the chief. McLaughlin, it was rumored, had offered Sitting Bull a drink in his office, and Sitting Bull had grabbed the agent by the neck and had shaken him until his teeth rattled . . . . . ."Don't you ever offer me anything like that, to make a fool of me!" That was the story. And others came running to Sitting Bull, repeating what—they said—the agent and his Indian allies were saying about the chief. Though neither, probably, gave more credence to these stories than they deserved, the tale-bearers persisted; they saw that they were causing the dislike between the two men to grow.

Sitting Bull, it is said, never stepped into the Agency office. He always stood outside and requested the interpreter to tell the Agent to come outside and talk with him. Says he, "I do not care to go inside a white man's tipi. Under the roof of a white man's tipi are lies and intrigue. I wish to remain out in the open air. The air outside is pure, inside impure."

If these stories fairly represent the chief's attitude, it is hardly surprising that McLaughlin found Sitting Bull "not a pleasant person."

No. 39.
THE SWAN SONG OF THE SIOUX NATION

During the councils at Standing Rock Agency in 1889, when the United States commissioners were trying to induce the Sioux to sell their lands and break up the great Sioux Reservation into smaller, tribal reservations, Sitting Bull did all that he could to oppose the cession. Every evening, just before sunset, he would ride around the big camp circle singing, to remind the people of his authority, to hearten the discouraged, and to intimidate the wavering. He feared that some of the chiefs might sign the proposed agreement. The people, seated around the bright little cooking fires, drinking soup and chewing their temporarily increased ration of agency beef, listened to his song:

> "The Nation named me,
> So I shall live courageously."
> It is reported,
> Sitting Bull said this.

The music of this song will be found in Frances Densmore's "Teton Sioux Music," Bulletin 61 of the Bureau of American Ethnology.

No. 40.
GRASPING EAGLE'S REPORT OF SITTING BULL'S WORDS ON BEING TOLD THAT HE WAS TO BE ARRESTED

For a time he was silent, then broke out: "Why should the Indian police come against me? We are of the same blood, we are all Sioux, we are relatives. It will disgrace the nation, it will be murder, it will defile our race. If the white men want me to die, they ought not to put up the Indians to kill me. I don't want confusion among my own people. Let the soldiers come and take me away and kill me, wherever they like. I am not afraid. I was born a warrior. I have followed the warpath ever since I was able to draw a bow."

Indignantly, he went on, venting his suspicions: "White Hair (McLaughlin) wanted me to travel all around (with Buffalo Bill) and across the sea, so that he could make a lot of money. Once was enough; I would not go. Then I would not join his church, and ever since he has had it in for me." Sitting Bull smiled scornfully, "Long ago I had two women in my lodge. One of them was jealous. White Hair reminds me of that jealous woman."

Still the chief poured out his grievances: "Why does he keep trying to humble me? Can I be any lower than I am? Once I was a man, but now I am a pitiful wretch—no country, no fast horses, no guns worth having. Once I was rich, now I am poor. What more does he want to do to me? I was a fool ever to come down here. I should have stayed with the Red Coats in the Grandmother's country.

"I did not start this Ghost Dance; Kicking Bear came here of his own accord. I told my people to go slow, but they were swept into this thing so strong nothing could stop them. I have not joined the sacred dance since I was told to stop, away back."

The pent-up indignation of years had spent itself. Thereafter, Sitting Bull believed that his days were numbered. He went no more to the agency, but asked others to bring his rations. It was no surprise, this news; as early as the summer of '89 he had told his nephew, Chief Joseph White Bull, "Great men are generally destroyed by those who are jealous of them." Bear Ribs, Spotted Tail, Crazy Horse, plenty of examples rose up from the past to give warning. For Sitting Bull was a soldier, and had many people jealous of him.

No. 41.
NOTE ON SITTING BULL'S PIPE DURING THE GHOST DANCE EXCITEMENT

Many stories were current during and after the Ghost Dance at Standing Rock. One to the effect that "Sitting Bull broke his pipe of peace which he had kept in his house since his surrender as prisoner of war July 1881" and that he declared "that he wanted to die and wanted to fight," gained some notoriety. This story is repeated in Major McLaughlin's book *My Friend the Indian*, and again in Mooney's *Ghost Dance Religion*, in the 14th Annual Report of the Bureau of American Ethnology. Mooney, as he frankly stated, was unable to get the Sioux to talk of the Ghost Dance and had to print what he could learn from officials at the agency. McLaughlin also seems to have been deceived. For I have been unable to find any Indian who had ever heard or could believe that Sitting Bull broke his pipe or expressed any wish to die.

In the first place no one seems to remember that Sitting Bull smoked a pipe when he surrendered. He was so distrustful of white Americans that he regularly refused to smoke with them unless they were "Black Robes" (Roman Catholic priests). He feared they would break faith with him and that he would be perjured before his gods if he smoked with them. Granting however that Sitting Bull may have smoked a pipe on his surrender, it is very unlikely that any Indian under any circumstances would have broken or destroyed the most sacred symbol of his religion and the altar of his burnt offering. The destruction of such a sacred object was an act so violent and sacrilegious as to be totally foreign to the chief's deliberate and pious character. Who can believe that a man who was risking his freedom and his life rather than give up his religion would wantonly destroy the most sacred object connected with his religion?

As to his wanting to die and wanting to fight, the old men say it is false. They say, "If he had wished to die fighting, he could have satisfied his desire any day. He had only to take his rifle, ride to Fort Yates, and begin shooting at the soldiers." Almost every ration-day after the Ghost Dance began, the troops were paraded, and the guns fired at Fort Yates, to impress the Indians. Had Sitting Bull wished to die shooting, it would have been made easy for him. But the chief had responsibilities, and in 1890 he did not wish to throw away his life, like a peevish child, any more than he did when Crazy Horse got obstinate and went in to get himself killed. Plenty of Indians have done that, at Laramie, at Lame Deer, and elsewhere; but it was not in Sitting Bull.

This story was not officially published until August 1891. The yarn was then brought forward, possibly, in order to give an appearance of hostility to a man who had been killed in opposing the suppression of liberty of conscience in his camp.

No. 42.
NOTE ON THE SO-CALLED "SQUAW-MEN"

In the early days, before the Indian country had been occupied by white settlers, many of the pioneers—trappers, scouts, hunters, traders, Indian agents—married Indian women. Their reasons were various, no doubt, as reasons for marriage are everywhere. At that time, Indian women were the only women in the region, and every man who had a wife had an Indian wife. The foremost men had Indian wives: men such as William Bent and Kit Carson, for example.

Later, when the country was settled with white immigrants from the States, these newcomers, who knew nothing of and cared little for Indians, dubbed the husbands of Indian wives "squaw-men," and made the term one of reproach. No doubt some of these "squaw-men" were no better than they should have been. The pioneers, generally, were a rough lot, trained to live in an epic world. But a little consideration will make it clear that the term "squaw-man" in itself contains nothing derogatory.

Indeed the squaw-man was a better man than many who lived in the Indian country with Indian women, and abandoned them when they found the country changed. Many an Indian girl was taken as a wife—as she supposed—by some trader, Indian agent, Army officer, or trapper—and then found herself deserted when her white husband drifted away. The squaw-man, at any rate, had honorable intentions, married in good faith, and was willing to accept the responsibility for his family. As a rule, he was considerate of his wife, remained with her to the end of their days, and brought up a number of respectable children.

Such men as Ben Clark, William Bent, Kit Carson, Jim Bridger, need not fear comparison with those who have followed their trail into the West. They were all "squaw-men," and their children Indians. There were hundreds of others of the same type. One suspects that the term "squaw-man" was invented by some spinster from the East, who came west to find a husband, only to discover that the Indian women had married all the best men.

III. NOTES ON INDIVIDUALS

No. 43.
NOTE ON CHIEF MAKES-ROOM (KIYU KANPI)

During my research among the Sioux Indians, Chief One Bull conferred upon me the name of his father, Makes-Room, which might better be translated Make-Room-For-Him or Welcome. Because of this honor done me and because Makes-Room was an hereditary chief of the Minniconjou Sioux and Sitting Bull's brother-in-law, I wish to include some account of him here. His name will be found in the records of every council of importance between the United States Commissioners and his people, and his career illustrates the nature of an hereditary chieftaincy. Makes-Room was born the son of Chief White Bull I (Pte San Hunka I) in 1825. He died in 1905 at the age of eighty.

Among people of European ancestry, great men are often strikingly different from the mass of their fellows. So much so, in fact, that they are not generally appreciated until after they are dead. Also our people often have a suspicion that a great man cannot have become powerful without some crookedness, some shady deals, in his past. Our ethics and our practice do not mix well, and we have to wink at the weaknesses and even the crimes of our great men, in consideration of their tremendous services to mankind. This unhappy condition of affairs is due, of course, to the hybrid culture of Europeans, with its Greek art and philosophy, its Roman law, its German science, its Semitic religion, its American business, its Gallic refinements. No man can possibly make a perfect synthesis of such diverse materials. He is bound to sacrifice some elements to others, he has to compromise. And so we have our specialists: great statesmen, great thinkers, great poets, great men of action, but mighty few—if any—men who are great in four directions. Our great men are not evenly balanced, not representative.

This was not true of the American Indian, because his culture was entirely his own and uninfluenced by outside forces. It had been growing up for perhaps ten thousand years, all by itself, and it fitted him like a glove. He was geared to the soil, to the climate, to the conditions of his life. He had long ago found out the best way to meet every emergency of his existence, and he was not cursed with legal precedents and outworn creeds to keep him from changing when change was necessary. And so, among the Sioux, a great man was not a freak, or a rebel. The test of a great man was not oddity, but perfection and completion in fulfilling the laws and customs of his people.

Makes-Room's career must be seen in the light of these facts. Here follows a statement by his son Chief Joseph White Bull, (Pte San Hunka II), now living, as to Makes-Room's war record.

"This story is about my father Makes-Room, what he did in his days:

1. When Makes-Room was seventeen years old (1842), they had a fight with the Skutani (Kootenay) at the head of Thick Timber River (the Little Missouri). He struck one of the enemy first and he struck another one second. In this fight they captured a lot of the enemy's women and some of them married Sioux men. They raised their families amongst us. After this fight

the Kootenay got scared and moved away to the west where they cannot see any more of the Sioux.

2. The Crow Indians camped along Powder River on the west bank. The Sioux entered their camp in the daytime and captured a lot of horses. Right at this moment one of the Crows was out looking for his horses, so they got this Crow. Makes-Room struck him first. Right after this the Crows got on their horses and started after them. When they caught up they had a big fight. Makes-Room captured eleven head of horses that day.

3. Below the mouth of Powder River they had a big fight with Crow Indians on the Yellowstone. One of the brave Crows was out in front, coming, trying to scare the Sioux. But Makes-Room started for him. The Crow took a shot at him but missed him, so Makes-Room took his lance and speared him off his horse and captured his horse. Good thing that he was missed by that enemy.

4. Along Red Water near the mouth they had a fight with Hohe (Assiniboine) Indians. One of them was brave, coming in front. The Sioux were afraid of him because he had a good gun. Finally Makes-Room got mad and started for him. When he rode him down Makes-Room yelled just to hurt that enemy's feelings! Makes-Room was then (1848) twenty-three years old. Sitting Bull was in this fight too.

5. At the mouth of Yellowstone River they had a fight with the Hohe again. Makes-Room was twenty-four years old then (1849). One of the enemy was out in front like a brave man. He had a bow and arrows. Makes-Room got mad again. He ran this man down and rode over him. He yelled because he was not shot.

6. Near this same battle ground Makes-Room was twenty six years old (1851) when they had another fight

with the Hohe. Makes-Room was first to strike a woman and second to strike a boy.

7. Along the Rosebud River Blackfoot and Crow Indians were having a fight. The Blackfoot had stones or rocks for protection so the Crows finally gave up and sent a message to the Sioux (Minniconjou) camp. So they turned out and ordered the Crow Indians to stand back and watch them, what they were going to do. When they made a start at the enemy Makes-Room was leading. He got there first and struck one first. He was twenty-five years old that time (1850).

Makes-Room was high among his people, doing many brave deeds. He also did many good deeds that other people could not do. But at last the old men said to him, 'See here. You are born a chief. You must give up the warpath and look out for your people.' After that Makes-Room seldom went to war and fought only when it was necessary."

(Signed)
Chief White Bull.

No. 44.
NOTE ON CHIEF FOUR HORNS (HE-TOPA)

Four Horns was Sitting Bull's uncle, the elder brother of Returns-Again or Jumping Bull, Sitting Bull's father. He was a tall man of light complexion and serious mind, who took his responsibilities as head man much to heart. Some white authors say that chiefs among the Sioux Indians were an invention of the Hudson's Bay Company's factors, who created them in order to have a central authority to deal through in trading with the tribesmen. This seems doubtful, though undoubtedly the traders did name certain head men to act as their agents among the Indians. The Hunkpapa Sioux say that they originally had no chiefs, but were governed by a council of warriors or "Soldier Lodge" presided over by an old man named Little Bear. As the Sioux nation began to fall to pieces under the impact of the white man the Indians made repeated efforts to tighten up their loose federation. In 1850 the Hunkpapa named four chiefs, of whom Four Horns was one.

Chieftaincy, of course, was a position of honor rather than of power, and such powers as the chiefs had were strictly conditioned by the wishes of the soldier bands, and for the most part delegated to others. Chieftaincy was hereditary by custom, but not necessarily in the direct line. The chieftaincy was as often passed from uncle to nephew as from father to son. The fact is that a Sioux hardly thinks of his uncle as different from his father; I have heard an interpreter use the phrase "one of his fathers" when an uncle was meant.

In one of the Sioux calendars (Lone Dog's Winter Count),[1] Four Horns is mentioned as making medicine in the winter of 1856-7 (that is, he adopted Noisy-Walking-Elk and another young man in the Calumet ceremony) and owing to a mistake of the interpreter, has been indentified in the white man's books with Sitting Bull. This, of course, is an error. Four Horns was born about 1800 and died in 1887. His death was hastened by a wound received in the fight with General Sully at Killdeer Mountain, July 1864. In 1845, also, Four Horns was wounded and left for dead in a fight with the Crows. He took a prominent part in the treaty council with General Harney at Fort Pierre, 1856.[2]

After the Custer Fight he preceded Sitting Bull into Canada, and when Sitting Bull arrived, complained

---

1. See Mallery, in Tenth Annual Report, Bureau of American Ethnology.
2. For this council, see House of Representatives, 34th Congress, 1st Session, Vol. XII, Executive Document No. 130.

because the officers of the Mounted Police dealt with Sitting Bull instead of with Four Horns. Because of this some historians have assumed that Sitting Bull was no chief. However, the point of Four Horn's complaint lay in the fact that Sitting Bull was a war chief, or leader of the warriors, whereas in Canada the Red Coats had forbidden fighting. Four Horns very naturally felt that he, as the principal *civil* chief there, should be deferred to.

Four Horns surrendered with Sitting Bull in 1881 and was held prisoner of war at Fort Randall until May 1883. He appears to have taken great interest in his nephew's career and taught Sitting Bull to seek popularity and to think for himself. Four Horns had several nicknames, of which the best known was Moccasin Top and another, which cannot be translated, being the name of an old game long since obsolete. After Sitting Bull, Four Horns is regarded by the Hunkpapa as the most remarkable of that remarkable family of chiefs (Sitting Bull, Four Horns, Looks-For-Home, Makes-Room, Black Moon, White Bull, One Bull.)

Robert P. Higheagle adds:

"Four Horns was considered to be a very good chief. I came to hear about him in this way. There was a young man, an ex-service man. He was particularly kind to old men. He would invite them to dinner and give them tobacco. The old men called him to one of the meetings of their White Horse Society. They told him it was their wish to give him a name as a sort of honor so they gave him the name of Four Horns. One of them got up and said he was related to Four Horns and was a near relation of Sitting Bull. He told the ex-service man that Four Horns was always kind to old men and always kind to everybody and that he had been selected as chief mostly on that account. Therefore they gave this young man that name."

No. 45.

NOTE ON CHIEF CRAZY HORSE

Crazy Horse (Ta Sunka Witko) was a prominent head man and chief of the Oglala Sioux. He was one of the four hair-shirt or scalp-shirt men of the tribe at one time. He was born in 1844 and was killed in 1877. During his short life he became one of the most famous of the Sioux war leaders and was prominent in many battles. His exploits included leadership in the Fetterman fight and the Wagon Box fight, both of which have been erroneously credited to Chief Red Cloud.

Little has been published about Crazy Horse from the Indian point of view and the Indians say that the "photograph of Crazy Horse" which appears from time to time does not represent him at all, but some other Indian. Crazy Horse would not face the camera and seldom talked to white men.

Chief Joseph White Bull, of the Minniconjou, knew Crazy Horse well and makes the following statements regarding him. "When in battle Crazy Horse preferred to wear a plain white buckskin suit. He let his hair hang loose and wore no feathers in it. I never saw him wear the red horsehide cape which you say white men claim he wore. I fought with him many times from 1865 to 1876 and I never saw that. Before entering a fight Crazy Horse painted his face with white spots by dipping the ends of his fingers into the paint and lightly touching his face here and there. Some warriors painted their faces like that to show they had been brave in some fight in a snow storm or when snow was on the ground, but

Crazy Horse used that paint for his protection in battle (*wotawe*).

"I have told you already some of the deeds of Crazy Horse to put in your books about me and my uncle, Sitting Bull.[3]

"Now, my friend, I will tell you of the other deeds which he performed to my knowledge.

"1. Crazy Horse was in a fight with the People-Who-Live-in-Grass-Houses west of the mountains and struck third. It is not true that Crazy Horse was never wounded. In this very fight he was hit in the calf of his left leg. I cannot tell the time and place of this fight.

"2. Crazy Horse fought with the Skili (pronounced Skeélee).[4] Those Indians then lived near the city of Omaha or somewhere down there. In this fight he struck a woman first.

"3. In a fight with the People-Who-Live-in-Grass-Houses (who live where the Shoshoni do now) Crazy Horse had a horse shot under him. Crazy Horse started back on foot. An enemy tried to head him off, but Crazy Horse killed the man, took his horse, and came home.

"4. In a fight with Crows Crazy Horse struck second and third.

"5. On Powder River Crazy Horse fought the Crows. His horse was shot under him.

"6. On the Big Horn River Crazy Horse's mount was shot in two places.

"7. At two different times his horse was shot in fights on the Yellowstone river. I have told you about one of these.[5]

---

3. See *Sitting Bull* and *Warpath*, passim.
4. Perhaps this refers to the Skidi band of the Pawnee tribe.
5. The Baker fight at the mouth of Pryor creek, August 14, 1872, described in *Warpath* and in *Sitting Bull*.

"Crazy Horse was about as tall as I am (five feet ten inches) but slim, with a light complexion and a small, sharp aquiline nose. He was a quiet man and a good fighter. Now I have told you about Crazy Horse."

Crazy Horse has been much praised as a great strategist and tactician. Therefore a word upon Indian strategy and tactics may be opportune here.

The Plains Indians were universally recognized by military officers who fought with them as the best cavalrymen in the world. They were excellent horsemen, good shots, as they made their living shooting running buffalo from the bare backs of ponies, and daring fighters, as well as unequaled scouts. However, they lacked entirely the discipline and organization of white soldiers. They fought as volunteers, each man to distinguish himself. They could never act together for long or in large numbers.

Therefore they could never follow up a victory. If their first attack failed, they abandoned the attempt, as a rule. If the first attack succeeded, they were content to go home and celebrate. When they acted together they did so voluntarily and therefore any complicated manœuvres, due to a change in conditions, were impossible. Their strategy was elementary.

It consisted for the most part of surprise, ambush, attack and flight. Owing to the ease with which they could outride the soldiers and avoid fighting when outnumbered, they seldom fought unless they had the advantage of numbers. Their battles were generally ended when darkness fell or at dinner time. A rainstorm or a cold wind was enough to make them end the battle. They might have issued rain-checks like a baseball team. For they could always ride away to fight again some other day.

Indeed, what the white man knows as Indian strategy was often enough accidental. The ambushes of Indian warfare were often quite unplanned. The young men simply slipped off and attacked before the less active warriors could arrive. Then, being forced to retreat, they naturally led their enemies back to the main body of warriors. In questioning Chief White Bull about such exploits I asked him if young men who disregarded the wishes of their elders and made the first attack were not censored or punished for disobedience of orders. The chief's lips curled in scorn and his eyes flashed as he replied, "No! We were not white men!" He considered it idiotic to punish a man for showing more courage than his comrades.

The simplest tricks are remembered with satisfaction by old warriors as triumphs of military strategy. In one of his early battles Crazy Horse went with a war party against the Crows, and the Sioux scouts found them on the Yellowstone. The Crows were resting, and their horses were fresh, while the Sioux ponies were fagged by an all-night ride. The leader of the Sioux party was one of Crazy Horse's relatives and as soon as he saw the Crows, he decided to rush them. For in Indian warfare there was rarely any stalling for position. It was fight or fly, the moment the enemy was sighted. The Sioux were delighted: now the fun was about to begin.

But Fine Weather knew that if the Sioux charged the Crows, they would run away. They fought like wolves: run, and they follow; follow, and they run. And he knew that the Sioux ponies could not catch them, and that the Sioux would soon be all scattered out and then killed man by man.

"Cousin," he said, "their ponies are fresh. Let us run from them and keep together. Then, when they catch up with us, we can turn around and have them at our mercy." The leader saw the sense of this suggestion. "Friends," he said to the others, "let us do as my cousin says." The others agreed, and away they went, loping easily along across the flats, in plain sight of the Crows, who came whooping and yelling, hot on the trail of the fleeing Sioux. In a very short time they had come close on the heels of the fagged Sioux ponies. Then the leader of the Sioux gave a yell, "*Hopo!* Let's go!" The Sioux wheeled around, and lashed their ponies back into the astonished faces of their enemies. Before the Crows could check their mounts, wheel, and dart away, the Sioux were among them. Fine Weather rode side by side with a Crow riding a bay horse and armed with a bow. The Crow did not attempt to defend himself, but tried to get away. His horse had more speed than Fine Weather's but before he was out of reach, the Sioux caught him in the left shoulder-blade with the point of his lance, and one hard jab sent the man reeling to the ground. Fine Weather rode over him, and dashed on. The Crow, however, survived, and bluffed the Sioux who followed, until he could run and swing himself up behind a comrade and ride away.

No. 46.
NOTE ON CHIEF RED CLOUD

Chief Red Cloud of the Oglala Bad Faces was one of the most outspoken of the Southern Sioux, who had first to bear the brunt of white invasion after the discovery of gold in California, Montana, and Idaho. The Oglala was the largest tribe of the Teton or Prairie Sioux then living west of the Missouri. Their home was along the Platte and the Oregon Trail and near the Black Hills. They therefore were first to come into serious conflict with the white pioneer. Because of this fact and because Red Cloud was so outspoken in his defiance of the white man, most of the hostilities in the 60's were laid at his door, and the war ended by the Treaty of Laramie in 1868, is known as Red Cloud's War. During these wars, when Sitting Bull was far to the north and engaged in fighting Indian enemies, newspaper men, perhaps under the prompting of military officers who may have wished to drag the whole Sioux nation into the wars, created a legend according to which Red Cloud was the great war chief of the Sioux nation and Sitting Bull was represented as the medicine man who misled his people into opposing the occupation of their hunting grounds. Red Cloud, the war chief, Sitting Bull, the medicine man, that was the legend, and of course, a mere legend. As a matter of fact, Red Cloud seems to have begun his career as a medicine man.[6] Sitting Bull was not a doctor, though he knew how to use the remedies of his doctor father. Sitting Bull was, however, a prophet, and had far more foresight than Red Cloud, who signed on the dotted line only to find later that he had been swindled by the whites.

Undoubtedly Red Cloud's Bad Faces were very active against the southern forts on the Bozeman Trail during the 60's, but Red Cloud was *not* the leader in *any of the major combats* with United States troops in those wars, unless possibly he was leader of the Sioux who destroyed Sergeant Custard and twenty-three men in the summer of 1865. Crazy Horse was the principal chief and leader of the Indians when Colonel Fetterman was destroyed on December 21, 1866, though Red Cloud's name adorns the monument on that fatal field. Red Cloud was not present. Red Cloud has also been

---

6. See 33rd Annual Report of the Bureau of American Ethnology, page 64.

given credit for leading the Indians in the Wagon Box Fight, August 2, 1867, though here too Crazy Horse was leader and principal war chief. Red Cloud was present in this fight and no doubt was valorous as an individual fighter, but Crazy Horse deserves the credit of starting this battle. As the Hayfield Fight took place a hundred miles to the north of the Wagon Box Fight on the previous day, it is certain that Red Cloud could have had nothing to do with the Hayfield Fight. He was *not* present in *any* major fight following the Treaty of 1868, and therefore had nothing to do with the major battles of his people, the Baker Fight, Reynolds Fight, Battle of the Rosebud, Custer Fight, Slim Buttes, and the engagements with General Miles and Lieutenant Baldwin. There is no doubt that Red Cloud had many valorous personal exploits to his credit, but he was *not* the great war chief of the Sioux and *never* the leader in any conflict of the first rank, according to Indian testimony. He was therefore not a political rival or military rival of Sitting Bull. The Sioux laugh at the notion, and Captain James H. Cook, for many years Red Cloud's most intimate white friend, considers the idea ridiculous. Red Cloud and Sitting Bull lived too far apart to have more than casual contact. In the main they were in agreement until 1868, and after Red Cloud surrendered and became an agency Indian they lived in different worlds. The Oglala who hunted and fought with Sitting Bull's people, were led by a younger man than Red Cloud—Crazy Horse.

Nevertheless Red Cloud will retain a prominent place in history. Though brave as a lion, he was by no means the tough-minded thinker Sitting Bull always remained. Red Cloud gave in early and became an agency Indian to his lasting sorrow and misery, thirteen years before Sitting Bull surrendered. Too late Red Cloud realized that he and his people were to be swindled and humiliated and that treaties were only scraps of paper. For when Red Cloud and Spotted Tail, taken to Washington, found that the treaty they had signed was not the treaty as explained by the Commissioners, Red Cloud said sadly, "The Whites, who are educated and civilized, swindle me, and I am not hard to swindle, because I do not know how to read and write."

When Sitting Bull heard of this treatment of Red Cloud's, his comment was "Well, what did he expect?"

Red Cloud and his delegation were so despondent over the deception practiced upon them that they planned to kill themselves at Washington, and had to be prevented from taking their own lives. Red Cloud's speech on this occasion is one of the loftiest and most touching pieces of Indian oratory on record.

It was not Sitting Bull, but Red Cloud who played the diplomat and begged and flattered, traveling around the country rigged out in a Prince Albert coat and posing as a sort of clerical Hiawatha. When Sitting Bull traveled to the East he wore Indian costume and spoke straight from the shoulder. It is time the legend of Sitting Bull, the medicine man, contrasted with Red Cloud, the war chief, should be laid aside.

No. 47.

NOTE ON CROW KING

Crow King (Kangi Yatapi) or Patriarch Crow, was also known as Burns-the-Medicine-Bundle. In *My Friend the Indian* Major James McLaughlin gives a story to account for this name, stating that Crow King, having been cured by the agency doctor, became disgusted with Indian medicine and threw his medicine bundle on the fire. There seems no reason to doubt the Major's story, but the Hunkpapa old men nevertheless insist that Burns-the-Medicine-Bundle was Crow King's boyhood name, and state that he was made a chief and given the name Crow King in 1858, in his manhood.

Crow King was a valiant warrior and a man of very quick and passionate temper, as will be recognized in the light of the following anecdotes.

During the late '50s, while the chiefs made by General Harney were trying to hold their people steady in spite of the failure of the government to fulfill its promises, there was much jealousy between the agency Indians and those on the Plains. The hunting bands resented the presents given to the agency Indians and felt that these were selling them out to the whites. Accordingly, when agency Indians came out to hunt on the Plains, the hunting bands shot their horses, put them afoot, and told them to go back and live on their friends, the white men. This, of course, caused much hard feeling.

In 1860, when the Hunkpapa were encamped near Chalky Buttes, Crowg Kin came home one night late and found his best horse lying dead with an arrow in its body. Next morning all the best horses in camp were found similarly treated. The Hunkpapa did not know which of the men in camp had killed the horses. Therefore the whole camp scattered, each family by itself, until the affair should blow over. Though they have no proof, the old men now say that they suspected Crow King of killing the best horses. At any rate, this event was so unusual that the winter of 1860 is known as Killing-Off-the-Best-Horses in the Hunkpapa Calendar.

Whether or not Crow King was guilty, the fact that he was suspected is sufficient evidence that the Sioux considered him quick-tempered.

The Sioux nation was so large, and contained so many bands and tribes, that sometimes jealousies and rivalries were very bitter. This was particularly the case after some of the bands had settled at the agencies and lived on the annuities given them by the Grandfather of the white men. The hunting bands, free and independent, distrusted these agency folks, and referred to them scornfully as "captives of the white man." And as all Indians carried arms, the feeling sometimes resulted in serious strife.

Of all the Western Sioux, Sitting Bull's big camp was most warlike and independent. And when some of the Hunkpapa settled at Standing Rock Agency, the wild, hunting bands almost regarded them as strangers, instead of relatives.

In June, 1870, Sitting Bull's big camp stood on the bank of the Yellowstone, not far from the Shallow Crossing, about seventy-five miles below the mouth of Powder River. The camp was on the north bank, and the warriors had just returned from a raid against the Crows, bringing hair and horses. One day some agency Sioux dragged in from Standing Rock, and went into camp across the river. Their tipis could be seen pitched in a big circle, and before long the bullboats or coracles began to bob across the stream, and a party of fifteen or twenty men came up the path to the camp of Sitting Bull. Every man in the party was armed with a bow, gun, or lance, and they all marched in a body to Sitting Bull's tent.

Crow King, suspicious and quick-tempered, saw them coming. He was Sitting Bull's close friend, and he was annoyed by the way these men came marching into camp under arms, marching right up to the tent of the chief, all bearing arms. Crow King began to walk up and down, clutching his hatchet, gun, and bow in one hand. When a Sioux warrior began to walk up and down like that, everyone knew that he was getting ready for a fight.

Crow King began to scold these men: "When you come here, why don't you come peaceably? What do you pack those guns for? You ought to do everything in a peaceful way."

As he was talking, others saw that something was wrong, and came trooping up to be on hand. Just then Sitting Bull's nephew, Big-in-the-Center, rode up and slid from his pony's back. Jumping Bull, Sitting Bull's adopted brother, stood there. He stepped over to Big-in-the-Center, indicated Crow King and the crowd of visitors by a slight jerk of his thumb, and said in a low voice, "Nephew, get ready. It looks as if these men came here to make trouble. Be prepared." Both of them had their guns and knives handy.

While Crow King was talking, a number of Sitting Bull's body-guard came up and crowded around the bunch of visitors, and wanted to know what was up. The visitors stood close beside Sitting Bull's tipi, and the body-guard surrounded them. It was contrary to Sioux custom for a party to enter another band's camp bearing arms. It looked bad. But the visitors began to answer Crow King.

One of them said, "We came over here to bring Sitting Bull an invitation to our camp, and to carry him back with us. We have just gone into camp in a circle yonder to make the Sun Dance. That's why we came after him. Someone must have mistold you, Crow King.

You are walking back and forth as if you were getting mad."

Crow King was angry. Immediately he retorted, "If you mean peace, then why do you fellows come here packing guns?"

The agency Indians answered, "Well, we were a little bit afraid of you on our side, because you are just back from the warpath. We thought maybe you were on the warpath still. That is why we packed our guns along. We mean nothing by that. We came to help ferry you across."

But Crow King was not ready to back down. He was still angry, and hard to pacify. "All the same," he insisted, "you've got no business packing guns into our camp. Why do you do it?" Then he turned abruptly, and stooping, went into Sitting Bull's tipi. The visitors stood close together, watchful, and the watchful bodyguard stood close around them. Crow King was a chief, and a dangerous man.

In a few moments, they all saw the door-flap tossed aside. Crow King came out again, with Sitting Bull at his heels. Crow King was still angry, but said nothing. Sitting Bull spoke to the crowd.

"Friends," he said, "Crow King means no harm. But the way you came over here excited him. He thought you meant some harm by it. That's why he is getting crazy mad. But your suggestion is welcome to me. I accept your invitation. And so we are going to move across the river to your camp."

Then Sitting Bull called a herald, and gave his orders. Immediately the herald began to shout to the listening camp. "Pack up," he yelled, "pack up. We are going to cross the river and go into camp with our cousins."

In a moment all was bustle, and after a few minutes

the camp pulled out to the river bank, where the Standing Rock Sioux helped ferry it over in bullboats. The river was high, the young men had to swim the horses. And as soon as they got across the Yellowstone, they pitched their tipis in the big camp circle along with the Standing Rock Sioux, all ready for the Sun Dance.

Having invited Sitting Bull across, they honored him further by asking him to compose a song praying for fair weather for the duration of the ceremony. Accordingly, when the Sun Pole had been captured, cut down, and set up within the camp, he sang the song he had composed for them. The words are supposed to be those of the Sun, and represent the prayer as already granted:

> With visible face I come forth;
> Buffalo I have given you;
> With visible face, behold me!

As had been expected, the weather during the ceremony was blue and cloudless. Sitting Bull's prayers were strong.

That was a big Sun Dance. Many dancers came from all segments of the camp circle and when the Director had placed them, all wailed for mercy, shedding their blood. They danced that day, the night after, the next day and night, and on into the afternoon of the following day. A long time. Many of the dancers fainted from thirst. Some gave it up and quit.

It was at this Sun Dance that the captive Frank Grouard heard Sitting Bull re-count his valorous exploits. Frank had then been living with the Sioux for eighteen months, and had a good command of the chief's language. In his memoirs he says, "Some who have written of Sitting Bull, claiming that he was a medicine-man and not a warrior, are unacquainted with the circumstances surrounding his life among the Indians themselves. No man in the Sioux nation was braver than Sitting Bull, and he asked none of his warriors to take any chances that he was not willing at all times to share. I could recall a hundred different instances coming under my own observation to prove Sitting Bull's bravery, and in the first great Sun Dance that I ever witnessed after my capture by the Sioux, I heard Sitting Bull recount his "*coups* in action." They numbered sixty-three, most of them being victories over Indian enemies."

It was not caution that led Sitting Bull to quiet Crow King and accept the invitation of the Standing Rock Agency Sioux. He was a "mean warrior" in battle, but always a peacemaker among his own people. Always he tried to hold the Sioux together, and even to unite with other tribes against the common enemy—the white man. But after he went to the agency himself, he was not always able to placate the other bands. In the end he was not even willing, probably. For some of those same people who invited him to join in the Sun Dance were among those who shot him down at last.

That Sun Dance of 1870 was a great success. When it was over, the camps moved three sleeps up-river, found buffalo herds, made a surround, and killed plenty. Having waited a few days to jerk this meat and rest their horses, they rode on three sleeps farther, found more buffalo, made another successful hunt. Everybody was eating fat meat; they had so much meat that the pack-horses could hardly travel. Life in that camp was just one feast and dance after another. Big-in-the-Center says he stole a girl in that camp.

Those were the days!

After settling at the Agency, Crow King became an

Indian policeman, but his quick temper remained with him and finally, it is said, he killed an Indian in a fit of temper.

No. 48.

NOTE ON LITTLE ASSINIBOIN

Among the most famous warriors and admirable characters in the Hunkpapa Sioux tribe was the Assiniboin whom Sitting Bull captured in 1857 and adopted as his brother. On the Agency rolls and in old military records his name is given as Little Assiniboin. However, he was better known to the Indians by the name of Sitting Bull's father, Jumping Bull, or as Ota Ktepi, Plenty-Kill, or Kills-often. Owing to his refusal to leave Sitting Bull to rejoin the Assiniboin, he was given the name Stays-Back also.

Little Assiniboin was born about 1846, captured in 1857. The Assiniboin language being only a dialect of the Sioux tongue, he soon adapted himself to his new tribe and became one of the best liked and most successful hunters and warriors of the Hunkpapa.

About the year 1870 Sitting Bull prepared a series of drawings of his own exploits and encouraged Little Assiniboin to do likewise. Afterward Chief Four Horns, uncle to the young men, began a set of copies of these drawings in an old roster book of an infantry regiment. Four Horns had completed 54 drawings and was working on the 55th when his book fell into the hands of some Indian who sold it to James C. Kimball, Assistant Surgeon, U.S.A. This was in the year 1870. The book of drawings afterward was placed in the Army Medical Museum in Washington, D.C. and later was transferred to the archives of the Bureau of American Ethnology, where it is filed under the title, *Hieroglyphic Autobiography of Sitting Bull, Number 1929*.

The title given this book by the man who obtained it is, in full: *The War Record of the Noted Sioux Chief Sitting Bull, From Age of Fourteen, to Year 1870*. With the drawings was a key, or interpretation (highly inaccurate and incomplete), provided by the Indian who sold the book to Surgeon Kimball.

While Sitting Bull was prisoner-of-war at Fort Randall, this book was brought to him for verification. At that time Sitting Bull pointed out that fifteen of these drawings (in the original series, Nos. 39 to 51 inclusive, and Nos. 53 and 54) represented exploits performed by Little Assiniboin, and not by himself. It is of these exploits we wish to speak here.

In these drawings Little Assiniboin is shown on horseback in every case. Like his brother Sitting Bull, he seldom went to war on foot. His equipment in most of these drawings is the same. He wears his hair loose, flowing down his back, with a black feather rising like a horn from his forehead. His face was painted all over red with a black crescent or curved line passing from the eyebrow to the jaw following the line of the jawbone. He carries a bow-lance, evidently the insignia of his warrior society. This bow-lance is a cupid's-bow with a lance-head on the end, and a bunch of eagle feathers attached above and below the hand-hold. The blade of the bow-lance is painted blue. Little Assiniboin also wears a thong about his neck to which is tied a small pouch containing his "medicine" or war-charm (*watowe*). He sometimes wears a bone breastplate such as was common among the Sioux.

In Number 39, the first of the drawings given here, he is shown as a chief of the Strong Hearts, capturing a mule in an engagement on Powder River with white men.

Number 40. Carrying a bow-lance, Little Assiniboin captures two horses in a fight on the Montana Trail with white men. In this engagement his own horse was wounded in the shoulder.

Number 41 shows him capturing a horse in a general engagement.

Number 42 shows him bringing home an Army mule.

Number 43 shows Little Assiniboin capturing two horses. In this fight his own mount was shot in the leg.

Number 44. Little Assiniboin, mounted on a branded Government horse, captured from the troops in a fight on the Montana Trail, pursues and captures a white man. In this picture he carries a holster and wears yellow buckskin leggins and a powder horn. A pistol is shown dropping from his hand.

In Number 45 Little Assiniboin steals two horses.

Number 46. He wears a dark shirt or coat with tails, probably captured from some white man, and runs off four mules from a wagon train. In this fight his horse was shot in the hip.

In Number 47 and in Number 48, Little Assiniboin is shown mounted on a branded buckskin, a horse given him by Sitting Bull. In each of these two pictures Little Assiniboin counts *coup* on a white man.

Number 49. Little Assiniboin steals a government horse. In this picture he is shown wearing a bone necklace.

Number 50. One of his principal exploits is shown. Little Assiniboin wears a single head-feather, dark clothing, and a powder horn supported by a broad red flannel baldric. He has thrust his lance upright in the ground, tied his horse to it, and attacked his enemy, a white man, on foot. The ground is shown covered with black marks to indicate that it was fought and trampled over. Little Assiniboin here kills the white man with the white man's own gun.

Number 51 represents Little Assiniboin's part in the fight on the Big Dry River in the winter of 1869-70, when thirty Crows were killed. This battle has been described in my *Sitting Bull*, Chapter XVI. In this drawing Little Assiniboin is shown charging the rock fort of the Crows, who maintain a hot fire. He is shown wearing the trailing red sash of a Strong Heart chief.

Number 53 shows Little Assiniboin capturing a drove of mules.

Number 54 shows a second exploit in the battle with the thirty Crows. Little Assiniboin leads the charge against the Crows in order to get them to empty their guns, so that his comrades may charge in and kill them.

These exploits, heretofore generally credited to Sitting Bull, should be credited to his brother, Little Assiniboin, or Jumping Bull II.

Chief White Bull describes Little Assiniboin as a strong, brave, all-around man, a chunky warrior of medium height, always laconic but good-natured, who performed many brave deeds, was wounded in the hip in battle, and had horses shot under him. One of his exploits is mentioned in Finerty's book, *Warpath and Bivouac*. He also figures in General Baldwin's account (diary) of the campaign against Sitting Bull in the winter of '76, and reference is made to his treatment when captured by Major Ilges elsewhere in this book.

Owing to the fact that he did not surrender with Sitting Bull but was captured at another time, he was not sent to Fort Randall as prisoner-of-war, but to Standing Rock Agency. There he appears to have led a law-abiding, quiet life, loyal to his "brother," with whom he died at last. The Hunkpapa remember Little Assiniboin with affection and respect.

No. 49.
A NOTE ON MRS. EUBANKS

In the middle 60's a number of white persons were captured by the Sioux in retaliation for outrages upon their people. On the southern plains the Kiowas and Comanches had developed the capture and sale of Mexican and American persons into a regular industry, but in Sioux country such kidnaping for profit was comparatively rare. Among the most notorious of these captures was that of a Mrs. Eubanks, who was brought into Fort Laramie in a very bedraggled condition by two Sioux chiefs who had bought her from her captors and restored her to her friends at no little trouble and expense. The officer in command of the post, however, instead of rewarding these chiefs, ordered them hanged in chains. An account of this wretched business will be found in *The Bozeman Trail*, and in Grinnell's *The Fighting Cheyennes*. It appears that the thing which particularly enraged the white soldiers at Fort Laramie was the fact that Mrs. Eubanks had been hauled across the river behind a pony by means of a lariat tied around her waist. The officers were ignorant of the fact that this was the usual Indian method of getting women across streams when they could not be trusted to ride a pony or when ponies were scarce. I believe reference is made to this custom in Mr. Niehardt's recent book *Black Elk Speaks*, and also in one of the books by Chief Standing Bear. The Indians treated Mrs. Eubanks as they would have treated one of their own women.

No. 50.
NOTE ON FRANK GROUARD

Members of Sitting Bull's family remember the captive Frank Grouard, whose Indian name was Sitting-with-Upraised-Hands. He was quick to learn, soon spoke Sioux, and became an excellent hunter and scout. Though he was descended from a woman of the Sandwich Islands and a white man, Sitting Bull's nephews will not believe that he was not an Indian.

They like to tell a joke on this young man. It happened one day that he was to start early next morning on a hunt, and asked Sitting Bull's sister to put up a lunch for him. She did so, tying the bundle to one of the tipi poles above his bed. Nearby was tied another bundle containing some materials used in tanning hides. In the darkness, next morning, Grouard took the wrong bundle, and when he opened it to eat, found a most unpalatable lunch! So long as he remained in Sitting Bull's tipi, he never heard the last of that!

No. 51
NOTE ON ISAIAH

Isaiah was a Negro who came up the Missouri River to Standing Rock before or about 1871 and married a Sioux Indian woman. He cut wood for Major Galpin, the trader, as described in Lewis F. Crawford's excellent book *Rekindling Camp Fires*. At one time Isaiah had a woodyard about half a mile north of Fort Yates. The remains of the dugouts he made can be seen there now. Isaiah joined the Custer command in the summer of '76 because he loved the wild country and said he wished to see that western land once more before he died. He was with Major Reno when the troops charged the Sioux camp on June 25. He was shot in the breast and mortally wounded. The Sioux remember Isaiah with affection. He spoke their language fluently and was known to them by a Sioux word meaning Teat, because the Sioux word for teat sounds much like the name Isaiah.

No. 52.
NOTE ON CHIEF RUNNING ANTELOPE, BY ROBERT P. HIGHEAGLE, SON OF CHIEF HIGHEAGLE

"Running Antelope was an orator, a chief and a warrior, a better orator than John Grass. He had such dignity that you could not help feeling that he was a chief and a man of high standing. He had some qualities which Sitting Bull lacked. Sitting Bull listened to too many people, too many dictated to him. Running Antelope struck me as being more independent and always good humored."

No. 53.
NOTE ON KICKING BEAR

Kicking Bear brought the Ghost Dance to Standing Rock. He came of his own accord. He was never invited to come. Crazy Walking, chief of the Indian Police, was sent down to order Kicking Bear away. Major McLaughlin sent him down, but Kicking Bear refused to go. Up to that time Kicking Bear had scarcely been heard of. His name was hardly known. He was not much of a warrior. Chief White Bull mentions him only once in his story of the Sioux wars. When a medicine man was needed he would be one known to be qualified for the particular occasion. So it was at the time of the Ghost Dance.

Chief One Bull makes the following statement as

COURTESY, BUREAU OF AMERICAN ETHNOLOGY

Running Antelope, Hunkpapa Sioux Chief

to what happened when Crazy Walking ordered Kicking Bear away in October, 1890: "I, One Bull, in company with Crazy Walking and Catka, were all serving on Indian Police Force. McLaughlin ordered us to stop the Ghost Dance. Crazy Walking told the dancers to stop. Sitting Bull answered him as follows: 'The education of my children is uppermost. I have a school in my locality. This dance is not the most important undertaking. They will, eventually, stop.' This is what we reported to McLaughlin upon our return. Crazy Walking is still living."

No. 54.
NOTE ON CHIEF JOHN GRASS

John Grass is said to have taken himself very seriously. He was an eloquent man and a mouthpiece for the agents at Standing Rock, as well as a chief of the Blackfeet Sioux. Therefore he was frequently sent to Washington as a member of Indian delegations.

John Grass did not like to be teased and could not take a joke on himself very gracefully, they say. It is seldom that an Indian gets bald-headed unless as a result of sickness, but John Grass was partly bald. Once when in Washington his brother-in-law was with him. Brothers-in-law among the Sioux are very intimate and are privileged to tease each other. One day when the delegation was seated at the dinner table John's brother-in-law said: "The very idea that my brother-in-law should be ashamed of being bald-headed. If you go to Congress over there you will see those white men proud of their bald heads. They polish their heads and dress up. John, why don't you cut off your hair on the sides and polish your bald head like those Senators and Congressmen?" John Grass was very much embarrassed.

He did not like that remark. This is said to have happened in 1914.

In one of the printed reports of the Indian Councils of 1883, the name of this Chief is incorrectly spelled Glass!

No. 55.
NOTE ON SERGEANT SHAVEHEAD

At most Indian agencies in the last decades of the nineteenth century it was the practice to engage for service as Indian policemen the fiercest and most hard-boiled scrappers on the reservation. In this way the agent gained a stout ally and lost a possibly dangerous enemy. At Standing Rock Agency Shavehead was one of the fiercest of the younger men and soon became First Sergeant of the Standing Rock Indian police. He was evidently idolized by the agent, Major James McLaughlin. In the first draft of his book, *My Friend the Indian*, he devoted Chapter Fifteen to an account of Shavehead and entitled it "Shavehead's Code of Honor; The Story of a Man of the Hunkpapa Sioux Who Fought Fiercely, Hated Thoroughly, and Died For the White Men." This chapter (deleted on the advice of the publishers) represented Shavehead as a man of vindictive temper. McLaughlin described how Shavehead, at a beef issue, fell into a dispute with an Indian whom he calls Crooked Neck, but is better known to the Indians as Red Thunder. At the time Shavehead was Ration-chief. Unfortunately, some beeves are fatter than others and portions even of the same beef are not always equally desirable. Red Thunder thought that Shavehead was appropriating more than his share. According to McLaughlin Crooked Neck twice fired at Shavehead with his shotgun, whereupon Shavehead shot and killed Crooked Neck, and having pumped fifteen bullets into the dead body, reloaded his Winchester and defied the dead man's relatives to do their worst. According to the story of Red Thunder's relatives, his gun was empty and was never fired at all.

Red Thunder, or Crooked Neck, was laid to rest on a burial scaffold near the mouth of Cat Tail Creek, which flows into the Missouri almost opposite the Standing Rock Agency. The dead man's relatives made no attempt to retaliate upon Shavehead, probably because he was a policeman. All the same, the Indians say that the dead man haunted Shavehead and terrorized him both day and night. Shavehead dared not drink from a tin cup, for whenever he did so he would see Red Thunder's face looking up at him from the shiny bottom of the cup. Shavehead had to get a cup made of black buffalo horn to be rid of that curse.

McLaughlin says that every payday when Shavehead drew his wages he immediately bought cartridges, and taking his Winchester, he went down to Red Thunder's grave. The people at the Agency could hear him shooting as he pumped the whole magazine of his Winchester into the dead body of his enemy. Shavehead kept this up until Red Thunder's remains had disintegrated and dropped from the scaffold. It is apparent from McLaughlin's story, told with some gusto, that Sergeant Shavehead was a hardboiled, quick-tempered man who never forgot a grudge. He was mortally wounded in the attempt to arrest Sitting Bull, December 15, 1890.

No. 56.
NOTE ON BLACK BULL
Various amusing things occurred at treaty councils with the Indians at Standing Rock Agency. One of the

amusing characters who showed up at such times was an old scout named Black Bull, who is usually mentioned in the reports of the commissions as coming forward to present a huge bundle of papers. It appears that this Black Bull made a habit of collecting testimonials certifying that he was a chief and deserved special consideration. He also tried to induce every white man he met to give him such a paper or to add his signature to one already prepared. These were the papers which he invariably presented to the commissions.

Black Bull was known in the tribe as a wag and a wit, and on one occasion made a speech to the commission which has never been forgotten by the Indians and is still repeated as often as the name of Black Bull is mentioned. On this occasion Black Bull got up and said: "Of course I am not a smart man. I am only the chief of a band here. Yet all this talk about the value of our land and how it should be sold does not strike me. So I intend to speak my mind now. Whenever we go to the store to buy from the traders we find that they have a scale and weigh everything. They base the value of everything on that scale. Now you say we should be like white people. So I have a proposition to make which will, I am sure, please all my people. You want to buy our land and we are willing to sell it at a fair price. I suggest that you bring here a big scale. We will weigh the earth and sell it to you by the pound."

No. 57.
NOTE ON SITTING BULL'S BOYHOOD NAME

In most of the accounts of Sitting Bull's life one finds the statement that his boyhood name was Jumping Badger. None of his family or intimate friends have any recollection of any such name being given him.

As a boy he was known as Hunkesni (pronounced Hungkeshny) meaning "Slow." This name was given him because of his deliberation, apparently, and had nothing to do with any inability to run. Little Soldier and Young Eagle state that Sitting Bull, before he was wounded in the foot in 1856, was the swiftest runner (for any distance) among the Hunkpapa Sioux. The only man who could give him a close chase was Crawler (Slohan). Crawler was very tall and long-legged and occasionally beat Sitting Bull.

Even after Sitting Bull was lamed he was still swift of foot. Frank Zahn, the son of William Presley Zahn and a woman of the Yanktonais Sioux, gives the following account of a famous footrace in which Sitting Bull ran against a white man after he came to the agency. This story has been told me by more than a dozen Indians. Zahn says: "There was a cowboy, a white man, at Standing Rock known as 'Sport' Whitsell. 'Sport' had married a Hunkpapa woman and was employed in one way or another at the agency. He challenged Sitting Bull to a footrace. It happened on one ration-day here in Fort Yates. Sitting Bull bet his celebrated circus horse (the one Buffalo Bill gave him). 'Sport' Whitsell bet a sorrel horse. The soldiers of the garrison bet money, while the Indians bet horses. I can point out to you the exact spot where the race took place. Sitting Bull left the white man in the dust. . . . beat him badly. 'Sport' Whitsell however, did not live up to his name. He did not give up his horse to Sitting Bull. Said Sitting Bull, 'A white man has no business to challenge a deer.' That is to say he was as fleet as a deer. I think my father bet a carbine that time. He saw the race. Naturally he bet for the white man, and lost."

No. 58.
NOTE ON INDIAN PORTRAITS

Photographs of famous Indians must be studied with a realization of the conditions under which they were taken. Very often the Indian was afraid of the camera and had to be bullied or bribed into sitting for his portrait. This fact and the fact that the sitter's head was, in those days, steadied by an iron contrivance behind him, will account for some of the curious expressions to be seen in Indian photographs.

Those taken outdoors generally have a more authentic quality, at least as regards costume. The agency Indians, or indeed Indians of any sort, did not go about dressed up in war-bonnets and buckskin shirts, as a rule. Such costumes were for dress occasions. Professional photographers, therefore, usually kept a war-bonnet and tomahawk and perhaps a buffalo robe or other similar accessories in the studio, and dressed up their sitters in these as often as a photograph was made. The fact that a man is shown wearing a war-bonnet is therefore no indication that he had any right to wear one, and it is obvious in studying the photographs taken in any single studio that the same costume was used for nearly all sitters. Very often it did not fit, and the Indian felt awkward and uncomfortable when wearing it.

Photographs taken by Mr. D. F. Barry of Superior, Wisconsin, are among the best for the early period of Sioux agency life, particularly at Standing Rock. The Bureau of American Ethnology also has a large collection of excellent photographs of Indians taken soon after the wars ended, and many of the local photographers in Montana and the Dakotas had, and have, very good collections of Indian portraits. Some of those taken of the early Wild West Shows are very good and authentic for costume, for in those days the chiefs would not permit one of their warriors to wear any honor feathers to which he was not entitled, no matter how much Buffalo Bill proposed to dress them up.

Sitting Bull and Red Cloud were more photographed than any others, probably. Crazy Horse would never permit his photograph to be made. As a result, photographs of other Indians have been palmed off upon the public as those of Crazy Horse. Indeed there is considerable confusion as to the identity of Indians in certain well known photographs. Thus in the much-reproduced family group of Sitting Bull, showing him seated between two women, one of whom holds a child, the usual legend is "Sitting Bull and his two wives." However, on showing this photograph to Chief One Bull and other members of his family, I learned that the old woman on Sitting Bull's right in this picture is his mother, Her-Holy-Door, while the woman on his left holding the child, is his favorite daughter, Has-Many-Horses. The child was named Tom Fly.

Mrs. Catherine Weldon painted Sitting Bull's portrait three or four times in oils during her sojourn at Standing Rock in 1890. Two of these portraits were lost with the rest of her household goods in shipment from Standing Rock to Brooklyn, as recorded in one of her letters to the chief. The third portrait was recently sold at auction among the effects of Mrs. Van Solen, I am told. The fourth, reproduced here, was found in Sitting Bull's smaller cabin after his death, and almost destroyed by one of the engaged policemen. Colonel Matthew F. Steele of Fargo, North Dakota, prevented its destruction and purchased it from Sitting Bull's wives. I believe he still has it. Our reproduction is made by courtesy of the U.S. Signal Corps.

IV. CHRONOLOGY

No. 59.
A HUNKPAPA SIOUX CALENDAR

1831 *Itazipa waunskati.* Yellow Eyes' accident. (A trader has an accident).
1832 *Titanka obleca kagapi.* Lodges with roofs were built.
1833 *Wicahpi Okecamna.* Shower of Stars. (Meteoric display, in November.)
1834 *Wapaha hetan kagapi.* War-bonnet with horns is made.
1835 *Wiciyela waniyetu wicakasotapi.* Yanktonais Sioux almost wiped out in winter.
1836 *Cara Kiciupi.* Carrying ice.
1837 *Wicahanhan.* Smallpox plague.
1838 *Sungleska Awicaglipi.* Spotted horses brought home.
1839 *Winkte Peji wan ici kte.* The Hermaphrodite committed suicide.
1840 *Unktomi heraka ecopey api.* Spider-Elk taken to his people.
1841 *Psa ohanpi.* Snowshoes worn.
1842 *Hohe cicala wan ktepi.* A small Hohe (Assiniboin) killed. (He had been scalped before!)
1843 *Hetopa glisni.* Four Horns did not return, (from a fight with the Crows. Left for dead, he came in later.)
1844 *Nawica sli.* Severe skin eruption. (Epidemic).
1845 *Igmu sakowin wicaktepi.* Seven mountain lions shot.

1846　*Pabobo alowanpi.* Pabobo's adoption ceremony.
1847　*Wojun econpi Ota.* Many contests.
1848　*Peji Wanica.* No grass. (Drouth.)
1849　*Womase te natanhi.* Hunters charged upon by enemies, (while killing buffalo.)
1850　*Kewoyuska ta.* Turtle-Catcher dies.
1851　*Canhasah oju el okiju.* The Indian nations assemble at Birch Grove. (Treaty at Fort Laramie.)
1852　*Psaloka Okiju.* Crow Indians assemble. (Treaty with Crows.)
1853　*Hetopa Ktepi.* Four horns (i.e. an enemy wearing a bonnet with four horns attached) killed.
1854　*Tuweni Oyuspi sni wacapa.* Nobody-Catches-Him stabs (his sister-in-law).
1855　*Putinhinska waaksije.* White Beard (General Harney) seizes the Sioux. (At Ash Hollow).
1856　*Wapaha wan yuksapi.* War-bonnet torn. (On Tongue River, Loud Bear tears an enemy's war-bonnet.) See *Sitting Bull*, Chapter IV.
1857　*Ota ktepi Agli.* Kills-Plenty (Little Assiniboin, Sitting Bull's captive "brother") brought home.
1858　*Patopi pte san wan o.* A man named Four Heads (Patopi) shot a white buffalo. (Near Slim Buttes.)
1859　*Kangitanka ktepi.* Big Crow (elder son of the Minniconjou Chief, Breast) killed (by Crows on Cheyenne River.)
1860　*Sunkakan karnirnir tewicayapi.* Killing off the best horses.
1861　*Itunkasan luta ktepi.* Red Weasel (Hunkpapa chief) was killed, (by the Hohe on Heart River.)
1862　*Hohe wichemna-numpa wicaktepi.* Twenty Hohe

(Assiniboin) killed, (by Hunkpapa and Blackfeet Sioux on Heart River, in winter.)

1863 *Horpa wica sota.* Severe cough epidemic.

1864 *Wasicu winyan wan aipi.* Rescuing a white woman. (Mrs. Fanny Kelly.) See *Sitting Bull*, Chapter X.

1865 *Wojupi Ota.* Much planting.

1866 *Wasicu opa-win-ge wicaktepi.* One hundred white men killed. (The Fetterman "Massacre," December 21, 1866. See *Warpath*, Chapter VI.)

1867 *Carsu.* Sleety season.

1868 *Akezaptan wicaktepi.* Fifteen persons killed (by Crows.)

1869 *Psa wichemna-yamini wicaktepi.* Thirty Crow Indians killed. (Near Spoonhorn Butte. See *Sitting Bull*, Chapter XVI.)

1870 *Saglasa ahi.* French Canadian Indians (traders) from Canada visit.

1871 *Tiwoksan sunk okuwapi.* Chasing Horses in camp. (See story elsewhere in this book. Part II, No. 10.)

1872 *Sunk hinto akanyanka wan ktepi.* The Sioux killed an enemy riding blue-colored horse.

1873 *Maka qa ob kici zapi.* Fighting in trenches (with Red River Breeds. See *Warpath*, Chapter XVI.)

1874 *Psa cepa wan ktepi.* A fat Crow Indian killed. (Near Tongue River. See Part II, No. 12.)

1875 *Sunka ska hi.* White Dog (Hohe Chief) visits (and makes peace with the Sioux.)

1876 *Pehin hanska ktepi.* Long Hair (Custer) killed. (See *Sitting Bull* and *Warpath*.)

1877 *Oglesa Okiju.* Red Coats assemble. (Refugee Sioux make treaty with Red Coats in Canada.)

1878 *Poge hloka ahi.* Nez Percés visit. (Refugee Nez

Percés join Sitting Bull in Canada. See Part II, No. 29.)

1879 *Wichapi wanjila ktepi.* One Star killed (by the Crows.)

1880 *Sunk ha kte.* Mange among the horses (in Canada.)

1881 *Ouwica-tapi.* Sioux fired over. (Major Guido Ilges attacks the Sioux. See Part II, No. 30.)

NEW SOURCES OF INDIAN HISTORY, 1850-1891, by Stanley Vestal is composed in Monotype 337, popularly known as Caslon Old Face, a faithful modern recutting of one of the world's most famous type faces. The text is set in twelve point with two point leading. The famous Caslon type had its origin in 1722. Two years earlier William Bowyer, the elder, observed a signature which William Caslon appended to a font of Arabic type. The freshness and solidity of the letter compelled Bowyer's admiration and he encouraged young Caslon to complete the alphabet. Accordingly, in 1722, Caslon Roman was born. The letters were modelled from Dutch types but they had a variety of design and a delicacy of line which few Dutch types possessed. The letters analyzed separately are at times awkward and apparently unwieldy but in mass their effect is pleasing. They reflect the Anglo-Saxon temperament—sturdy honesty, ingenious practicality—and are particularly fitted for the printing of "common-sense" material. Caslon and modified forms of it were popular during the greater part of the eighteenth century when they fell into disfavor. Caslon was revived again in 1844 by Pickering and Whittingham at the Chiswick Press. In 1859 the Johnson Type Foundry of Philadelphia brought to this country strikes of the Caslon punches, and the type was used sporadically for a few years. It was not until 1915 that a good version of Caslon became popularly used in America. In that year the Lanston Monotype Machine Company produced the "337 Caslon," which generally follows the traditional Caslon design. The long ascenders and descenders are faithfully produced, especially in the twelve point as used in this volume.

THE PRINTED PAGE IS   EVERYMAN'S UNIVERSITY

UNIVERSITY OF OKLAHOMA PRESS : NORMAN

www.ingramcontent.com/pod-product-compliance
Lightning Source LLC
Chambersburg PA
CBHW020827160426
43192CB00007B/554